D0770626

An Immigration of Theology

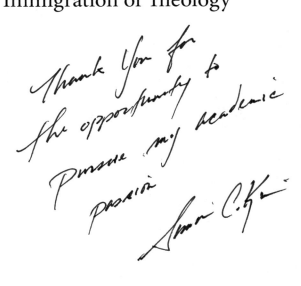

Thank you for
the opportunity to
pursue my academic
passion

Simon C.K[...]

An Immigration of Theology

Theology of Context as the Theological Method of Virgilio Elizondo and Gustavo Gutiérrez

Simon C. Kim

Foreword by
Daniel G. Groody, CSC
and
Timothy Matovina

PICKWICK *Publications* · Eugene, Oregon

AN IMMIGRATION OF THEOLOGY
Theology of Context as the Theological Method of Virgilio Elizondo and
Gustavo Gutiérrez

Pickwick Publications
An Imprint of Wipf and Stock Publishers
199 W. 8th Ave., Suite 3
Eugene, OR 97401
www.wipfandstock.com

ISBN 13: 978-1-978-1-61097-636-7

Cataloging-in-Publication data:

Kim, Simon C.

An immigration of theology : theology of context as the theological method of
Virgilio Elizondo and Gustavo Gutiérrez / Simon C. Kim ; foreword by Daniel G.
Groody and Timothy Matovina.

xxvi + 280 p. ; 23 cm. — Includes bibliographical references.

ISBN 13: 978-1-978-1-61097-636-7

1. Emigration and imigration—Religious aspects—Christianity. 2. Elizondo,
Virgilio P. 3. Gutiérrez, Gustavo, 1928– I. Groody, Daniel G., 1964– II.
Matovina, Timothy M., 1955– III. Title.

BR115.C8 K555 2012

Manufactured in the U.S.A.

This book is dedicated to the *mestizos* and the poor of the world.

Mestizos have helped me to better understand who I am as a child of God while the poor have allowed me to encounter Christ in my brothers and sisters.

Contents

Foreword

IT IS AN HONOR to write these lines welcoming readers to Simon Kim's book, though it scarcely needs any words of introduction. He has clearly delineated his goal of examining the importance of doing theology in context through a comparative analysis of the works of Gustavo Gutiérrez and Virgilio Elizondo. Then he masterfully achieves that goal through a careful exposition of the contexts, contents, intersections, and divergences of their respective theologies. Many readers will recognize the influential dialogue partners Kim appropriately chose for his study: Gutiérrez is the founding figure of liberation theology in Latin America and arguably one of the most influential theologians of the twentieth century, while Elizondo is the premiere U.S. Latino theologian whose influence also stretches to all continents around the globe. Fewer readers will note at first glance that Kim has produced the most comprehensive comparative analysis of these two leading theologians to date. Since many theologians and scholars from related fields tend to conflate the theologies of Latin Americans and those of U.S. Latinas and Latinos, this comparative analysis alone makes Kim's book a valuable contribution to contemporary theological scholarship.

But there is more. Kim brings out the value of the method Gutiérrez and Elizondo employ for doing theological reflection. He captures beautifully how his subjects' life experiences and pastoral leadership have deeply shaped their theological insights and, at the same time, how those insights have shaped their pastoral vision and that of numerous others whom they have inspired. Both of these theologians are pastors who never had a permanent university appointment before they reached their 65th birthday. In the early church, of course, nearly all theologians were pastors. On the contemporary scene, however, particularly in the West, the tendency is precisely the opposite as theology has become more specialized and university-based. In this circumstance Gutierrez and Elizondo provide an important model for pastoral theology. They enable a new generation of theologians like Kim to offer constructive theological interpretations from new vantage points. Thus it is not surprising that the significance of a vital link between the academy and pastoral life is woven into the fabric of Kim's text. At one level his exposition is a testimony—along with an accompanying critique—about the need for theologians today to learn from and contribute to the pastoral life of ecclesial communities. Yet Kim doesn't merely dwell on this aspect of the theological vocation with admonitions and pious platitudes. Explicitly and implicitly, he relentlessly demonstrates it by concretely showing how embedded it is in the singular contributions of his two subjects.

Kim himself is a pastor-theologian strongly committed to the ideals he illuminates. More specifically, he is a Korean American priest who observes the profound resonance between Elizondo's concept of *mestizaje*—the dynamic and often violent mixing of cultures, religious systems, and peoples—and the obstacles and opportunities for ministries among his own Korean American people. In particular, he is concerned about the challenges of generational transition, through which numerous Korean Americans pass amidst the accompanying process of adapting to life in the United States as immigrants or the children of immigrants. Like Elizondo, Kim perceives potential pitfalls such as the loss of identity or active practice of their faith to which his people might succumb during this process of adaptation. But he also sees and seeks to promote the *mestizaje* possibility of his people embracing the best of both Korean and U.S. cultures. The primary insight he gains from Gutiérrez is his emphasis on the preferential option for the poor in theology and in the life of discipleship. Kim notes that this preferential option is good news for displaced immigrants and racial minorities like Korean Americans who do not always feel welcome or at home in the United States, but are assured in faith that they are fully members of the household of God. At the same time, the option for the poor challenges them to be agents of that same good news in the lives of their own communities and beyond.

As Kim makes clear, the option for the poor is not merely a social ideology with a religious mask. Many tend to see Gutiérrez only in light of social categories. But as important as these are, they are shaped first and foremost by the theological notion of gratuity. In their pastoral outreach and theological reflection, both Gutiérrez and Elizondo draw on the notion that God first loved us. They seek to understand what this means within their respective contexts of Latin America and the Mexican-U.S. borderlands. Neither Gutiérrez nor Elizondo set out to create a new form of theology. Rather, like Kim, they seek to answer the questions of their people in light of the Christian tradition. In the process they offer fresh perspectives on enduring issues that speak across cultures and generations. Though each of their writings has a unique particularity, they touch on themes that are universal.

There is an admirable humility in Kim's decision to write about theologies in other contexts before presuming to develop a theology from his own background. At the end of this volume he briefly sketches out a plan to address in a forthcoming project such a Korean American theology aimed at enhancing pastoral ministries in Korean American communities. The profound integration of life experiences, faith, pastoral concerns, and theological reflection he demonstrates in this current work provide a solid foundation for that future endeavor. It will be a natural and welcome extension of what he has already accomplished so splendidly in the work you now hold in your hands. Welcome to this important volume on two of the foremost theologians of our day and to Simon Kim's outstanding analysis of what they offer the theological craft and the life of faith.

Daniel G. Groody, CSC
editor of *Gustavo Gutiérrez: Spiritual Writings*

Timothy Matovina
editor of *Virgilio Elizondo: Spiritual Writings*

Preface

IN MANY WAYS THE theological reflections of Virgilio Elizondo and Gustavo Gutiérrez are examples of the ecclesial fruitfulness of the second half of the twentieth century. Following the directives of Pope John XXIII and the Second Vatican Council, Elizondo and Gutiérrez present the Gospel message in relevant terms to their own people by engaging the world as the Church of the poor. Inspired by this moment in Church history, while at the same time recognizing the plight of their people in their poor and marginal existence, Elizondo and Gutiérrez discovered a new way of doing theology by asking a specific set of questions based on their local context. By investigating where God is present in the border-crossers of Southwestern United States and the poorest of the poor in Latin America, both theologians have uncovered a hermeneutical lens in re-reading scripture and deepening our understanding of ecclesial tradition. Their particular investigations have, in turn, benefitted the universal Church and overall society by prophetically reminding us of God's intent, the *mestizo* future of humanity through our encounters and the preferential option for the poor.

Elizondo's *mestizaje* and Gutiérrez's preferential option for the poor arose out of a theology of context, a theological method that takes seriously the contextual circumstances of their locale. By utilizing the common *loci theologici* of scripture and tradition in conjunction with context and their own experience, Elizondo and Gutiérrez illustrate through their theologies how every group must embrace their own unique theological reflection. Examining their theological method and relating them to other situations such as my own has been the impetus for this book. Through the monumental efforts of Virgilio Elizondo and Gustavo Gutiérrez, we are able to reflect in a similar theological manner locating the blessings of different worlds coming together in a *mestizo* manner while at the same time locating the poor and entering into solidarity with them to enjoy true communion with God and God's own. The moment we are able to accomplish this particular, yet universal task, the Kingdom is truly ours.

Acknowledgments

W HEN I FIRST BEGAN this project I never imagined the conversion that would take place through the encounter of theologies rooted in a particular context outside my own immigrant, minority experience. Therefore, I am most appreciative to The Catholic University of America for giving me such a wonderful opportunity to grow both academically and pastorally. Academically, I was challenged to verbalize in theological categories the unique journey of Korean Americans as I walked with them pastorally during this time of studies. The interaction of pastoral and theological investigations has renewed my sense of mission in the Church and for this I am extremely thankful to the many theologians who have entered my life and nurtured this vocation.

First of all, I am extremely grateful to Virgilio Elizondo and Gustavo Gutiérrez for the interviews as well as their time and friendship. I am indebted to John Ford, who first introduced me to Hispanic/Latino theology and the works of Virgilio Elizondo. Without his encouragement and direction this book would not be possible. I am also thankful to Patrick Granfield, who deepened my understanding of liberation theology and the theological contributions of Gustavo Gutiérrez. Last, but not least, I would like to express my deep appreciation to Brian Johnstone and Paul McPartlan for their comments and encouragements in refining this work.

Since this theological investigation would be incomplete without a pastoral element, I am appreciative of the Korean American communities who have allowed me to nurture them as an immigrant Church while also nurturing me to continue my work on behalf of the next generation. In addition to the support received through various theologians and Korean American communities, this theological endeavor would not have been possible without the many benefactors who believed in me and my desires to serve the local church. During this time, both moral and financial support came in miraculous ways as is always the case within God's economy. I am grateful for the friendship, encouragement, and support from my brother priests and other religious, especially to Bill Barman, who continues to introduce me to the poor around the world; to Alejandro Solalinde, whose work with the migrant train-riders from Central America is a true inspiration to what priests are able to do with a courageous vision; to the Sisters of the Korean Martyrs who have opened their convents to me throughout the world. Friendship and support have also come through many families including my own. There are too many to list but they have always welcomed and shown me *hospitalidad* and for that I am truly grateful.

Introduction

INTRODUCING MYSELF AS A Korean American with interests in Hispanic/Latino and Latin American theology invariably elicits many questions. Two of the most common questions revolve around the connections between immigration and theology and the interest a Korean American has in theologies done outside his own minority context.

In regards to the first inquiry, I make a distinction between a theology of migration, which focuses on the departure from one's country of origin and entrance into a country of destination, from an immigration of theology, where the context of the locale gives rise to better understanding of our faith tradition and scripture. The two theologies are not in conflict, but rather complement one another. A theology of migration illustrates human mobility and thereby, the movements of God's revelation to different places and peoples. An immigration of theology illustrates the depth of God's revelation as understood in a particular cultural context.

Out of need for survival and preservation, humans have migrated from the beginning of their history. Although modern reasons for uprootedness, displacement, and reestablishment in differing locales have become more complicated due to cultural, generational, political, and economic circumstances, the same instinctual basis for survival and self-preservation still remains true. People carry with them to foreign encounters their set of beliefs; among these beliefs, their religious system gives deeper meaning to their perilious journey. Therefore, through population's movement God's revelation becomes fluid and dynamic. Rather than simply being a static set of religious tenets transferrable from one locale to another, scripture and tradition are more deeply comprehended within a specific context. Thus, an immigration of theology parallels human migration since God's revelation is not only transmitted through a specific context, but just as important, it is received and understood within a specific context.

As for the second inquiry, I believe that the theological method utilized by Virgilio Elizondo and Gustavo Gutiérrez illustrates the need for scholars to reflect seriously upon their own cultural context as they do theology. Hispanic/Latino theology and liberation theology has impacted my academic and pastoral outlook in three signficant ways. First, the works of Virgilio Elizondo and Gustavo Gutiérrez inspired me to look more intensely at myself and the people I address. No longer could I see Korean Americans simply in generic terms as another group of immigrants or a religious group subscribing only to the tenets of a faith brought over from a foreign land. I began seeing my own experience and the experiences of those around me as a hermeneutic lens in understanding God's presence among us. Second, Hispanic/Latino and Latin American liberation theology's focus on the poor, marginalized, and excluded allowed me an opportunity to see the "little ones" who receive God's preference within my own context—the poor, marginalized, and excluded through the immigration process—as well as the unique issues facing subsequent generations. Third, the theologies emerging from the Americas challenged me to imagine the possibilities of a theology specific to the Korean American experience: a theology grateful to Korea and the European influences that helped the Church overcome great obstacles in the lives of Koreans, but at the same time cognizant of the need to broaden immigration theology by incorporating Korean Americans' unique immigration history.

Thus, writing about Elizondo's *mestizaje* and Gutiérrez's preferential option for the poor in this book is absolutely relevant for minorities like my own. Because of the universal truths regarding human beings, their work speaks not only to their own in Church and society but to all immigrants especially in the Americas. The *mestizo* experience of the Mexican American people, the source of Elizondo's theological endeavors, speaks volumes since all immigrants can identify with being caught between the two worlds contained within the country of origin and the country of destination. The preferential option for the poor reflected upon by Gutiérrez throughout his writings provides the framework for identifying the poor caused especially by displacement through various forms of migration and illuminates God's grace active in their and in our solidarity with the least among us. Both theologians' contributions to their people highlight not only the hope and liberation of their unique oppressive situation, but also the universal aspects of our faith, emphasizing the hope and liberation for all humanity as God's gift of salvation.

The uniqueness of this book is bringing the works of these two theologians together, comparing and contrasting their theological endeavors, and uncovering the same theological method undertaken in a particular theological reflection. Naively, I assumed with the current immigration from Latin America to the United States, that Hispanic/Latino theology immigrated with the people as well. However, the two theologies grew independently of one another while paralleling and producing many similarities. Originally encountering the works of the two theologians in books and articles, I later had the privilege of meeting both Elizondo and Gutiérrez, learning from them in their lectures and through personal contact. One of the highlights of writing this book has been the encouragement and friendship I received from both men.

By utilizing the same theological method that seriously examines the context of one's own people and situation in light of the traditional sources of theology, namely scripture and tradition, Elizondo and Gutiérrez have made unique contributions to their people and in turn, significant contributions to the universal Church and all humanity. In brief, they have prophetically called us to perceive the world through the eyes of the poor, marginalized, and excluded. The preference these "lowly ones" receive simply for who they are gives us a glimpse of God and the reign of God. In turn, these authors' theological and pastoral endeavors allow others to enter into solidarity and fully realize God's economy for liberation and salvation. The path set by these theologians also allows others to reflect on their unique and privileged positions.

The pastoral challenge set forth by Elizondo and Gutiérrez is to denounce the injustices facing those on the margins of society, to announce the Good News contained in the poor person because of God's preference, and to celebrate the beauty contained in those often overlooked. The theological challenge posed by Elizondo and Gutiérrez is for an ongoing theological reflection where theology is not static, but rather continuously refined through the reflection on praxis of a certain group, in a particular locale, at a concrete moment of history. Through this theological reflection on God's activity within us, a particular theology is born with the poor, marginalized, and excluded as its central concern, a theology always unique and particular to one's own people.

Elizondo's and Gutiérrez's pastoral and theological endeavors are both vivid illustrations of a theology of context in which theology is always a reflection on pastoral endeavor and continuously undergoes refinement since pastoral commitments never cease. The uniqueness of a theology of context is that it makes relevant cultural influences, making theology incarnational. Thus, a theology of context is necessary and vital for all in every corner of the world. A theology of context is not an isolated endeavor, but one where engagement of the other is necessary. It is a *teología de junto*, a theology undertaken together. Before reflections and the tenets of our faith can be written, oral communication verbalizes the struggles and hopes, the sadness and joys of a people. In journeying and listening to their people—in particular, the cries of the voiceless and insignificant among them—both Elizondo and Gutiérrez have developed theologies locating the preferential option of God in their midst and calling others to solidarity with those whom God has championed. By specifically identifying how God communicates today and who is being addressed, their theologies of a particular locale have unveiled universal tenets of our faith. This universality invites us to engage and identify with the endeavors of Virgilio Elizondo and Gustavo Gutiérrez and the masses of poor, marginalized, and excluded who are always at the forefront of their minds.

The first chapter begins with a brief biographical introduction of Elizondo and Gutiérrez. Their biographical background includes the educational development that would later serve both men in their pastoral pursuits. Included in this section are the major works which have opened the door for others to enter into the world of the poor, marginalized, and excluded. Also considered within the first chapter is the ecclesial development that inspired Elizondo and Gutiérrez to reflect on their pastoral endeavors. The ecclesial situation leading up to the Second Vatican Council provided the backdrop of where such theologies irrupted. Due to the lack of philosophical and theological understanding and the Church's isolationist position in society during the Neo-Scholastic period, the Second Vatican Council was called to bring the Church up-to-date with the world and find relevant ways to communicate the Gospel message. Pope John XXIII and his desire for *aggiornamento* for the Church were an invaluable catalyst for change during this period.

In particular, John XXIII advocated for the transmission of the Gospel message in relevant terms and, most importantly, for the Church to be the Church of the poor. The sixteen documents produced at Vatican II along with the many debates on the Council floor, in the corridors, and behind closed doors fueled the imaginations of churchmen such as Elizondo and Gutiérrez. Through their understanding of Vatican II—diachronically, synchronically, and in its reception—both theologians were inspired and challenged to address the needs of their own people in their respective locales.

Due to several factors, John XXIII's call for the Church to be for all the Church of the poor never truly materialized. Rather than being discouraged, churchmen like Gutiérrez and Latin American bishops who attended the Council began making plans to live out John XXIII's vision of a Church of the poor. Through their episcopal gatherings, the *Consejo Episcopal Latinoamericano* (CELAM), particularly at Medellín and Puebla, the reception of the Second Vatican Council, understood as an ecclesial commitment to the poor, was realized. The first chapter concludes by introducing a theology of context as the theological method utilized by both Elizondo and Gutiérrez.

The second chapter is an exposition of Virgilio Elizondo's life work as "the father of Hispanic/Latino theology." In looking to his own history, a history similar to many in the Southwestern United States, Elizondo develops a *mestizo* theology which speaks to those on the borders of two worlds. To understand his own being, Elizondo reflects on the events that produced his reality today. Beginning with the Spanish conquest of Mexico in the sixteenth century, Elizondo describes how *mestizaje*, the cultural, social, and biological mixture between the Spaniards and the indigenous people, created a new offspring referred to derogatorily as *mestizos*. These neglected and oppressed offspring would eventually find their dignity in God through the appearance of Our Lady of Guadalupe, the Mother of God who appeared as one of them to one of their own, Juan Diego.

However, simply reflecting on the sixteenth century conquest was not enough for Elizondo and descendents like him since they were living on the borders of two worlds. Mexican Americans needed further historical reflections—this time regarding the conquest of the nineteenth century. Expansion westward according to the doctrine of *Manifest Destiny* led to the conquest of the indigenous people by Euro

Americans. Similar to the clash of the sixteenth century, the nineteenth century encounter produced another *mestizo* group, intensifying the cultural, social, and biological exchange and thus, furthering the people's marginalization and exclusion from society. Within this reality, a chaotic and multi-faceted existence, Elizondo is able to re-read the Gospels and uncover a previously overlooked revelation of God in the humanity of Christ.

Elizondo refers to the Galilean region where Jesus was born to make connections between the modern day *mestizo* existence of Mexican Americans and the Galilean existence of two thousand years ago. Jesus lived in a *mestizo*-type environment where his cultural, social, and biological surroundings were influenced by the many different nations that occupied the Galilean region. In this context, Elizondo defines Jesus' ministry to those on the fringes of society, in particular, those alienated because of cultural, social, biological, or religious impurities, the last of these being of primary importance to the Jewish people. The scope of Jesus' ministry to restore those living in marginalized and excluded circumstances because of their *mestizo*-type existence afforded Elizondo great hope in reaching out to Mexican Americans, who are a part neither of the United States nor Mexico, a part neither of society nor the Church. Rather than succumbing to the derogatory view of *mestizaje* of the past, Elizondo is able to find the privileged position of his reality through the understanding of God's revelation. By examining his own reality, Elizondo is able to continue the ecclesial traditions of conveying the Good News in relevant terms for his generation. Jesus is the *mestizo*-type messianic figure who calls those once considered nothing to be something valuable in God's Kingdom. Similarly, the Marian encounter in Our Lady of Guadalupe reveals the *mestiza* Madonna who appears to her children as one like them. In both these central figures of our faith, *mestizaje* becomes a constitutive element in relating the Gospel message of God becoming one of us.

The third chapter is an exposition of Gustavo Gutiérrez's life work as "the father of liberation theology." The constant underlying theme of Gutiérrez's writing is the preferential option for the poor. More commonly known for his insistence on orthopraxis and questioned for his orthodoxy, Gutiérrez has quietly left a legacy of always siding with the poor. This solidarity has led him to develop a theology and help formulate some of the social teachings of the Church in embracing the preferential option for the poor. Pastorally, Gutiérrez served in a barrio in Rimac outside of Lima, Peru. Serving the poorest of the poor for twenty years allowed Gutiérrez to reread the Gospels through their eyes. In doing so, a new understanding of God irrupted with the irruption of the poor where our activities on earth mattered in bringing about the Kingdom of God. Although earth and heaven are not identical, Gutiérrez emphasized the constitutive connection between the two, and thus the need for our action in the world. Following the ancient notion of discipleship or simply following Christ, *la sequela Christi*, Gutiérrez insists we must first live out our spirituality—a spirituality that requires us to imitate Christ in reaching out to the poor and oppressed. Only then can we achieve proper reflection allowing for true theological reflection.

Rereading scripture through the perspective of the poor, or the "underside of history," allowed Gutiérrez to conceive a Christian life that includes both the secular and the religious. Due to the massive poverty in his country, no longer could one simply dismiss the plight of the poor in hopes for a future reward in heaven. Rather, every action allowing those insignificant in society to be recognized realizes the reign of God here on earth. Suffering becomes a central theme throughout Gutiérrez's life, one exemplified by the suffering of Job in the Old Testament. Breaking away from the model of temporal retribution, the Book of Job reminds us there are those who are sinless, not guilty; yet suffer great iniquities like Job. Therefore, poverty, sickness, and immense struggles are not signs of faithlessness; like Job, the masses of those living in poverty in Latin America suffer unjustly. Job's breakthrough during his plight is not the ability to suffer or to endure patiently, but to realize there are others who also suffer unjustly around him. Through this understanding of solidarity with those around him in similar straits, Job becomes a figure interceding on behalf of others, thereby becoming a prefiguration of Christ in his own passion.

Along with his scriptural reflection, Gutiérrez has also looked to other figures in Church history for personal encouragement and theological support. The sixteenth century Spanish Dominican, Bartolomé de Las Casas experienced a conversion during his early missionary activities that led him on a great quest to defend the indigenous poor of Latin America. Through his theological defense of why the indigenous people have certain rights and his pastoral practices giving dignity to the local population, Las Casas has been singled out as a great defender of the indigenous peoples of the Americas. Gutiérrez has leaned upon him as a stalwart Church figure and a model of one who defends the poor throughout his life. Similar to Elizondo's use of the Galilean Jesus and Our Lady of Guadalupe, Gutiérrez utilizes Job of the Old Testament as the prefigurement of Christ and Bartolomé de Las Casas as embodiments of the ecclesial tradition to enter the world of the poor and live out our lives on their behalf.

The last chapter compares and contrasts Elizondo's and Gutiérrez's body of work, the geographic locales they occupy, and the specific people being addressed by these two theologians. In addition, outside critiques and further examination of the central themes of their lifework are examined. With regard to Elizondo's *mestizo* outlook, his scriptural interpretation and use of Galilee in describing the *mestizo*-type Jesus, deeper understanding of the sixteenth century Spanish conquest, and the development of our understanding of the role of Our Lady of Guadalupe for those in the past and those who still adhere to her figure and message are further examined. A closer examination of Gutiérrez's themes revolving around the preferential option for the poor, his theological understanding of the distinction of planes (the relationship of nature and grace), his identification with Bartolomé de Las Casas, and scriptural and theological interpretations in the Latin American context are also further explored.

Further examination of Elizondo's and Gutiérrez's lifework also requires a look at the future of their respective theologies. Being "fathers" of their respective theologies are only worthwhile titles if their legacies impact the next generation and continues to inspire the lives of those who come afterwards. An example of such inspiration from Elizondo's work is the carry over of the theme of *mestizaje* into the literary field in the works of John Phillip Santos. Gutiérrez's impact on other theologies emerging from the local context of the poor and oppressed can be seen in feminist, Asian, and *dalit* theology. Finally, a fairly recent field, gaining popularity in theology because of current global issues in immigration, is a theology of migration. This theological reflection on the current displacement of people has captured the imagination of many all over the world since immigration is today a global reality and crisis. Therefore, a theology of migration can be used to further highlight and illustrate the methodological schema of a theology of context along with the contribution and relevance of Elizondo's and Gutiérrez's theological offerings.

Liberation theology provides the foundation for a theology of context such as migration since those migrating are usually poor and insignificant. How does God journey with migrants and where is liberation to be found? Migration naturally means that individuals must leave their country of origin for the country of destination. No longer are migrants in their homelands; as foreigners they experience the *mestizo* realities that Elizondo often describes—being accepted neither in the country of destination nor back in their country of origin. Thus, Elizondo's theological perspective offers hope to those who are now caught in between two realities. How does one's unstable position in life bring them to a closer identification with Jesus' own humanity? A theology of migration is a pastoral necessity and as a recent theology of context illustrating the theological method of a theology of context confirms the ongoing contributions of Elizondo's and Gutiérrez's respective theologies.

In sum, Virgilio Elizondo and Gustavo Gutiérrez became pioneering theologians in their field because they began asking questions, questions not previously asked in Europe or in theology. By asking how do we speak of God to the poor, marginalized, and excluded, Elizondo and Gutiérrez have been able to respond in their own unique way. They found particular and universal answers out of their own identity and experience. Knowing and understanding one's identity allows God's communication to enter one's life in a unique, meaningful, and powerful way. Without first understanding who we are, our theological endeavor is incomplete. After all, Jesus became a human person in a specific time and locale proving our *Sitzen in Leben* also have something to convey as part of God's revelation. Therefore, our own being, whom God is addressing, is constitutive of receiving God's gift of Christ, the Church and equally important, the poor among us.

1

Movement Towards a
Theology of Context

THIS CHAPTER BEGINS WITH brief biographical introductions to
Virgilio Elizondo and Gustavo Gutiérrez. After sketching the ac-
complishments of these two pioneering theologians in their respective
fields, a brief overview regarding the state of Catholic theology leading
up to the Second Vatican Council (1962–1965) provides the backdrop
to the next section. Certain aspects of the Council are considered; in
particular, the *desiderata* of Pope John XXIII in convoking an ecumenical council along with Vatican II's impact on local theology and theologians, especially the impact of *Ad Gentes* § 22 on Elizondo's *mestizo*
theology and *Gaudium et spes* § 39 as an impetus for Gutiérrez's liberation theology. Next, CELAM (*Consejo Episcopal Latinoamericano*:
Latin American Episcopal Conference) and its conferences at Medellín
and Puebla are discussed as a continuation of John XXIII's vision for
the Church; special attention is given to the comments of both Virgilio
Elizondo and Gustavo Gutiérrez regarding these meetings. This chapter
concludes with a section on the theology of context as a prelude to the
more detailed study of the theologies of Elizondo and Gutiérrez in the
second and third chapters.

1

INTRODUCTION TO VIRGILIO ELIZONDO

This is the very paradox of church:
local yet universal, traditional yet contemporary.
The church is not an either/or, but the mystery of the unity
of the past with the present, the particular with the abso-
lute, and the finite with the infinite.[1]

This paradoxical mantra—the more local we are, the more universal we become—has been repeated throughout the life and work of Virgilio Elizondo. As a theologian, priest, and Mexican American living on the borders of two worlds—Southwestern United States and Mexico—Elizondo has consistently labored to discover his identity within a particular locale, a labor that has enriched the universal aspects of the Church and all of humanity. Through the discovery of his own marginalization in society, in the Church, and in the world, Elizondo compares his people to those who are despised and on the fringes of society in the Gospel accounts. In particular, Elizondo equates the person of Jesus surrounded by a similar set of cultural, social, and biological circumstances with those of the Mexican Americans living in the southwestern United States.[2]

This commonality allows Elizondo to reflect on the situation of the poor and outcast of the New Testament as being in a privileged position for communion with the historical Jesus. Elizondo finds Mexican Americans living in the Southwestern United States in a situation similar to those of the Gospels and thus, the Mexican Americans of today have become the privileged ones gaining insights into the Good News and the reign of God. Therefore, the paradoxical mantra—the more local we are, the more universal we become—rings true in our self-discovery in our own life situations.

> We are more and more convinced that *all* theological reflection is socially and historically conditioned. Thus we do not consider our thought to be any less authentic than that of any other theological tradition. It is just that we are very clearly aware of the point of departure of our own reflection. And we feel that this type of conditioned theological reflection is not only more honest but even more universal. For at the core of the Judeo-Christian

1. Elizondo, "Cultural Pluralism," 72 (italics added).
2. Elizondo, "Jesus the Galilean Jew," 262.

tradition is the fact that through the particular, determinate actions of a people and a person, God wrought salvation for all humankind."[3]

The localization of our reality reveals a fundamental human truth that may then be applied to the universal truth found within the Church. In other words, the local discoveries shed valuable insights on the sometimes abstract universal truths we hold. The local insights highlight the universal currents of our faith. Self-discovery, however, is not what makes the particular universal. There is a unique self-discovery that allows it to become universal. When the marginalized and excluded aspects of our lives are discovered, embraced, and reflected upon as the hermeneutic key to our existence, the universal aspects of our particular lives can be comprehended. For Elizondo, the marginalization and exclusion that exist in his world revolve around the theme of *mestizaje*:

> "Mestizo" is the Latin American expression for the English "mixed race." In Latin America it started with the European-Amerindian encounter of the 15th century when race-mixture became the regular practice throughout the land. It comes through the conjugal and spiritual encounter between persons of different ethnic groups. The process is called "*mestizaje*." In the Caribbean and in some parts of Latin America the mixture with Africans has been referred to as "*mulatez*." The Mestizo/mulatto tends to be rejected as "impure" by both parent groups. This process of racial/ethnic mixing had been prohibited in the United States, and even now is feared and abhorred by many. Mexican Mestizos in the United States were considered undesirable mongrels and inferior in every way.[4]

The *mestizo* is a person central to Elizondo's writings. It is not enough to consider the *mestizo* in his or her current environment. Rather, an intense and complex examination of the originating culture and society must be understood in relation to the current culture and society. To ignore or to separate these two worlds that give birth to

---

3. Elizondo, "American-Hispanic Theology," 54.

4. Elizondo, "Jesus the Galilean Jew," 263, footnote 2. In contemporary Spanish, *mestizo* commonly refers to a person of European and Amerindian parentage; *mulato* commonly refers to a person of European and African parentage. Other terms were used in the Spanish colonies in the Americas to describe various types of miscegenation; for example, *zambo* referred to a person of African and Amerindian parentage.

mestizaje mutilates one's identity.[5] One world cannot exist without the other and so it is also the case for Elizondo with his priestly ministry and theological writings. The underlying theme of *mestizaje* has been and presumably always will be the coming together of two worlds; contained within this "mixture" is a wealth of experiences that produce something more vibrant and life-giving for their own people and the Church.[6]

Mestizaje is not simply a conceptual notion in Elizondo's writings, but more importantly, it is a reality he lives every day. On August 28, 1935, Virgilio Elizondo was born not only into the world of San Antonio, Texas, but he was born into a world characterized by *mestizaje*. At the time of his birth, some residents of San Antonio still understood their city as the northern reaches of Mexico, while others struggled to reconcile their Latino neighborhoods with their usually well-to-do Anglo neighbors. What would eventually prove to be the fertile ground for his theology was the neighborhood and people with whom Virgilio grew up. Early in life, Virgilio was nurtured by the world that revolved around the *tienda* (store) his father owned and operated and the local church, the hub of neighborhood activities, which was literally across the street. From the beginning, the economic and religious characteristics of his neighborhood along with the political treatment of Mexican Americans in the Southwestern United States would leave their imprints on Elizondo and eventually guide his pastoral and theological endeavors.

As one of the first of his generation as well as of his family to attend college, much was expected from Virgilio. Although initially interested in the sciences as a student at St. Mary's University in San Antonio, graduating with a bachelor's degree in chemistry in 1957, Elizondo used his collegiate period to discern a priestly vocation geared towards service especially on behalf of the Mexican American population. In being true to what became his life motto—the more local, the more universal— Elizondo's formation at the seminary led him to become more aware of the treatment of Mexican Americans in the Church and society at large. Ordained to the priesthood in the Archdiocese of San Antonio in 1963, Elizondo had the experience of pastoral ministry in several local

5. *Mestizaje*—a substantive derived from *mestizo*—has the basic meaning of "mixing" or "mixture" and is used in a wide variety of contexts: biological, cultural, political, social, etc.

6. In this respect, *mestizaje* resembles the biological phenomenon of "hybrid vigor"—the superior qualities that result from crossbreeding genetically different plants and animals.

parishes and served as the academic dean at Assumption Seminary in the Archdiocese before continuing his studies abroad.

In the late 1960s, Virgilio Elizondo continued his educational formation in the Philippines where he began honing his theological and catechetical skills. In 1969, Elizondo received an M.A. in Pastoral Studies from the Ateneo de Manila and a diploma in Pastoral Catechetics from the East Asian Pastoral Institute. He then returned to San Antonio to implement this new catechetical approach in the archdiocese as well as to mentor others on behalf of Mexican Americans. In 1972, Elizondo established the Mexican American Cultural Center in San Antonio with the help of PADRES, an association of Mexican American priests who embraced a similar vision of outreach and training of Hispanic leaders in the Church.[7]

Soon afterwards, Elizondo embarked on another educational journey; this time his theological formation led him to Paris, France. During his doctoral studies, Elizondo refined the notion of *mestizaje* that he had experienced in the United States into a theological category which would define the rest of his ministry. In 1978, Elizondo received his doctoral degree from the Institut Catholique for his work on *mestizo* Christianity: *Mestizaje: The Dialectic of Birth and the Gospel*. This dissertation was eventually revised and became one of his seminal works, *Galilean Journey: The Mexican American Promise*. The theme of *mestizaje* was also prominent in Elizondo's other theological writings—especially *The Future is Mestizo: Life Where Cultures Meet*.

Virgilio Elizondo was very active in the formation of the *Ecumenical Association of Third World Theologians* (EATWOT), a group that brought together theologians from Asia, Africa, Latin America along with minorities residing within the United States during the mid-seventies. While serving on the editorial board of *Concilium*[8] from 1979 to 1999, he also served as rector of San Fernando Cathedral, the oldest cathedral in the United States. There he had the opportunity of implementing a pastoral plan for Mexican Americans, the culmination of years of worldwide theological education. Although some felt Elizondo's skills

7. PADRES—an ancronym for *Padres Asociados para Derechos Religiosos, Educativos y Sociales*—began as an advocacy movement among Hispanic priests around 1969 but went out of existence a couple decades later.

8. As an editor of *Concilium*, Virgilio Elizondo edited such diverse editions as "Women in a Man's Church," "Any Room for Christ in Asia," "1492–1992: The Voice of the Victims," "Tensions between the Churches of the Third World and First World," etc.

as a theologian would be lost by serving as rector of a cathedral filled with elderly parishioners, Elizondo returned to his roots as a pastor first, theologian second, by taking on the challenges of this downtown parish. Soon his love for the people—meeting them where they were and welcoming them to the cathedral—manifested itself as one of the most amazing transformations of the Church in the United States. By embracing the people with all their customs and heritage, Elizondo was able not only to revive the cultural and religious celebrations of the past but also to transform them into a new reality relevant for Mexican Americans today. The popularity of Elizondo's pastoral approach led to national acclaim as the celebrations of San Fernando Cathedral were broadcast internationally.[9]

Elizondo's efforts have transcended the walls of Catholicism bringing him attention as a Mexican American pioneer recognized and honored by many outside the Church. For instance, in 2000, TIME magazine recognized Elizondo as one of the century's leading spiritual innovators, while other groups ranging from Hispanic educators to science foundations have honored him for his untiring work in linking faith and culture. Elizondo has received numerous awards based on his theological writings as well as his pastoral and catechetical work. A few worthy of mention are: the Laetare Medal (1997), the University of Notre Dame's highest honor; the Johannes Quasten Award (1997) for excellence and leadership in theological development presented by The Catholic University of America; the President's Award of the National Federation of Priest's Councils (1992) for outstanding priestly leadership in the United States; and the John Courtney Murray Award (2008) by the Catholic Theological Society of America for his theological contributions.

The praise and acclaim that Virgilo Elizondo has received for his work illustrate its relevance and importance for both Church and society. The reality Elizondo writes about stems from his personal experience as a Mexican American, as a Catholic, and as a priest living in the southwestern region of the United States. However, his personal and

9. Because his work with the *mestizaje* of San Antonio involved the interaction between life and culture, evangelization, and Church, Elizondo has been invited to teach in Europe, Asia, Africa, Australia, and Latin America on subjects such as "evangelization and inculturation." Elizondo mentions his amazement at how others have seen value in discerning their own situation out of a very local experience such as his.

individual heritage transcends the regional locale, for his theology and pastoral actions resonate within human beings worldwide regardless of their location. Simply stated, the truth—the more local we are, the more universal we become—is evident in the life, work, and passions of Virgilio Elizondo, while his message of *mestizaje* reveals the true nature of our humanity. The truthfulness of this humanity reveals: the past, where we have come from; the present in the struggles of embracing who we are; and the future, where we need to go in religion and society.

INTRODUCTION TO GUSTAVO GUTIÉRREZ

My book is a love letter to God, to the Church,
and to the people to which I belong.
Love remains alive,
but it grows deeper and changes its manner of expression.[10]

This response—which was given by Gustavo Gutiérrez to a journalist when asked almost two decades later whether he would still write *A Theology of Liberation*—reveals his commitment then and now to God, the Church, and to the poor. Gutiérrez was not willing to revise his seminal work for its anniversary printing; instead he insisted that what was born not only from his theological endeavors but, more importantly, from his solidarity with the poorest of the poor years ago remains true today. Although situations, concepts, and language undergo development, for Gutiérrez, what allows for those changes to occur is the foundation on which they are built. A theology of liberation or more appropriately, a spirituality of liberation, is a foundation, one that cannot be changed without affecting everything else that has occurred in the history of Latin America. This foundation, with all its wonders and distresses, is essential for what has since developed within the mind of Gutiérrez and for the theology that is being done on behalf of the Latin American poor.

Regardless of whether Gutiérrez is seen as a theologian, a priest, or a Latino, his love for God and the poor within the Church is never in doubt. How deep must love and conviction run in a person in order to endure the years of questioning regarding one's orthodoxy and fidelity

---

10. Gutiérrez, *Teología de la liberación*, translated by Inda and Eagleson as *A Theology of Liberation*, xlvi (italics added).

to the Church? The willingness of Gutiérrez to defend his beliefs, then and now, indicates an intimate connection between his thoughts and the people with whom he identifies as the privileged ones of the Kingdom. As he continues to defend his theology, Gutiérrez is not just pained by the criticism of his theological concepts, but more importantly, is moved by the fact that the poor are being forgotten economically, politically, and theologically by the developed world: "Recent years have witnessed an important debate on the theology of liberation in the context of the Catholic Church. It has meant some painful moments at the personal level, usually for reasons that eventually pass away. The important thing, however, is that the debate has been an enriching spiritual experience. It has also been an opportunity to renew in depth our fidelity to the church in which all of us as a community believe and hope in the Lord, as well as to reassert our solidarity with the poor, those privileged members of the reign of God."[11]

Gustavo Gutiérrez Merino, whose work has impacted not just the theological world but the lives of many in all walks of life, was born on June 8, 1928. The location and manner he came into the world defined his identity and the direction of his theology. Gutiérrez was born with a Hispanic and Quechuan heritage. As a *mestizo*, Gutiérrez is identified with those living on the fringes of his culture. Being born in the barrio of Monserrat in Lima, Peru, also located Gutiérrez on the economic fringes of society. His humble beginnings would be important later in life especially after his ordination to the priesthood when Gutiérrez felt most distant from the world of his origin. Having an education and being ordained removed Gutiérrez from the impoverished world of his birth. From that point on, he would work diligently to remain in solidarity with the poor. No longer was Gutiérrez automatically in the world of the poor, but he would have to commit daily to live in solidarity with them.

In his early years, Gutiérrez was stricken with polio. Spending much time in bed allowed the young Gutiérrez time to engage in studies which would later aid his education abroad. At first, Gutiérrez pursued a career in medicine, perhaps inspired by his childhood illness. However, his study of medicine would eventually steer him to the priesthood. After his philosophical training at the seminary in Santiago, Chile, Gutiérrez's capacity for learning landed him in Europe where he continued his education: first at Louvain, Belgium, where he furthered his

11. Ibid., xxiii.

philosophical education along with studies in psychology, then at the Université Catholique de Lyon and the Gregorian University in Rome for his theological studies.

In 1959, Gustavo Gutiérrez was ordained to the priesthood in Rome and returned to Peru to begin his pastoral ministry in the slum areas of Rimac, a barrio on the outskirts of Lima. There Gutiérrez began developing his theology addressing the situation of the poor. During the sixties, the parish *Iglesia Cristo Redentor* (Church of Christ the Redeemer) would provide the venue for Gutiérrez to re-read the Gospel in light of the situation of his people. This interpretation of the Gospel would eventually bear fruit in his writings that verbalize the struggles of the people and is known today as a theology of liberation.

In 1968, Gutiérrez's article "Towards a Theology of Liberation" was published in preparation for the Latin American Episcopal Conference (CELAM) at Medellín (1968). In 1971, Gutiérrez's seminal work *Teología de la liberación* continued the theme of his initial article and further illustrated the dynamics of the Church in the barrios of Peru. Standing at the forefront of this new way of thinking, Gutiérrez became known as "the father of liberation theology;" however, he would be the first to shy away from this title. As a pastor, he insists that the real founders of liberation theology are the people who struggle to live out the Christian faith in their daily lives. He maintains he is primarily a pastor and theology is something he is able to do in his spare time. Although desiring more time for theological exploration and writing, his heart as a parish priest is always directed to the lives of his parishioners. Gutiérrez is quick to point out that he had never been on a university faculty fulltime until his recent appointment at the University of Notre Dame; until then, he has always considered his pastoral calling as his vocation.

Gutiérrez continued to add to his body of works in the following decades by developing the themes found in *Teología de la liberación*. He has written many articles following his seminal work; however, most of his major themes have appeared in book form. Between 1979 and 1992, he published the following works that complement the original: *La fuerza histórica de los pobres: selección de trabajos*[12]; *El Dios de la vida*[13]; *Beber en su propio pozo: en el itinerario espiritual de un pueblo*[14];

---

12. Translated by Barr as *The Power of the Poor in History*.

13. Translated by O'Connell as *The God of Life*.

14. Translated by O'Connell as *We Drink from our own Wells: The Spiritual Journey*

La verdad los hará libres: confrontaciones[15]; *Hablar de Dios desde el suf-rimiento del inocente: una reflexión sobre el libro de Job*[16]; and *En busca de los pobres de Jesucristo: El pensamiento de Bartolomé de Las Casas*[17]. In 1985, he defended the body of his earlier works for his doctorate at the Université Catholique de Lyon.

Gutiérrez would be the first to mention that the theology of liberation occurs in the people struggling in poverty and oppression and not necessarily in the theologians, clergy, or other professionals who report on the activities of the masses. Since the starting point of liberation theology is to address the non-person, those who are considered insignificant and less than human because of the injustices of society, and because the real work of liberation occurs on this level, it seems only appropriate for Gutiérrez to broaden his outreach to the poorest of the poor in his pastoral ministry. In 1974, Gutiérrez, with other supporters, created the Instituto Bartolomé de las Casas-Rimac to respond to the atrocities committed against the economic poor as well as against the native Indians, the original inhabitants of Latin America. Named after Gutiérrez's hero in Latin America's Catholic history, Bartolomé de las Casas, a defender of native Indians during the Spanish conquest in the sixteenth century, the institute has become a vehicle in publicizing the realities of the poor through the writings of Gutiérrez and others.

In addition to growing as a priest, theologian, and a leader in the Latin American community through his pastoral experience in serving the local community of Rimac, Gutiérrez also grew by serving the Church through various ministries. For instance, Gutiérrez served on the faculty at the Pontifical University of Peru, as a chaplain to the National Movement of Catholic University Students (UNEC), and as a member of the Peruvian Academy of Language. On the international scene, Gutiérrez was instrumental in drafting the documents of the Latin American Episcopal Conference (CELAM) at Medellín (1968) and Puebla (1979) and served as an advisor to the Committee on University Pastoral Problems.

Gutiérrez has served as a visiting professor in several universities. Currently, he is the John Cardinal O'Hara Professor of Theology at the

---

of a People.

15. Translated by O'Connell as *The Truth Shall Make You Free: Confrontations.*

16. Translated by O'Connell as *On Job: God-Talk and The Suffering of The Innocent.*

17. Translated by Barr as *Las Casas: In Search of the Poor of Jesus Christ.*

University of Notre Dame. He has also served as a member of the board of directors of the international journal, *Concilium*. Whether in the trenches of the barrios of his homeland or in the classrooms of developed nations, his work on behalf of the poor has not gone unnoticed. He has been awarded honorary degrees by some twenty universities and in 1993, he received the Legion of Honor from the French government for his lifework on behalf of the poor and the oppressed.

It has not been a smooth journey for Gutiérrez and other liberation theologians working with the poor within the context of their respective governments and societies, as well as within the Church. The thousands of martyrs and extensive violence during this time reveal the tension not only in society but also within the Church. Liberation theology and liberation theologians were also targeted by the Vatican. In 1984, the Congregation for the Doctrine of the Faith (CDF) published its first official statement, *Libertatis nuntius*,[18] regarding the theology of liberation. While maintaining that the "theology of liberation" contains "a grain of truth," *Libertatis nuntius* stated that there are many variants of this theology whose "novel interpretations" of the Christian faith and adherence to the Marxist fundamental option "constitutes a practical negation" of some of its positions by its inner discontinuity.[19] Then, in 1986, the Congregation's *Libertatis conscientia*[20] criticized the Marxist influence while attempting to sooth the harsh tone of *Libertatis nuntius*. *Libertatis conscientia* asserted that the Congregation's two documents must be read together in an "organic relationship".[21] In recent years, the Vatican's tone about liberation theology has been much more neutral. At the 2007 Latin American Episcopal Conference (CELAM) in Brazil, Pope Benedict XVI presented a balanced view of the oppressive situation in Latin America by pointing to the destructive errors and false notion of reality of both the Marxist and capitalist system.[22]

Speaking over two decades earlier, Gutiérrez prophetically stated: "The passage of time has caused essentials to become clearer. Secondary elements have lost the importance they seemed to have at an earlier period. A process of maturation has been under way. But the temporal *factor*

18. CDF, "Instruction on Certain Aspects,"; hereafter cited: *Libertatis nuntius*.

19. See Ratzinger, "Liberation Theology," 174–75; *Libertatis nuntius*, VI: 9.

20. CDF, "Instruction on Christian Freedom"; hereafter cited: *Libertatis conscientia*.

21. Ibid., 2.

22. Benedict XVI, "Brazil Visit: Address to CELAM," 3.

is not the only one affecting the course of liberation theology during these years. There has also been a *spatial* extension."[23] Today, Gutiérrez considers Benedict XVI's address at Aparecida as being more favorable and supportive than any other pontiff's address at CELAM: "Oh certainly, I think the speech of Benedict is the best speech addressed today in the Latin American Bishop Conference—is better than the speech of Paul VI [at Medellín]; is better than the speech of John Paul [at Puebla]."[24]

IMPETUS FOR A THEOLOGY OF CONTEXT

Prior to the Second Vatican Council, the Church was entrenched in the ideals of medieval Christendom advocating a Neo-Scholasticism in opposition to modernity: "The era is marked by a desire for Restoration, and it is medieval Christendom, insofar as it realized the proper relationship between the Church and civil society, whose restoration is desired."[25] Not only was the Church hostile to modern society, but it also sought to impose an earlier relationship of the Church upon the world, one which existed in the Middle Ages. This period was not simply Tridentine Catholicism, but a time that encapsulated a specific movement of the Church, closed to the world and seen as relevant only to herself. "This modern Roman Catholicism took the form of a counter-society, legitimated by a counter-culture, as a response to and in opposition to the emerging liberal culture and society which advanced with such apparent inexorability throughout those years."[26] This attitude was found at all levels of the Church, from the hierarchy to the faithful in the pews, insofar as Catholic associations in the nineteenth century "not only multiplied and flourished but began also to take on the social and political goals of opposing the spread of liberalism, of safeguarding Catholic rights, and of supporting Catholic identity and solidarity in an increasingly alien world."[27]

During the time between the First and Second Vatican Councils, papal authority became increasingly more centralized. This was a shift

23. Gutiérrez, *Theology of Liberation*, xix.

24. See Appendix B.

25. Komonchak, "Modernity," 361.

26. Ibid., 356.

27. Ibid., 369.

from the earlier period of decentralization when national Churches and Gallicanism gained popularity. The decentralized Gallican movement gave way to centralized Roman authority as the French Revolution revealed the ineffectiveness of national Churches and their religious leaders.[28] The external turmoil surrounding the Church, particularly in Church-state relations, also led to internal turmoil as theological endeavors in this period became irrelevant: "The Church did not emerge from the theologically mediocre eighteenth century and from the politically disastrous experiences of the Revolution with great intellectual resources. Catholic philosophy and theology for the most of the first half of the nineteenth century were for the most part uncritical and eclectic . . . As the century moved on, it saw an unprecedented increase in the claims of Rome over the intellectual life of the Church."[29] The lack of intellectual integrity and uses of outmoded philosophical and theological approaches contributed to the need for an ecumenical council to address the position of the Church, both internally and externally, in a different light.

POPE JOHN XXIII AND THE SECOND VATICAN COUNCIL

> It is this modern Catholicism which was seriously challenged at the Second Vatican Council. Briefly stated, the hypothesis is that in three respects the Council called into question the logic of modern Roman Catholicism. It produced a much more positive assessment of modernity in its intellectual, social and political aspects. It called for an *aggiornamento* and reform of Church worship, devotion and practice, which in effect called into question the procedures by which the Church had always, at least within anyone's memory, reproduced itself. And it encouraged local Catholic Churches to engage in an active effort to achieve culturally distinct and relevant realizations of Catholicism in their several areas.[30]

More importantly, the vision for the ecumenical council presented by Pope John XXIII was not a separation of the Church and the world, but a rather a healthy relationship between the two in which the Church was

28. Ibid., 371–72.
29. Ibid., 373–74.
30. Ibid., 384.

able to communicate to the world the Gospel message in relevant terms. In a speech prior to the opening of Vatican II, John XXIII addressed the new political world: "The ecumenical council is about to assemble 17 years after the end of the Second World War. For the first time in history, the Fathers of the Council belong, in reality, to all peoples and nations. Each of them will bring his contribution of intelligence and of experience, to cure and heal the wounds of the two conflicts which have changed profoundly the face of all countries."[31] And in his opening speech at the Second Vatican Council, John XXIII emphasized both religious and secular unity so the Council might speak to all people and nations: "Venerable brothers, such is the aim of the Second Vatican Council, which, while bringing together the Church's best energies and striving to have man welcome more favorably the good tidings of salvation, prepares, as it were, and consolidates the path toward that unity of mankind which is required as a necessary foundation in order that the earthly city may be brought to the resemblance of that heavenly city where truth reigns, charity is the law, and whose extent is eternity."[32]

Although Elizondo and Gutiérrez have been relatively silent about the period leading up to the Council other than their vindication of the *Nouvelle Théologie*, the inspiration they gained from the Council and its vision illustrates the conciliar impact on their theological endeavors.[33] Both Elizondo and Gutiérrez studied in Europe and were taught by theologians such as Yves Congar[34] and Marie Dominique Chenu,[35] theologians who were influential in shaping the discussions at Vatican II. Thus, it is no surprise that both Elizondo and Gutiérrez followed and

31. John XXIII, "Pope's Address to World," 20.

32. John XXIII, "*Gaudet mater ecclesia*," 28.

33. *La Nouvelle Théologie*, which emerged in France after the Second World War, advocated a renewal of theology, and thus the Church, by a return to biblical and patristic sources (*ressourcement*); criticized by its opponents as a "new theology" that purportedly distorted the Church's traditional theology, *la Nouvelle Théologie* gained acceptance at the Second Vatican Council.

34. Yves-Marie-Joseph Congar (18 April 1904–22 June 1995), ordained a Dominican priest in 1930, served as a French Army chaplain in World War II and was a prisoner of war (1940–1945); forbidden to teach or publish during the latter part of the pontificate of Pope Pius XII, he was a *peritus* at Vatican II and was named a cardinal-deacon by Pope John Paul II in 1994.

35. Marie-Dominique Chenu (6 January 1895–11 February 1990) entered the Dominicans in 1913; after studying at the Angelicum in Rome, he taught at Le Saulchoir, but was eventually relieved of his teaching post; later, he was a *peritus* at Vatican II.

then went beyond their mentors: "[f]rom about 1930 to Vatican II Latin American theological liberals were content to follow French theology, enthusiastically if not creatively, for French theology then represented the Catholic avant-garde."[36] As Richard Gaillardetz has observed: "The true import of the Second Vatican Council, however, goes far beyond any of its documents. As with every ecumenical council, Vatican II was an ecclesial event. By this I do not mean merely that it was the twenty-first in a series of ecclesiastical meetings of bishops and other Church leaders. Vatican II was an ecclesial event in the sense that in the planning and conduct of the council we see the nature of the Church itself in microcosm."[37]

Soon after his election as Roman pontiff, John XXIII surprised both the ecclesial and secular world by calling for a general council—a surprise to those who did not see a need for another council after the First Vatican Council (1869–1870). "Pope John envisioned a Church to be poised for a dramatic outpouring of the Holy Spirit that would be, in his term, a 'New Pentecost.'"[38] To move the Church towards this vision, John XXIII called for an internal and external renewal by placing the Church in a positive relationship with the world. To foster this relationship, toward which the Church had been so hostile in the past, a new way of presenting the Gospel was needed. During the period of preparation for the Council, John XXIII expressed three *desiderata* in order for the Church to communicate effectively the Gospel: first, a renewal of the relationship of the Church to herself; second, a renewal of the relationship of the Church to the world; and third, becoming the Church of the poor—these were the vehicles the pope envisioned for the faithful transmission of the Gospel message to the current generation.

First, by examining the internal relationships of the Church, the Church would have the internal fortitude to proclaim the Gospel to the faithful. "The Church wishes to be sought again as she is, in her internal structure—vitality in her own behalf—in the act of presenting anew, above all to her children, the treasures of enlightening faith and of sanctifying grace, which take their inspiration from those final words of Christ. They are words which express the preeminent task of the Church, her titles of service and of honor, namely, to vivify, to teach and

36. Gutiérrez, "Two Theological Perspectives," 245.
37. Gaillardetz, *Church in the Making*, xiii.
38. Twomey, *Preferential Option for the Poor*, 42.

to pray."[39] Second, by examining the "signs of the times" and dialoguing with the world, the Church would be able to communicate the deposit of faith in a relevant manner. "It is from this sense of responsibility before the duties of the Christian called to live as a man among men, as a Christian among Christians, that so many others, who, although not Christians, in reality ought to feel themselves drawn by good example to become Christians . . . The world indeed has need of Christ, and it is the Church which must bring Christ to the world . . . The ecumenical council will be able to present, in clear language, solutions which are demanded by the dignity of man and of his vocation as a Christian."[40] Third, by becoming the Church of the poor, she would gain credibility proclaiming the Gospel in the world. A month prior to the opening of the Council, John XXIII stated: "Confronted with the underdeveloped countries, the Church presents itself as it is and wishes to be, as the Church of all, and particularly as the Church of the poor."[41] Again, "[t]his concern was categorically and prophetically expressed by Pope John XXIII at the Vatican Council: in the call for the Church to become the Church of all, and in particular the Church of the poor (11 September 1962)."[42]

Although, John XXIII remained behind the scenes for most of the Council's first session, his reasons for gathering the Council Fathers need to be kept in mind in order to appreciate the discussions (or lack thereof) on the Council floor. Two of John XXIII's three *desiderata* were addressed by Cardinal Leon-Joseph Suenens[43] of Belgium, who proposed an approach taken from trinitarian theology:[44] "Near the end of the first session, he proposed that the Council consider the Church under two aspects: the Church *ad intra*, or its inner life, and the Church *ad extra*, its relationship to the world."[45] The first *desideratum* of John XXIII was achieved in one of the principal documents, *Lumen Gentium*, where

39. John XXIII, "Pope's Address to World," 19.

40. Ibid.

41. Ibid., 19.

42. Gutiérrez, "Task and Content," 25.

43. Leo Jozef Suenens (16 July 1904–6 May 1996) ordained a priest in 1927, was named: auxiliary bishop of Mechelen (Belgium) in 1945, Archbishop of Mechelen, 1961–1979, and a cardinal in 1962.

44. Gaillardetz, *Church in the Making*, 14.

45. Ibid.

the Council Fathers examined the Church's internal relationships, for example the collegiality of the bishops along with the *sensus fidelium* of the laity. The second *desideratum* was achieved in *Gaudium et spes* at the close of the Vatican Council. Looking at the Church's relationship with the world, the Council Fathers set the Church on a course to dialogue with, to learn from, and to contribute to the world.

The third and final *desideratum* did not materialize as John XXIII had hoped. Although efforts were made by Cardinal Giacomo Lercaro[46] of Bologna to bring to the Council floor the theme of the Church of the poor for discussion, there was not adequate reflection on the Church of the poor. The only remnant of Lercaro's efforts appears in *Lumen Gentium*, § 8:

> Just as Christ carried out the work of redemption in poverty and oppression, so the Church is called to follow the same path if she is to communicate the fruits of salvation to men. Christ Jesus, "though He was by nature God . . . emptied Himself, taking the nature of a slave" (Phil. 2:6,7), and "being rich, became poor" (2 Cor. 8:9) for our sakes. Likewise, the Church, although she needs human resources to carry out her mission, is not set up to seek earthly glory, but to proclaim, and this by her own example, humility and self-sacrifice. Christ was sent by the Father "to bring good news to the poor . . . to heal the contrite of heart" (Lk. 4:18), "to seek and to save what was lost" (Lk. 4:18). Similarly, the Church encompasses with her love all those who are afflicted by human misery and she recognizes in those who are poor and who suffer, the image of her poor and suffering Founder. She does all in her power to relieve their need and in them she strives to serve Christ.[47]

On the one hand, most of the bishops and theologians active at the Council were from either Europe or the United States, and thus unfamiliar with the poverty of the Third World at that time. On the other hand, the Council documents were primarily intended for the western industrialized First World, and thus the countries most affected by poverty took a secondary position.

---

46. Giacomo Lercaro (28 October 1891–18 October 1976), ordained a priest in 1914, served as Archbishop of Ravenna e Cervia (1947–1952) and Archbishop of Bologna (1952–1968) and was named a cardinal in 1953.

47. Quotations of Vatican II are from Austin Flannery, ed., *Vatican Council II*, Volume 1, *The Conciliar and Postconciliar Documents*.

Gutiérrez has recalled the joy and sadness that arose within him during the Council, especially at its close: "I remember well the last two days of this session—December 7 and 8, 1965. One side of myself was very happy because finally the theology that I had studied in France was being well received."[48] However, the vindication of theological approaches that Gutiérrez called his own did not address the realities of his people in Latin America. This dichotomy between the recognition of theology being done in France by the Council Fathers and the lack of recognition of his own reality back home weighed heavily on Gutiérrez: "But it was also a difficult year in Latin America in the struggle of many popular groups for justice and liberation. I felt during that year what the French call *sentiments mélanges*, or mixed feelings. I was happy, yet at the same time I saw that it was not enough for my reality. My theology belonged to the Western world, but myself belonged to another world."[49] This sadness overwhelmed the vindications of Vatican II and Gutiérrez remained by himself as others celebrated the close of the Council: "I was not present for the conclusion of Vatican II. I was in Rome, but I preferred to stay in my room and listen by radio because it felt like a kind of contradiction for me. I was happy, but on the other hand, it was not enough."[50] His loneliness in his room in Rome over the Council's failure to address the situation in Latin America became one of the motivating factors for his life's work. "This moment was my starting point for many things, including the first seeds of liberation theology. Certainly at that moment I didn't have the exact idea of liberation theology in my mind, but I began to perceive this Western theology as not enough for the reality of my people."[51]

The meaning and impact of the Second Vatican Council are still debated today. Recently, Pope Benedict XVI has insisted that Vatican II should be read, not as an isolated event, but as a continuation of the Church's tradition in promulgating documents regarding the deposit of faith.[52] Advocating a proper hermeneutical lens in understanding the Second Vatican Council, the pope contrasted the "hermeneutics of discontinuity and rupture" with a "hermeneutics of reform." "Well, it all

48. Gutiérrez, "Opting for the Poor," 12.

49. Ibid.

50. Ibid.

51. Ibid.

52. Benedict XVI, "Christmas Greetings" (22 December 2005).

depends on the correct interpretation of the Council or—as we would say today—on its proper hermeneutics, the correct key to its interpretation and application. The problems in its implementation arose from the fact that two contrary hermeneutics came face to face and [quarreled] with each other. One caused confusion, the other, silently but more and more visibly, bore and is bearing fruit."[53]

Benedict XVI's contrasting of two hermeneutic lenses in comprehending the Second Vatican Council is reminiscent of the theological division that emerged with regard to the Council's final document, *Gaudium et spes*—a division that would continue to affect the Church in interpreting the Council. What emerged from the debates about the final document and continued to grow in the reception of the conciliar documents were two schools of thought regarding *ressourcement* and *aggiornamento*:

> This *ressourcement* led to a recovery of a more theological understanding of the Church grounded in baptism and Eucharist rather than in law and jurisdiction. It meant a return to the liturgical spirituality of the first millennium in preference to the arid mechanistic view of the liturgy and sacraments that dominated in neo-scholasticism . . . The work of *aggiornamento* demanded a policy of active and respectful engagement with the world out of a confident expectation that the hand of God was at work in the world. It called for a new ecumenical impulse. This theological perspective, with its relatively greater confidence in God's action in the world, reflected not so much the patristic theological vision of the first millennium as the theological vision associated with the thirteenth-century Dominican, St. Thomas Aquinas.[54]

In spite of the differing schools of thought regarding the Council's texts or the debate over which hermeneutical lens bears fruit, a healthy and comprehensive approach to Vatican II is to look at the Council diachronically, synchronically, and by its reception. Diachronically, Vatican II is understood by the developments in preparing the conciliar documents. Conciliar documents, prepared prior to the gathering in Rome, underwent major or minor revisions and sometimes even outright rejection by the Council Fathers before reaching their final form. Therefore, each document must be understood in its context of development:

53. Ibid.
54. Gaillardetz, *Church in the Making*, xvii.

from inception, through discussion on the Council floor, to revision, and finally to final form. "[A diachronic] reading requires a careful consideration of the sources from which a text draws, the history of its development, and a consideration of the questions it was intended and not intended to address. Such a reading will also identify an emerging trajectory of development that may in fact point beyond the council."[55]

Synchronically, Vatican II is understood when viewing the conciliar documents in relation to one another. Each conciliar document becomes a hermeneutic key in understanding another text since the "whole corpus of conciliar documents [may] shape the way that a particular text is read".[56]

Third, in terms of the reception of Vatican II, it is important to examine what has been emphasized or neglected in the post-conciliar instructions especially regarding the different cultures in which the Church is situated. "Vatican II, for reasons that are well known and easy to understand, did not fully take up John XXIII's proposal, even though this concern was at the fore during much of the work of the Council . . . Alongside the fact of the new presence of the poor, the idea of a Church of the poor stimulated considerable theological reflection."[57]

One of the ways the Latin American Church has been a blessing to the universal Church is to illustrate the reception of Vatican II in the Third World and to continue the vision of John XXIII as being the Church of the poor. Although forty-five years have passed since the close of Vatican II, the time needed to understand its full impact may be two or three times this length—as history has shown in the case of past ecumenical councils. Nonetheless, the fruits of Vatican II are being realized in various parts of the world, especially in Latin America. As Gutiérrez has observed: "As time passes and the conciliar event comes into better perspective, the stature of John XXIII also increases. Not everything has yet been said about his reasons for calling the Council or about the tasks he meant Vatican II to carry out."[58]

Both Virgilio Elizondo and Gustavo Gutiérrez were inspired and motivated by Vatican II. In part, their mentoring by theologians of *la Nouvelle Théologie* naturally led them to a feeling of vindication of the

55. Ibid., xviii.

56. Ibid., xix.

57. Gutiérrez, "Task and Content," 25.

58. Gutiérrez, "Church and the Poor," 173.

theological method in which they were educated. However, as Gutiérrez pointed out in his personal reflections, the Second Vatican Council also raised mixed feelings as it fell short of John XXIII's vision of the Church of the poor. Rather than allowing this to hinder their theological investigations, Elizondo and Gutiérrez took the instructions of Vatican II—even in its limitations when speaking to people with Latin American heritage—to develop pastoral plans which spoke to their unique situations. Instead of lamenting the shortcomings of the Council, both Elizondo and Gutiérrez feel compelled to carry on the work of the Council by proclaiming the Gospel in a relevant manner for today especially in light of the struggles of their people.

Ad Gentes § 22: The Conciliar Foundation for Elizondo's Mestizo Theology

In his classes at the University of Notre Dame, Elizondo teaches how *Dei Verbum* influenced his understanding of scripture and how he reads the bible culturally through the lens of the Mexican American struggle. The Old Testament recalls how God spoke to the chosen people through prophets. In the New Testament, Jesus is God's communication *par excellence*. Taking these precedents from scripture, *Dei Verbum* presented God's Word as being communicated in the past yet continuing today as well. Accordingly, Elizondo looks to his own historical past to see how God speaks to the Mexican American people today: if God used signs, symbols, and stories relevant to the people in scripture, then God continues to use human elements to communicate the divine today. By examining closely the lives of the Mexican American people, Elizondo is able to locate where God is present and to communicate the hope that comes from the presence of the divine in the midst of his people: "The Council did not call for a cultural *mestizaje* as such, but if we carry out its instructions, a cultural *mestizaje* will take place."[59]

To locate a cultural *mestizaje* that would serve as a hermeneutic lens for understanding revelation, Elizondo uses the evangelical directives of Vatican II, especially *Ad Gentes § 22*: "Vatican II in its decree on missionary activity returned to the earliest Christian tradition of evangelisation. It spoke about its mission to evangelise without destroying the

---

59. Elizondo, *Future is Mestizo*, 105.

native cultures, thus giving birth to truly local Churches."[60] *Ad Gentes* §
22 stated:

> The seed which is the word of God grows out of good soil wa-
> tered by the divine dew, it absorbs moisture, transforms it, and
> makes it part of itself, so that eventually it bears much fruit. So
> too indeed, just as happened in the economy of the incarnation,
> the young Churches, which are rooted in Christ and built on the
> foundations of the apostles, take over all the riches of the na-
> tions which have been given to Christ as an inheritance (cf. Ps.
> 2:8). *They borrow from the customs, traditions, wisdom, teaching,*
> *arts and sciences of their people everything which could be used to*
> *praise the glory of the Creator, manifest the grace of the saviour, or*
> *contribute to the right ordering of Christian life.*

By seeing the Mexican American community as one of the young
Churches, rich in custom and tradition, Elizondo sees *mestizaje* as part
of the vision of the Council Fathers: "Our task in going to serve is not to
destroy what is there but gradually, through patient dialogue, becoming
one with what is there, and out of the position of unity, assist the people
in discovering that which is good and beautiful in them, and then begin
to ennoble it, to perfect it, and to carry it beyond its present limitations."[61]

Although it could be argued that *Ad Gentes* was a document addressing foreign missionary territories where Christianity is unfamiliar,
Elizondo argues that the premise of such evangelization is still rooted in
the Incarnation and is thus, applicable to every situation. The question
of how to incarnate the human Jesus in a particular culture and people
is relevant not only for mission territories but for all communities trying
to identify their own history with salvation history. The Incarnation is
at the heart of *Ad Gentes*. The Incarnation was also at the heart of John
XXIII's reason for calling a Council to present the Gospel in a manner
relevant to the world. And the Incarnation is at the heart of Elizondo's
mestizo theology where the Mexican American situation becomes the
fertile soil for spreading the Gospel:

> [I]t is not a question of merely translating or adapting the the-
> ologies of the North Atlantic into the native languages, but of
> allowing the new community of believers to grow and develop
> in the Christian faith alive in them . . . The theological questions

60. Boff and Elizondo, "Editorial," xii.
61. Elizondo, "Biblical Pedagogy," 537.

will emerge out of the common needs, struggles, questions and tensions of the community. The fundamental books to be consulted will be the life-tensions of the community. The language to be used will be that of the people as conditioned by their own historical-cultural identity. The theologian becomes the person of analysis, dialogue, and creative (prophetic) proclamation.[62]

The evangelical zeal of Vatican II to reach out to all humanity marked a shift in the audience targeted from previous ecumenical councils. "For the first time in the history of Ecumenical Councils, a Council addresses itself to all men, not just members of the Catholic Church. In the following year, Pope John XXIII added, for the first time, the salutation "and to all men of good will" as the opening of a papal encyclical (*Pacem in Terris*, Apr. 11, 1963)."[63] Vatican II's evangelical outreach also had another underlying aspect that Elizondo develops in his writing. Not only is there encouragement for young churches to develop a unique connection between their local culture and the customs and traditions of the older churches, but the older churches should also understand the reality of the younger churches as being truly Church as well. "At this moment of history it is the mission of the young churches to come forth with new creativity which will enrich not only their own local churches but the entire communio of Churches. They should not waste their time seeking to be legitimised by the theologians of the old Church, but should strive to produce something truly new which is both in fidelity to the core of the Christian message and in fidelity to the 'genius and disposition of each culture.'"[64]

The challenge of *Ad Gentes* is to assist in the development of younger churches in their rightful status as Church and for older churches to acknowledge the movement of the Holy Spirit allowing ecclesial expression on earth to differ from locale to locale while maintaining the deposit of faith in its new soil. For Elizondo, this is a real challenge for established churches:

> I suspect that their own personal acceptance of the reality of their own church as local will be much more difficult. They are encumbered by centuries of tradition of seeing themselves as THE Church and their missionaries carried their model of Church to

62. Elizondo, "Conditions and Criteria," 20.

63. Abbott, ed. "Message to Humanity," 3, footnote 2.

64. Elizondo, "Conditions and Criteria," 20.

many parts of the world as if it were the one and only model of the Church . . . the 'mother churches' (the original missionary-sending churches which gave birth to new churches) will now have to begin learning from their children churches who have now come of age and have joined the *communio* of churches as equal partners.[65]

Encompassing the interaction between older and younger churches is the Church of Rome. Standing as the symbol of unity, a unity found in diversity, Rome has the special distinction of protecting the relationship between the local and the universal, between the local expressions of the faith and the universal tenets, a combination which allows the Incarnation to be fully realized. "In summary, there are three ecclesial conditions that are fundamental pre-requisites for an authentic intercultural theological dialogue: (i) For the young churches to be firmly secured in their own identity and in their own style of theologizing; (ii) for the old churches of the North Atlantic nations to discover that they too are local churches with the need to de-universalize themselves and begin to enjoy their own unique local status; (iii) for the local church of Rome to rediscover in practice what it means to be the centre of unity versus the centre of control, imposition and regulation."[66]

Gaudium et spes § 39: The Conciliar Foundation for Gutiérrez's Liberation Theology

With the bittersweet conclusion of the Second Vatican Council, Gustavo Gutiérrez's own journey from Rome back to his home country of Peru illustrated his commitment to the struggles of his fellow Peruvians and also to John XXIII's vision of the Church of the poor. The theme of the Church of the poor raised by John XXIII prior to the opening of the Council was not forgotten by the Latin American Church and the neglect of this discussion on the Council floor only motivated the episcopal leaders of Latin America to continue this necessary dialogue. Although the Latin American Episcopal Conference (CELAM) came into being prior to the Second Vatican Council in 1955 at its first meeting at Rio de Janeiro, Brazil, the passion and direction of CELAM can be considered a continuation of the work at Vatican II. Surrounded by

65. Ibid., 21.
66. Ibid. 21–22.

poverty and supported by Church leaders, Gutiérrez was then able to develop a theology of the reality already being lived out as Church. As a theologian stressing his own context, Gutiérrez has not been theologizing in a vacuum but rather in "organic communion with the people" and as a militant theologian (one who actively engages), Gutiérrez has been "working with the pilgrim people of God and engaged in their pastoral responsibilities".[67]

The Church of the poor was one of the "signs of the times" described in the final document of Vatican II, *Gaudium et spes*;[68] however, because the text addressed rich nations and not poor, Gutiérrez finds it difficult for the Church to be truly present in the world of the poor.[69] Hotly debated by the Fathers on the Council floor, this text revealed the theological tension dividing theologians. Regardless of the position taken, *Gaudium et spes* was approved with optimism by both traditionalists and progressives. However, the apparently unified theological mind dominating the Council discussions grew apart as disagreement grew fiercer regarding the role of the Church in the modern world:

> From the left the criticism is that the Council worked within a framework defined largely by the challenges and problems of the encounter with the liberal modernity of the Northern Hemisphere. The "modern world," in the singular, was taken to mean the world that liberalism had created, and so eager was the Council to show that the Church could have something to say to it and something to learn from it that it failed to address the failures of liberal modernity, in particular the price at which it achieved its progress, a price paid by the exploited classes and countries of the world. This criticism is often found among representatives of political theology and of liberation theology.[70]

For those on the right, the optimism in the easy and natural relationship between the Church and the world was seen as naïve. What troubled those making stronger distinctions between the Church and the world was how these two realities connected so easily with each other. A bridge was necessary for the Church to engage the world, this bridge being the

67. "Organic" and "Militant" are terms used for liberation theologians by Clodovis Boff and Leonardo Boff, *Introducing Liberation Theology*, 19.

68. Gutiérrez, "Latin American Perception," 58.

69. Gutiérrez, "Church and the Poor," 184; "Spirituality for Liberation." 42.

70. Komonchak, "Interpreting the Council," 23.

cross. At times, the enthusiasm of *Gaudium et spes* blurred not only the "distinction" of the Church and the world, but also the assertion that the two had "no separation."

Gutiérrez has reflected on the impact of this debate on the reality of the Church in the world through the reality of poor. Since his spirituality is based on the following of Christ, *la Sequela Christi*, active engagement with the world is just as much a part of prayer as is contemplation. Christianity apart from the world is impossible for theologians such as Gutiérrez. Although Gutiérrez may adhere to the Church and the world much more closely than others, he does not cross the line of collapsing the two realities or identifying them. However, without the two, the true Kingdom is not realized. This reading of *Gaudium et spes*, the "distinction, but not separation" of the Kingdom of God and the earthly Kingdom is derived from *Gaudium et spes* § 39: "Far from diminishing our concern to develop this earth, the expectancy of a new earth should spur us on, for it is here that the body of a new human family grows, foreshadowing in some way the age which is to come. That is why, although we must be careful to distinguish earthy progress clearly from the increase of the Kingdom of Christ, such progress is of vital concern to the Kingdom of God, insofar as it can contribute to the better ordering of human society."

Gutiérrez is careful, however, not to limit himself to interpreting Vatican II through this one paragraph. Although *Gaudium et spes* § 39 plays a foundational role in Gutiérrez's understanding of liberation, particularly in the chapter on the "Distinction of Planes" found in his seminal work, *A Theology of Liberation*, he is also aware of John XXIII's vision for the Council along with the Council debates and texts. In a real sense, Gutiérrez is reading the conciliar event both synchronically and diachronically and he turns to CELAM and the Latin American Church in her struggles against poverty to understand the reception of the Council.

Synchronically, Gutiérrez stresses the stronger identification between the Church and world in the preparatory schema of *Ariccia*.[71] *Gaudium et spes* shied away from this schema and attempted to appease the dividing factions resulting from this discussion. Diachronically, Gutiérrez identifies the continuing theme of the Church in the modern world throughout the Council's sixteen documents. Finally, in terms

71. Gutiérrez, *Theology of Liberation*, 98–99.

of reception, Gutiérrez turns to the situation of Latin America and the response of its episcopal leaders as the living out of the attitudes of John XXIII and Vatican II. All of these factors contributed to Gutiérrez's understanding of Vatican II and of the path it set for the rest of the world. "Of the three themes [internal unity, external openness, and the church of the poor] singled out by John XXIII, the necessity of dialogue with the world was the one that received the most extensive and profound treatment in the Council. It was this issue that accounted for the great turnabout toward the end of the first session and opened up pathways along which the work of the Council would advance very fruitfully. I have in mind here not only the document eventually to be known as *Gaudium et spes* but the entire body of documents."[72]

As previously stated, the Church's openness to the world is not without criticism regarding its naïve outlook. Although the theme is present in all sixteen conciliar documents, the shortsightedness of the theme is its location in the realities of rich countries, mainly in North America and Europe. Without a world perspective, focusing on the impoverishment of the Third World, the internal and external renewals called for by the Council could not be realized because the proclamation of Vatican II is not only a message directed to the Roman Catholic Church, but to all peoples of the world. Rather than adhering more closely to the intentions of John XXIII and his specific vision of the Church of the poor as the motivation for renewal in the Church's internal and external outlooks, the Council Fathers focused more generally on the outward expression of the Church in the modern world. The complex reality of the themes generated by John XXIII and the redirection of discussion by the Council Fathers is apparent in the opening discussion between influential bishops on the Council floor. "In the final days of the first session of the council, [Giacomo Lercaro] cited Pope John's idea in an intervention that startled us then (and now): Poverty and the evangelization of the poor must not be only one of the many subjects, but *the* subject, the central theme, of Vatican II . . . But speeches by Cardinal Giovanni Battista Montini (Later Paul VI) and Cardinal León Joseph Suenens were more influential; both argued for the necessity of taking into account the question of the presence of the church in the world."[73]

72. Gutiérrez, "Church and the Poor," 175–76.
73. Gutiérrez, "Church of the Poor," 12–13.

The three *desiderata* of John XXIII were not optional themes, but constitutive elements complementing each other. Gutiérrez does not linger with the developments of Vatican II. Rather, he uses Vatican II and the openness of the Church to the modern world, and in particular, the Council's final document, to continue his own theological endeavors faithful to the *desiderata* of John XXIII. For Gutiérrez, Vatican II laid the foundation for continuing the vision of John XXIII to be the Church of all, especially the Church of the poor. Thus, it is important to look at the developments of CELAM as well as the liberative writings of Gutiérrez to understand the growth of the post-conciliar Church.

CELAM: CONSEJO EPISCOPAL LATINOAMERICANO

Gustavo Gutiérrez has summarized the situation of the Church in Latin America in the following terms:

> . . . the Latin American Church, like the base-level ecclesial communities, the theologians of liberation, and Medellín, has made its own the insights of John XXIII vis-à-vis the Church of the poor, and it has tried to interpret the great themes of the Council in light of this insight. The statements made at Medellín and the program it laid out are inexplicable without reference to the Council with all its complexity and all its varied languages and problematics. There is no question, however, of a simple, mechanical application of Vatican II. Rather, the Latin American Church is endeavoring in a profoundly mature way to be faithful, with the Council, to the Lord of history and to a Church that is beginning to become truly universal[.][74]

In addition, Gutiérrez has pointedly remarked: "The poor have always been relevant in the Christian perspective; we did not have to wait for the twentieth century to become aware of the important issue of poverty. At the same time, the issue seems new because the concrete situation of poverty is not the same as it was in the past. At Medellín it was possible in a region both poor and Christian to take seriously the intuition of Pope John that the church is and wants to be the church of the poor."[75]

One of the gifts of John XXIII and Vatican II to the Latin American Church was the discussion regarding the poor. The Church in Latin

74. Gutiérrez, "Church and the Poor," 193.
75. Gutiérrez, "Church of the Poor," 13.

America became more conscious of the poverty plaguing the people and began planting the seed of being the Church of the poor in the soil of Latin America. With further investigations into the nature of this impoverishment by using the tools of social science, the Latin American Church began speaking in relevant terms to people struggling to live out their Christian heritage in a humane manner by distancing the Church from its alliance with the wealthy class and siding with the majority who were poor. "For the first time, the Church had begun to be more fully aware of its Latin American reality, and the cruel reality abiding, inhuman poverty of the majority of our people became a major issue impossible to forget."[76]

With the theme of poverty dominating the agenda of the Church, social sciences became increasingly more valuable in understanding and approaching the impoverished conditions where many of the faithful found themselves. "The most significant outcome from Medellín was the Church's discovery of the world of the poor and opting to struggle on their behalf."[77] From this commitment to the poor, the Latin American Church illustrated the real life application of the teachings of the Second Vatican Council and the result—unique to the situation of Latin America—was a commitment to liberation. Thus, the CELAM conferences at Medellín and over a decade later at Puebla were preoccupied with the vision of John XXIII wanting the Church of all to be the Church of the poor.

What the Latin American episcopal leaders began at Medellín and brought to fruition at Puebla was the preferential option for the poor. Medellín did not use the phrase "preferential option" when speaking of the poor; however, the central theme of the Medellín documents is the poor, and the Church's alliance with the impoverished is undeniable. By addressing the Latin American community as a "community in transformation," Medellín set the tone for the three themes of justice, peace, and the poverty of the Church by appealing to the "multiplicity and complexity" of the situation. "Latin America appears to live beneath the tragic sign of underdevelopment that not only separates our brothers and sisters from the enjoyment of material goods, but from their proper human fulfillment. In spite of the efforts being made, there is the compounding of hunger and misery, of illness of a massive nature and

76. Ibid., 14.

77. Muskus, *Origins and Early Development*, 153.

infant mortality, of illiteracy and marginality, of profound inequality of income, and tensions between the social classes, of outbreaks of violence and rare participation of the people in decisions affecting the common good."[78]

By speaking about justice, peace, and poverty, Medellín did not avoid the preference for and the constitutive component of the poor in our faith life. Rather, the final documents addressing these themes formed the foundation for the Church in Latin America to grow into the preferential option. Based on the educational system developed by Brazilian Paolo Feire,[79] the Latin American bishops stressed the "task of conscientization and social education" in building a just society. By addressing multinational businesses, political systems, and base families, along with those living in rural as well as industrialized environments, Medellín promoted justice in all areas of life.

> The lack of political consciousness in our countries makes the educational activity of the church absolutely essential, for the purpose of bringing Christians to consider their participation in the political life of the nation as a matter of conscience and as the practice of charity in its most noble and meaningful sense for the life of the community . . . We wish to affirm that it is indispensable to form a social conscience and a realistic perception of the problems of the community and of social structures. We must awaken the social conscience and communal customs in all strata of society and professional groups[.][80"]

In addition, to bring about social transformation through conscientization, the Latin American Church, especially in her small basic communities, reached out to the most vulnerable at every level of society. "The Church—the people of God—will lend its support to the downtrodden of every social class so that they might come to know their rights and how to make use of them."[81]

Before presenting its "Christian View of Peace," the Medellín document described the conflicts in Latin America in three categories: (1) *Tensions between Classes and Internal Colonialism*, (2) *International Tensions and External Neocolonialism* and (3) *Tensions among the*

---

78. CELAM (Medellín), "The Church in the Present-Day Transformation," 90.

79. See Freire, *Pedagogy of the Oppressed.*

80. CELAM (Medellín), "Church in the Present-Day Transformation," 103–4.

81. Ibid., 104.

Countries of Latin America. Building on the foundations of *Gaudium et spes* of Vatican II, *Pacem in Terris* of John XXIII and *Populorum Progressio* of Paul VI, peace is described as a work of justice, a permanent task, and the fruit of love. As a work of justice: "It presupposes and requires the establishment of a just order in which persons can fulfill themselves as human beings, where their dignity is respected, their legitimate aspirations satisfied, their access to truth recognized, their personal freedom guaranteed; and order where persons are not objects but agents of their own history."[82] As a permanent task, "peace is not found, it is built": "A community becomes a reality in time and is subject to a movement that implies constant change in structures, transformation of attitudes, and conversion of hearts . . . It is the result of continuous effort and adaptation to new circumstances, to new demands and challenges of a changing history. A static and apparent peace may be obtained with the use of force; an authentic peace implies struggle, creative abilities, and permanent conquest."[83] As a fruit of love: "[Peace] is the expression of true fellowship among human beings, a union given by Christ, prince of peace, in reconciling all persons with the Father. Human solidarity cannot truly take effect unless it is done in Christ . . . Peace with God is the basic foundation of internal and social peace. Therefore, where this social peace does not exist, there will we find social, political, economic, and cultural inequalities, there will we find the rejection of the peace of the Lord, and a rejection of the Lord himself."[84]

Medellín's document on *The Poverty of the Church* also manifested the Church's commitment to the poor as CELAM looked to John XXIII's vision of the Church of the poor. The episcopal conference, thus, distinguished poverty in three ways—material poverty, spiritual poverty, and poverty as a commitment—as a way of being the Church of the poor. Material poverty described as "a lack of goods of this world necessary to live worthily as human beings" was characterized as "itself evil."[85] Spiritual poverty, based on Scriptural references, was described at Medellín as "the attitude of opening up to God, the ready disposition of one who hopes for everything from the Lord," where one values,

82. Ibid., 109.
83. Ibid.
84. Ibid., 110.
85. Ibid., 115.

but is not attached to earthly goods.[86] Finally, poverty as a commitment reflects the call for all Christians to live in evangelical poverty as a way of solidarity with those who live in real poverty. Solidarity comes when "one assumes voluntarily and lovingly the conditions of the needy of this world in order to bear witness to the evil it represents and to spiritual liberty in the face of material goods."[87]

The three descriptions of poverty found in the Medellín documents are the basis for the preferential (spiritual poverty) option (poverty as commitment) for the poor (poverty as a lack of goods) that would be described at the next CELAM conference at Puebla. Through its documents on justice, peace, and poverty, Medellín laid the foundation for pastoral and theological reflections leading up to Puebla as it continued the *desideratum* of John XXIII for the Church to be for all peoples by becoming the Church of the poor. "The poverty of the Church and of its members in Latin America ought to be a sign and commitment—a sign of the inestimable value of the poor in the eyes of God, an obligation of solidarity with those who suffer."[88]

Medellín and Puebla steered the Latin American Church, and in a sense the entire world, towards analyzing poverty through the tools of social science. In this way, the Church of the poor became fully rooted in the modern world and so had the ability to address the situation of poverty afflicting a majority of the population in Latin America. "Medellín and Puebla constitute two privileged moments in the life of the Latin American Church. History will consider them as two expressions of ecclesial discernment in which not only the bishops take part, but all people of God in Latin America. Both events mark the culmination of a process of intraecclesial maturation concerning the nature of the Church's evangelizing task in the different areas in which she carries out her mission."[89] As Gutiérrez has remarked: "The growing maturity of the Church is evident by going not so much *beyond* the texts of Medellín as *through* them. I think the maturity of the Latin American Church is expressed in the documents of Medellín, with all their limitations."[90] What the Church is unable to say is as important as her direct statements

---

86. Ibid.
87. Ibid.
88. Ibid., 116.
89. Poblete, "From Medellín to Puebla," 31.
90. Gutiérrez, "Church of the Poor," 15.

especially since Vatican II placed the Church on an eschatological path as a pilgrim Church on earth. "Cardinal Juan Landázuri Ricketts of Lima asked at the beginning of the Medellín Conference: Who are we? I think Medellín itself was an attempt to answer that question. More than an internal, private question, identity is a social situation: to be present, to be in the service of the poor. For the whole church being present in the world of the poor is a way to affirm our identity today."[91]

When the CELAM gatherings at Medellín and Puebla are considered together, the maturation of the Latin American Church is visible, especially in her identity as the Church of the poor. What occurred at Vatican II and was carried on at Medellín with its attention to poverty by placing the Church on the side of the poor was more fully refined and cogently defined at Puebla. The maturation of the Church's approach to the least in society is further realized in Puebla's description of the poor. The exploitation of the most vulnerable in society is highlighted in the Puebla documents which speak of the least in our midst, the poor, and recognize the reality of those who suffer multiple forms of oppression. Thus, the preferential option for the poor verbalized at Puebla reflects both the awareness that began at Medellín and a more mature understanding of poverty in Latin America.

The final outcome at Puebla furthered the commitment made by the Church at Medellín. However, this commitment did not naturally occur but continued the struggles of the poor, in particular, their struggle not only for recognition, but for being the center of both political and religious discussions as illustrated by the preparatory document. Medellín did not address, for example, the bourgeois class and modernism; the preparatory document for the conference at Puebla leaned away from the language and focus on behalf of the poor. This attempt at "inclusivity" in the preparatory document once again prevented the poor and indigenous from being recognized in the Church. A clear example of this is found in the preparatory document in the discussion of culture, especially in its focus on Latin American culture as an offspring of the West. "So whereas we might have expected that dominant groups and the oppressors of the majority—those who are at the other end of the social scale—would be excluded from being part of the Latin American people, we find that the definition tends rather to exclude the members

91. Ibid., 24.

of the oppressed cultures whose presence in Latin America is overlooked by the [preparatory document]."[92]

In trying to balance the statements of Medellín in a "more inclusive" way, the preparatory commission did so in fear of reductionism; a reduction of poverty to simply the material needs of the poor. Accordingly, poverty was addressed in much broader terms than found in the Medellín documents in two ways: first, a "new poor" was included to go beyond the economic, social, or political understandings in an attempt to include the alienated, the uncared-for, and the elderly. Second, the preparatory document presented poverty in strict categories of spiritual attitudes of Christian life. By focusing the boundaries of poverty in broader terms, the preparatory commission lost the universal aspect of Medellín's definition that was relevant to all humanity and limited it to the religious arena. Thus, the preparatory document of Puebla manifested the chasm between material and spiritual poverty and the fears of reductionism by those who saw Medellín as an aberration rather than a commitment to the poor. In the fear of reducing poverty to the material, the preparatory commission leaned heavily towards the spiritual without seeing their own efforts as reductionistic. "What we actually have here is the classic distinction between material and spiritual poverty. But the [preparatory document] fearing the "reductionism" to which the notion of the poor is susceptible, is so cautious that many of its statements are ambiguous. They reflect a great preoccupation that the notion of poverty will be reduced to a "mere objective, economic and social condition of deprivation." There is less concern that it might be reduced to a "new subjective attitude.""[93]

In addition to these limitations, the preparatory document failed to echo Medellín's concern for denouncing poverty: "It is particularly unfortunate that the [preparatory document] does not say, as was said in simple, clear, and biblical terms at Medellín, that material poverty is *evil*."[94] In many ways, what was so hopefully presented at Medellín as the Church's commitment to those living in poverty was replaced by a passive, hopeless acceptance of poverty as a result of humanity's sinfulness. "[The preparatory document] gives the impression that poverty is inevitable, caused by the human shortcomings of the poor, rather than

92. Gutiérrez, "'Preparatory Document' for Puebla," 213.

93. Ibid.

94. Ibid.

something against which we should protest and struggle. The detached language takes no account of *the concrete situation of the poor* of the continent, and opens the door to misunderstandings that Medellín had taken the trouble to clear up."[95]

What further dampened the momentum started at Medellín was the use of religion in a return to an ideology prior to the Second Vatican Council. Instead of building on the commitment made at Medellín to the poor, the preparatory document returned to a Christendom-like perspective where the concern of the Church is strictly on the spiritual plane, thereby separating the Church from the world. The strategic disregard of the exploitation of the poor in Latin America excuses the Church from making tough choices in the difficult circumstances of life. By placing the issue of poverty as the central theme only in spiritual terms and not in material reality and, more importantly, by failing to denounce it as evil, the preparatory commission opted out of condemning the wealthy elite for their oppressive practices in the guise of Christian behavior, while simultaneously opting out of hearing the earthly cries of the suffering and dying poor as the overall prerogative of our faith.

> If the great challenge to faith in Latin America is a secularist ideology rather than the brutal exploitation of the poor of the continent, then the providential God will replace the God who liberates, the God of the poor of Medellín. Popular religiosity (as understood by the [preparatory document]) will have the role that poverty had; the notion of culture will take the place of liberation; the People, formed by all those who establish one identical culture, will replace the poor exploited classes; the people, considered in their material poverty, will be replaced by the people who are spiritually rich. In such a situation the task of evangelizing will be to discern the values of the modern world in order to build a new civilization, rather than to *denounce* the scandalous conditions of social injustice in Latin America, or to *announce* the love of the Father who raises his arm against the oppressor and frees the oppressed.[96]

The preparatory document for Puebla in 1979 thus had a vastly different tone than the final documents at Medellín and the discussions raised by bishops and theologians prior to and at Puebla produced very different results. In a fashion similar to the beginnings of Vatican II,

95. Ibid.
96. Ibid., 218.

the preparatory documents, drafted by conservative minorities, were rejected in favor of a growing consensus of bishops and theologians. The final documents of the episcopal conference at Puebla not only continued the attitude of Medellín in the Church's commitment to the poor, but formalized that commitment as the preferential option for the poor. By so doing, Puebla rejected the claim that the Medellín statements of 1968 were an aberration in the life of the Latin American Church and so further manifested the maturation of the Church in its commitment on behalf of those exploited.

By the time of the third CELAM conference, Rome was very interested in the activities of the local church in Latin America especially with the rise of Marxist thought in world politics along with the increasing embrace of liberation theology. Fearing the communism that plagued Eastern Europe and his home country of Poland, Pope John Paul II was adamant about the Church's incompatibility with Marxism. Thus, the Vatican, more than ever, grew concerned about the so-called commitment to the poor arising in Third World countries. In his opening address at Puebla in 1979, John Paul II insisted that the "primary and irreplaceable duty" of pastors is to watch carefully "over purity of doctrine, basic in building up the Christian community."[97] John Paul II also reminded his audience that "the faithful of your countries expect and demand first and foremost a careful and zealous transmission of the truth about Jesus Christ."[98]

John Paul II's emphasis on the promotion and transmission of faith related to Christological concerns in Latin America, regarding, for example, portrayals of Christ within the local context in ways that questioned Jesus' divinity along with a human identity reduced to that of a political activist: "We find "rereadings" of the Gospel that are the product of theoretical speculations rather than of authentic meditation on the word of God and a genuine evangelical commitment. They cause confusion insofar as they depart from the central criteria of the church's faith, and people have the temerity to pass them on as catechesis to Christian communities."[99] John Paul II voiced similar concerns on the side of caution even with regard to the rapid growth of small base communities—a healthy sign of the local church—where much of the

97. John Paul II, "Puebla Conference," I, 1, 58.

98. Ibid., I, 2, 59.

99. Ibid., I, 4, 59.

reflections on the Word of God took place. "Against such "rereadings," therefore, and against the perhaps brilliant but fragile and inconsistent hypotheses flowing from them "evangelization in Latin America's present and future" cannot cease to affirm the church's faith: Jesus Christ, the Word and son of God . . . Any form of silence, disregard, mutilation, or inadequate emphasis on the whole of the mystery of Jesus Christ that diverges from the church's faith cannot be the valid content of evangelization."[100] The rationale for caution in the face of rapid growth and activity of the Church in society, according to John Paul II, was to ensure authentic evangelization. The enthusiasm with which the Latin American Church engaged the injustices of society raised concerns because of the collapse of the distinction between the Kingdom now and the Kingdom to come, since the former could so easily focus on human activities without any outlook for the latter. Accordingly, John Paul II warned against this collapse by echoing the words of *Lumen Gentium* and pointing to the Church established on earth as the initial budding forth of the Kingdom we all see with faith:[101] "Emptied of its full content, the Kingdom of God is understood in a rather secularist sense: that is, we do not arrive at the Kingdom through faith and membership in the church but rather merely by structural change and socio-political involvement. Where there is a certain kind of commitment and praxis for justice, there the Kingdom is already present. This view forgets that "the church . . . receives the mission to proclaim and to establish among all peoples the Kingdom of Christ and of God."[102]

Unlike Medellín, where both Virgilio Elizondo and Gustavo Gutiérrez were in attendance but do not recall meeting one another, at the Puebla conference, both men were well acquainted and familiar with each other's work. Admiring each other's pastoral commitments, Elizondo and Gutiérrez encouraged one another throughout the seventies. Their presence at both Medellín and Puebla would encourage their theological endeavors especially as they were just beginning to formulate the vision of the Church of the poor in their locales. Thus, by the late seventies, both theologians with their world-renowned reputations had much more to contribute to the gathering of Latin American bishops.

100. Ibid., I, 5, 60.

101. Ibid., I, 8, 62.

102. Ibid.

Elizondo's reflections on Puebla, especially on John Paul II's opening address, are quite valuable as he presents the pontiff's message in
a comprehensive manner. Some in Latin America felt Rome's intervention as restrictive and not in touch with the situation of the poor
in the Americas. However, for Elizondo, John Paul II's comments must
be taken as a whole rather than as isolated statements, especially in his
opening address at Puebla. "Hence, even though his Opening Address
to the bishops assembled in Puebla was certainly the major presentation of his Latin American journey, it can be properly understood only
when studied in the light of all his actions and words as they were lived
and spoken during his entire pilgrimage."[103] During his visit to Mexico,
John Paul II visited the Basilica of Our Lady of Guadalupe out of his intense devotion to the Blessed Mother. He also went to other areas of the
country experiencing civil and religious unrest. Thus, the collection of
statements Elizondo proposes which makes up the matrix of John Paul
II's message takes into account all of his speeches. Consequently, a more
balanced message emerges when one hears John Paul II's words to the
indigenous masses, especially in his Address to the Indians of Oaxaca
and Chiapas.

On January 29, 1979, John Paul II reinforced in a twofold manner
the Church's desire to be the Church of the poor which struggles against
exploitation with the masses. First, the pope recognized the beauty and
richness of the indigenous people and their contribution to overall society and to the Church: "My presence in your midst is meant to be a
living, authentic sign of this universal preoccupation on the part of the
Church. The pope and the Church are with you and they love you. They
love your persons, your culture, your traditions. They admire your marvelous past, encourage you in the present, and have great expectations
for the future."[104] Second, by affirming the work of his predecessor at
Medellín and continuing the commitment to the poor made at that moment in the history of the Church: "With [Paul VI in his memorable visit
to Colombia, and more specifically in his meeting with the peasants] I
would like to reiterate—with an even stronger emphasis in my voice, if
that were possible—that the present pope wishes to be "in solidarity with

103. Elizondo, "Pope's Opening Address," 47.

104. John Paul II, "Indians of Oaxaca and Chiapas," 81–82.

your cause, which is the cause of the humble people, the poor people" (Address to Peasants, 23 August 1968)."[105]

Viewing John Paul II's message as a whole, Elizondo does not find a dichotomy between the tone of the pope's message to the bishops and the tone of his message to the poor. Rather, Elizondo understands the cautious warnings at the opening of the Puebla conference—especially the warning against too closely identifying the *regnum Dei* with the *regnum hominis* as a call to faithfulness.[106] "Throughout his stay in Mexico, he spoke about fidelity to the whole and integral truth about God, Jesus Christ, the Church, tradition, and human beings in the fullness of their concrete needs and aspirations. The pope was not speaking about abstract or philosophical truth, but about the very real saving truth as it liberates humanity from any and every form of enslavement and oppression. Fidelity to God is fidelity to the dignity of every human person."[107] Furthermore, Elizondo highlights the pope's address at the Cathedral in Mexico City on January 26, as a sign of the Church commitment to the present situations of the poor and not just holding on to antiquity. "It is important to note that for the pope fidelity to tradition means neither a holding on to the secondary things of the past nor a mere defense of the status quo. In fact, this very fidelity to the tradition of the Church demands that we continue to work for the ongoing transformation of persons and society through bold, creative, heroic, and innovative action . . . The tradition of the Church is the progressive liberation of humanity as sinful hearts and structures are transformed into hearts and structures of grace."[108]

In spite of the pope's cautious instructions on evangelization and the preparatory document's movement away from the attitude of Medellín, the episcopal leaders at the Puebla conference were still able to maintain the commitment of the Church to the poor while maintaining the fidelity called for by the pope. They did so by producing three influential documents affirming both the poor and their liberation: (1) *Evangelization, Liberation, and Human Promotion*, (2) *Base-Level Ecclesial Communities (CEBS), the Parish, and the Local Church*, and (3) *A Preferential Option for the Poor*. These documents affirmed the commitment to the most

105. Ibid., 82.

106. Elizondo, "Pope's Opening Address," 47.

107. Ibid.

108. Ibid., 47–48.

vulnerable in society and continued the struggles of the Church against the exploitation of the poor.

The final document on *Evangelization, Liberation, and Human Promotion* supported many of the foundational themes of liberation theology by appealing to the social teachings of the Church found in scripture and in the decrees of the Fathers of the Church, as well as to the *sensus fidelium* of people and theologians along with the Church authorities. By appealing to such authoritative sources, the Latin American bishops called upon the whole Christian community to continue the foundational mission of the Church, namely, the task of evangelization: "Clearly, then, it is the whole Christian community, in communion with its legitimate pastors and guided by them, that is the responsible subject of evangelization, liberation, and human promotion."[109]

Where John Paul II spoke about authentic evangelization, the Latin American bishops presented an evangelical approach which would be incomplete without the commitment to persons facing structures of injustice and oppression. "The primary object of this social teaching is the personal dignity of the human being, who is the image of God, and the protection of all inalienable human rights."[110] Not fearing the claims of reductionism in their evangelical approach, the Latin American bishops also appealed to the Second Vatican Council, in particular *Gaudium et spes*, for support in sustaining the necessary connection and distinction of earthly progress advocated in light of the Kingdom to come. "But the aim of this doctrine of the Church, which offers its own specific vision of the human beings and humanity . . . is always the promotion and integral liberation of human beings in terms of both their earthly and their transcendent dimensions. It is a contribution to the construction of the ultimate and definitive Kingdom, although it does not equate earthly progress with Christ's Kingdom (GS § 39)."[111]

In regards to liberation, Puebla presented the original understanding of Christian liberation as twofold—consisting of two complementary and inseparable elements. "The first is liberation from all the forms of bondage, from personal and social sin, and from everything that tears apart the human individual and society; all this finds its source to be in egotism, in the mystery of iniquity. The second element is liberation for

109. CELAM (Puebla), "Latin America's Present and Future," 233.

110. Ibid.

111. Ibid.

progressive growth in being through communion with God and other human beings; this reaches its culmination in the perfect communion of heaven, where God is all in all and weeping forever ceases."[112]

Following the guidelines presented by John Paul II that evangelization must be based on the truth about Jesus Christ, the Church, and human beings, Puebla spoke about liberation, especially in the attitudes found in the evangelizers:

> At the level of content one must consider how faithful they are to the word of God, to the church's living tradition, and to its magisterium. As for attitudes, one must consider what sense of communion they feel, with the bishops first of all, and then with the other sectors of God's people. Here one must also consider what contribution they make to the real building up of the community . . . and how, discovering in these people the image of the poor and suffering Jesus . . . Thus liberative evangelization finds its full realization in the communion of all in Christ, as the Father of all persons wills."[113]

The final document on *Base-Level Ecclesial Communities (CEBs), The Parish, and the Local Church* formulated practical application for the Church's liberative approach in its preferential love of the poor. In contrast to Rome's fear of basic communities as disengaging from the wider Church, the Latin American bishops encouraged these small communities and saw each of them in fact as the Church. "As an ecclesial reality, it is a community of faith, hope, and charity."[114] "In small communities, particularly those that are better organized, persons grow in their experience of new interpersonal relationships in the faith in deeper exploration of God's word, in fuller participation in the eucharist, in communion with the pastors of the local Church, and in greater commitment to justice within the social milieu that surrounds them."[115]

The final document, *A Preferential Option for the Poor*, is perhaps the most important document as it envisions the work of Puebla as a continuation of the heritage of Medellín's work on behalf of the poor. First appealing to the Gospel accounts of Jesus' outreach to the poor—by his identification and solidarity with those most

112. Ibid., 234–35.
113. Ibid., 236.
114. Ibid., 251
115. Ibid.

impoverished—Puebla asserted that subsequent followers of Christ must behave in a like manner: "When we draw near to the poor in order to accompany them and serve them, we are doing what Christ taught us to do when he became our brother, poor like us. Hence service to the poor is the privileged, though not the exclusive, gauge of our following of Christ."[116] Jesus' ministry and attention to the poor and our calling to do likewise is the basis for the preferential option for the poor as described by Puebla: "For this reason alone, the poor merit preferential attention, whatever may be the moral or personal situation in which they find themselves. Made in the image and likeness of God (Gen. 1:26–28) to be the children of God, this image is dimmed and even defiled. That is why God takes on their defense and loves them (Matt. 5:45; James 2:5). That is why the poor are the first ones to whom Jesus' mission is directed (Luke 4:18–21), and why the evangelization of the poor is the supreme sign and proof of his mission."[117]

Shifting away from the preparatory document where poverty was defined in spiritualistic terms and not denounced as material evil, Puebla acknowledged the inclusive role of evangelical poverty as "the attitude of trusting confidence in God with a plain, sober, and austere life that dispels the temptation to greed and haughty pride".[118] However, evangelical poverty does diminish the real life situations of the poor, who are the focus of this document. The pastoral guidelines stated that the objective of the preferential option is, first and foremost, the proclamation of Christ the Savior. The means of this preference is found in living out Christian poverty as the encounter with the poor demands constant conversion. Finally, the concrete implementation of the preferential option for the poor requires a commitment to the poor through condemning "as anti-evangelical the extreme poverty that affects an extremely large segment of the population" and so Christians must "make every effort to understand and denounce the mechanisms that generate this poverty."[119]

116. Ibid., 255.
117. Ibid.
118. Ibid., 256.
119. Ibid., 257.

ALL THEOLOGY AS A THEOLOGY OF CONTEXT

It is difficult to speak about the contextual nature of theology without reference to the seminal work of Stephen Bevans, *Models of Contextual Theology*. Realizing that the theology being done in European circles could not speak to the realities found in Asia, Africa, and Latin America, theologians began engaging their own cultures and developing so-called indigenous theologies which would speak to the people living in differing conditions. The rise in theologies developed outside of the European continent allowed theologians such as Bevans to categorize these movements as contextual theology to indicate the different approaches in theological method.

In the 1992 edition of *Models of Contextual Theology*, Bevans described contextual theology as a way of doing theology that takes into account "the spirit and message of the Gospel; the tradition of the Christian people; the culture in which one is theologizing; and social change in that culture, whether brought about by western technological process or the grass-roots struggle for equality, justice, and liberation."[120] Along with this description, Bevans clarified the theological imperative and universality of this approach, walking a fine line between the newness of contextuality while maintaining continuity. "Doing theology contextually is not an option . . . the attempt to understand Christian faith in terms of a particular context—is really a theological imperative. As we understand theology today, contextualization is part of the very nature of theology itself . . . A contextual approach to theology is a departure from the notion of traditional theology, but at the same time it is very much in continuity with it. To understand theology as contextual is to assert something both new and traditional."[121]

In the tenth anniversary publication of *Models of Contextual Theology*, Bevans revised his description of contextuality in theology by beginning with a much stronger opening statement: "There is no such thing as "theology"; there is only *contextual* theology."[122] While still maintaining the twofold aspect of the contextuality, newness and continuity, Bevans' opening emphasis reflects his "rethinking" of this approach. The newness arising from contextuality, often foreign to those

---

120. Bevans, *Models of Contextual Theology* (1992), 1.

121. Ibid.

122. Ibid. (2002), 3.

adhering strictly to classical or traditional theology, made it difficult for those not engaged in Third World or missionary situations to identify this approach as a continuation. Rather than seeing contextual theology as a theological method in which all theologians are engaged, contextuality was often identified with Third World theologians or theological endeavors differing from their European or First World counterparts.

> They thought that their context was the world or should be the norm for the whole world, and hence their theology was considered universal. They were so contextual in their mind-set that they could not realize that they were only one context in a pluralistic world. They were so secure in these convictions and arrogant in their presumed monopoly of divine revelation that they thought they had the right and the duty to convert others to their faith and even annihilate persons of other persuasions along with their cults and places of worship and libraries. They did not realize that their theology, expressing itself in Greco-Roman categories, was basically syncretistic and of one context.[123]

To illustrate the contextuality of all theology, Bevans presented the universal *loci theologici* of all theologians. The first two theological sources—scripture and tradition—are readily accepted as the basis of all theological reflection. As the third *locus theologicus* constitutive in doing theology, Bevans pointed to present human experience. Since both scripture and tradition are culturally and historically conditioned, the present social and cultural conditioning must also be taken into account: "And so today we speak of theology as having *three* sources or *loci theologici*: scripture, tradition, and present human experience—or context."[124]

As we identify salvific history within our human history—the saving actions of Jesus Christ with that of the human condition—a theology of context becomes necessary in understanding the relationship of the two. "One way of approaching these commonalities of story and world is to speak of contextual theology. Of course, all theology is contextual, growing out of a particular situation, culture and community. Also, all theology should be incarnational, seeking to incarnate, and to live out the good news of God's action in the world."[125]

123. Balasuriya, "Contextual and Universal Dimensions," 28.

124. Bevans, *Models of Contextual Theology* (2002), 3–4.

125. Russell, "Universality and Contextuality," 23.

Communication of the Incarnation in relevant terms was also Robert McAfee Brown's preoccupation especially in regard to scripture, since reception of the Good News requires that the Gospel message be passed to succeeding generations via useful and familiar approaches. "The first is a statement of the content and power of the Gospel: "Jesus Christ [is] the same, yesterday, today, and forever" (Heb. 11:8b). The second is a statement about those who receive and transmit the Gospel: "For we have this treasure in earthen vessels" (2Cor. 4:7)."[126] We proclaim Christ who is eternal, yet because this proclamation is communicated in human terms, our theological language must continue to develop anew for each succeeding generation. The transmission of eternal truths is contained within our limited human transmissions which a theology taking into consideration the context incarnates for a specific locale and people.

> The very nature of the claim Christians make is inconceivable save contextually. For the Jesus Christ who is "the same yesterday, today, and forever" is not an eternal principle, a timeless truth, to be sought in some realm removed from time, contingency, mud, carnality, and power struggles . . . Faiths that proclaim epiphanies, that is stories of gods temporarily appearing before mortal gaze and then withdrawing, cannot afford to be contextual; they must record a vision of the eternal untrammeled by the trappings of mortality, or else they play their vision false. But a faith that proclaims incarnation, that is, the story of a God fully and completely indwelling a human life, so human that the one enfleshed gets tired, hungry, discouraged, weeps, loses faith (at least temporarily), and dies an ignominious death–such a faith by its very nature *must* be contextual, all wrapped up in the tendencies of the time and place within which it is set.[127]

Speaking about Elizondo's theological method during a class lecture, Timothy Matovina described Elizondo's approach as "a theology of context."[128] Rather than using the phrase, contextual theology, Matovina intentionally spoke of a theology of context for a twofold reason. The first purpose of rephrasing—contextual theology as a theology of context—is to avoid connotations or divisions of theology done by others as different or somehow inferior to those being done by so-called main-

---

126. Brown, "What is Contextual Theology?," 81.

127. Ibid., 82–83.

128. Class lecture at the University of Notre Dame, Fall semester, 2008.

stream theologians. The second purpose of rephrasing is to accentuate the constitutive nature of context in all theological endeavors. Thus, all theology is a theology of context.

The richness of embracing all three *loci theologici* in a theology of context is the ability to speak to a specific group of people in their concrete situation rather than in abstract principles. This ability to speak to the people arises from the questions being asked in differing locales, especially in their struggles for basic human existence. "All theology is the product of many influences in a given context . . . Different contexts raise different questions."[129]

As indicated in the following chapters, both Virgilio Elizondo and Gustavo Gutiérrez became pioneers in their theological endeavors precisely because of the questions they were asking on behalf of their people. As pointed out in the second chapter, for Elizondo, the theological question arising from the *mestizo* context is how to speak about God to those who are excluded and marginalized. As indicated in the third chapter, for Gutiérrez, the theological question arising from the context of poorest of the poor is how to speak about God to those who are insignificant or considered sub-human because of their impoverished world.

129. Balasuriya, "Contextual and Universal Dimensions," 24.

2

Virgilio Elizondo and *Mestizaje*

THIS SECOND CHAPTER TRACES the development of Virgilio Elizondo's theology based on his personal experience of *mestizaje* and its historical roots. Centered on the theme of marginalization and exclusion created by the clashing of two worlds, Elizondo formulates his theological reflection through questions about the conditions of Mexican Americans living on the border of Mexico and the United States and seeks answers in the historical Jesus as well as the ecclesial traditions of the Church. Accordingly, *mestizaje* which occurs culturally, socially, and biologically is first addressed in this chapter. From this understanding of *mestizo*, the historical developments of *mestizaje* for the Mexican American people are then explored. The historical reality of the twice conquered, twice *mestized* people provides the foundation for a theological reflection on *mestizaje* and its significance for not only Mexican Americans, but for all humanity. Next, *mestizaje* as a theological category is applied to the Galilean Jesus as an identification is made between the *mestizo*-type conditions of Galilee with the *mestizaje* of Southwestern United States. Further understanding of historical and theological *mestizaje* is then traced through the foundational ecclesial event of Latin America, the appearance of Our Lady of Guadalupe. Juan Diego's encounter with the *mestiza* Madonna upholds the *mestizo* characteristics of life and serves as a model for Elizondo's theologizing.

VIRGILIO ELIZONDO AND *MESTIZO* THEOLOGY

Mestizo theology—which traces its origin to Virgilio Elizondo's doctoral study—has become the hermeneutic key not only for Mexican Americans but also for many Christians in understanding both the figure of Jesus as depicted in the Gospels and the situation of Christians today. In the previous chapter, in the biographical introduction to Virgilio Elizondo, *mestizo* was defined as the social, cultural, and biological mixture of at least two different groups while *mestizaje* is understood as the process of that mixing.[1] Through the natural encounters of peoples across the world, a process of *mestizaje* occurs. Socially, culturally, and biologically, human beings come together to form a new creation that incorporates the reality of both parent groups. Rather than looking at the negatives often associated with descendants of differing heritages, Elizondo has been instrumental in highlighting the positive interaction that takes place through *mestizaje*, where the strengths of the parent groups are transferred to their offspring. Thus, the development of *mestizo* theology begins with the mixed social, cultural, and biological reality found within a specific group in light of God's revelation found in scripture and tradition. Elizondo's contribution to theology in general is the highlighting of his own *mestizo* background as a Mexican American and of the relevance of his self-identity in reading scripture and continuing the ecclesial tradition.

The basis of *mestizo* theology is incarnational, focusing on the historical reality of the figure of Christ. God became totally local in Jesus of Nazareth in Galilee in a very specific time; yet out of this particularity he became the savior of the world. His speech and actions were totally localized; yet Christians do not hesitate to find universal meaning in what he said and did. Jesus of Nazareth in Galilee—in particular, the image and metaphor of a wounded healer living in a specific region reaching out to certain people—has become the lens in understanding salvation and liberation today.

This perspective is what Elizondo often refers to as the hermeneutic or epistemology of the marginalized and excluded. The wounded healer gives meaning to our current suffering and mission because of the identification between our own marginalized and excluded status with that of our Savior's. Through this identification of the past with the present,

---

1. See Chapter 1, footnote 4; Appendix A.

we are called to continue the work of Christ—so others will not suffer what we have suffered. Since the local events and customs in Jesus' day brought about such universal implications of salvation to all, we must once again embrace the local context of our own being in order to understand better the universal dimensions of our faith. Thus, the incarnation—being born into a specific region and period—is the central basis for the local to have universal meaning and for *mestizo* theology to have an important function for the Mexican American people. In fact, the perspective of *mestizaje* seems applicable to all of humanity for *mestizaje* encompasses every aspect of our lives, not just religious categories:

> Mestizaje is simply the mixture of human groups of different genetic make-up, determining the colour and shape of our eyes, skin pigmentation and bone structure. The mestizo will thus be a person of undefined physical and cultural identity. It is the most common phenomenon in the evolution of the human species. Scientists state that there are few, if any, truly 'pure' human groups left in the world and that they are the weakest, because their genetic pool has been gradually drained. Through mixture, new human groups emerge and the genetic make-up is strengthened. Because the mixture is not just biological but equally cultural, it will be welcomed or abhorred, depending on the stereotype which the groups have of themselves and of others.[2]

By describing the progression of humanity as one of *mestizaje* where globally every group is affected by the interaction with the other, Elizondo not only points to the necessity and richness of *mestizaje* but also reminds us of the social responsibilities inherent with the coming together of differing peoples.[3] The "clashing" of differing groups often creates a richness overlooked initially. Instead, the initial reaction from *mestizaje* creates a marginalized and excluded reality. Thus, the social responsibility or the prophetic aspect of the *mestizaje* is to call for the recognition and the inclusion of the *mestizo* offspring.

This prophetic nature of *mestizo* theology reminds all humanity of its *mestizo* existence and its natural progression. Often, the initial encounter with this theme of *mestizaje* creates a division. Rather than seeing this progression as simply a given process in our humanity, people divide between the non-*mestizo* and the *mestizo*. When speaking of

2. Elizondo, "Mestizaje," 47.
3. Elizondo, "Jesus the Galilean Jew," 263.

mestizo theology or *mestizaje* in general, the initial reaction is to pre-scind from the reality; however, the fundamental basis of *mestizaje* is a reality that includes all of us since we cannot live in a vacuum and our encounters with the other always create a situation of *mestizaje*. Thus, *mestizos*—originally referring to Mexican Americans living on the borders of life—are part of all of God's creation, as we continue to discover, encounter, and interact with the others in our midst.

In many ways, social and cultural *mestizaje* is much more difficult for differing groups to accept than biological *mestizaje*. However, when the initial fears and barriers are overcome, this type of *mestizaje* is much more freely accepted. On the other hand, biological *mestizaje* where the offspring receive the genetic makeup of both of their parents is "easier" since it results from physical contact. While the initial physical encounter is simpler than the social and cultural, biological *mestizaje* entails many more and much deeper consequences. Through the physical contact of two differing groups, *mestizo* offspring come into being. "The contribution *mestizos* make is to break down the separations at the most sacred level, the level of the sexual."[4] But, as Elizondo points out, the new *mestizo* descendants—a creation sometimes discarded by one or both parent groups—are often unable to penetrate either of their parental realities; making the biological the easiest of the *mestizo* interactions to come to fruition yet the most difficult for society to accept.

> History clearly brings out there is no difficulty with the physical mixing of peoples, but it is a completely different story when it comes to the social and cultural mixing of persons and of peoples. Biologically speaking, mestizaje appears to be quite easy and natural, but culturally it is usually feared, threatening and often even prohibited. It is as common as human history itself, and yet it is the great taboo of human history. Mestizaje is the bodily and spiritual transgression of the ultimate human taboo. It comes through the most intimate penetration of the most sacred space of the other–the sexual.[5]

For Mexican Americans, the discrimination that follows from *mestizaje* has been all too real. Having been looked down upon by both parents' groups, Mexican Americans have developed as a people with a stigma of inferiority. Elizondo has illustrated this *mestizaje* in his own

4. See Appendix A.
5. Elizondo, "Mestizaje," 47–48.

life as a person caught between two worlds: "I was an inside-outsider to both. I was "Mexican" in the U.S. and *gringo/pocho* in Mexico."[6] "As mestizos, our flesh and blood identity has consistently marginated us from both parent groups. We have been too Spanish for the Indians and too Indian for the Spaniards, too Mexican for the United States, and too "Gringo" for our Mexican brothers and sisters. Our non-being has been our being! It is the multiple commonality of our people."[7] In addition to the status of non-being, a *mestizo* also incurs non-identity: "In the ideal order, the exchange of genes and cultures would be mutually beneficial and enriching. However, in the real order of life, mestizos usually suffer from the deep trauma of non-belonging, non-identity and often even shame and disgust at being who they are."[8] However, instead of giving in to the stereotypes and being overwhelmed by the stigma of inferiority, Elizondo has probed his current world and the worlds that gave birth to it to form a new understanding of his existence.

Without denying the current state of his people, Elizondo has sought to recover the positive aspects of *mestizaje* as a beacon of hope for all Mexican Americans: "Our being was actually our "non-being." This consciousness of "non-being" would deepen and broaden as I gradually moved from a very secure experience of being, to one of non-being, to one of new-being."[9] This formative process later provided Elizondo with a way to do theology. The movement of being, to non-being, to new-being in the development of his own identity is evident in Elizondo's theology as he characterizes his theological endeavor as threefold: re-jection—election—mission. He is careful always to remember the past, and with that memory comes the critique of present injustices; with the memory of the past and critique of the present, he is concerned always to point to the future—to a new hope and vision. With this newfound perspective on life, a positive outlook of *mestizaje*, and the richness it provides by incorporating the heritages of differing worlds, Elizondo has refocused his efforts on how Christianity must now take into account the factors produced by the process of *mestizaje* in real life situations.

Often in Judeo-Christian cosmology, the individual Christian is depicted as a universal creature—a generic human being—standing

6. Elizondo, *Future is Mestizo*, 21.

7. Elizondo, "Hispanic Theology," 281.

8. Elizondo, "Mestizaje," 49.

9. Elizondo, *Future is Mestizo*, 18.

before the Creator and in relationship to other creatures. Little consideration is given to social, cultural, and biological conditioning within this framework. In particular, our conditioning in the world is overlooked especially in relation to our spiritual lives. Reasons for holding such an uncomplicated view without human conditioning are numerous. However, as Elizondo prophetically reminds us, the fear that usually accompanies the *mestizo* encounter stemming from our so-called notions of purity perpetuates a worldview of religion void of humanity. "As human beings, we seem to have a natural fear of 'others' and of disturbing the unity of the group—whether family, clan or nation . . . Mestizaje is feared because it is the deepest threat to all the ordinary bonds of identity and belonging. It is a threat to the security of social belonging, that is to the inherited national/cultural/biological identity which clearly and ultimately defines who I am to myself and to the world."[10]

Theologically speaking, we sometimes categorize our spiritual progress in abstract universal terms void of any particular human conditioning. We fall into the temptation that our faith life is "universally applicable" if it does not take into account our language, culture, or any other situational upbringing. In this perspective, our condition as Christians is universal because it is strictly seen within the framework of abstract relationships: our relationship between Creator and creature and our relationship with one another as brothers and sisters without any serious consideration of time and space.

Elizondo's theological contribution is an awareness of how social, cultural, and biological circumstances play a central role in Christianity. These aspects of humanity are central in understanding ourselves as followers of Christ, just as the social, cultural, and biological factors are central in understanding the figure of Jesus, since he was a particular individual living in a particular space and time. Although common threads of humanity are found in each one of us (the general), the uniqueness of each person as a result of social, cultural, and biological conditioning provides further and necessary insights to our overall humanity (the specific). Through the specific we arrive at the universal and not necessarily vice versa. Thus, through the investigation of our particular life circumstances, we come to a fuller realization of humanity. This vital and necessary link between the particular and the universal aspect of

10. Elizondo, "Mestizaje," 48.

our lives, in discovering who we are in relation to our Creator and one another, is very apparent in Elizondo's theological writings.

In elaborating a theology faithful to his social, cultural, and biological heritage, Elizondo recalls several memories of his childhood; these examples are illustrations that both greatly serve and hinder the Mexican American community in their true appreciation of themselves. One positive influence was the neighborhood where Elizondo grew up. His father's *tienda* (store) and the local church across the street were the central gathering places of the neighborhood. Growing up in the hub of neighborhood activities afforded Elizondo care and support from the entire community: "Everyone knew each other by name and had a sincere interest in the needs and goings-on of people in the neighborhood. Many of the customers not only bought from us, but would help with the cleaning up and other aspects of the business."[11] Along with this neighborhood support, Elizondo grew up with the love of his extended family. In a Mexican American household, the parents and grandparents are the first teachers of their children, especially in matters of faith. Having the nurturing presence of his grandparents—"who carry within their hearts and minds the living memory of the family, its spiritual journey, and its faith history"[12]—provided Elizondo with the additional richness of his heritage and culture.

Stories that deface the dignity of Mexican Americans should also be mentioned. Elizondo tells stories of the shame Mexican Americans carry and pass on to younger generations. For example, a particular family would visit an elderly lady on an Indian reservation every Saturday; however, the little boy who tagged along every weekend had no idea who this little old Indian lady was. Only later in life, did the little boy realize that the lady the family visited was, in fact, his grandmother. The shame of being Indian in addition to the Hispanic background was considered too much of a burden for a young child. It is not uncommon for biologically mixed people to possess an inferiority complex, which makes them hide their true natures to the outside world and even to the next generation of their own families. A similar incident recounted by Elizondo concerned a college student whose mother wanted the first in the family to go to college to be able to invite his campus friends to his home. In order to hide the perceived embarrassment of their household,

11. Elizondo, *Future is Mestizo*, 5.
12. Loya, "Religious Education," 17.

an inferiority complex derived from a *mestizo* culture, the mother suggested that the son call her the housemaid instead of the mother—which he did.

These encounters found throughout the Mexican American community could have easily handicapped Elizondo, as they have so many others. However, instead of allowing the inferiority complex of the *mestizo* to overshadow his life, Elizondo prayerfully reflected on his own situation, on the situation of his people, and on the life of Jesus in Galilee to understand his position in life not as a detriment but as a privileged position from which to serve. Instead of seeing the Mexican American heritage as a setback, Elizondo views his background as opening the doors to understanding the figure of Jesus and our calling to be his followers. *Mestizos* have become a portal to understanding our true humanity. Thus, the story-telling of a specific people, recalling and understanding the true nature and impact of their social, cultural, and biological upbringing—in this case the stories that define Mexican Americans—becomes an integral part of both our Christianity and our humanity.

The inferiority complex pervasive within the Mexican American people did not develop overnight but was the result of centuries of conquest and domination. In his attempt to understand his own identity, and thus the identity of Mexican Americans living in the Southwestern United States, Elizondo began plunging through the depths of the history of the Americas to shed valuable insight on his current situation. Being of Mexican heritage living in the United States meant that Elizondo would have to explore not just the history of Mexico, but also the history of the United States to comprehend fully his *Sitz im Leben*. Through the study of this unique *mestizo* history, Elizondo came to the painful discovery of who he is not, rather than who he is: "It has been easier to say who we are not than who we are . . . we are not Mexican . . . we are not USA American . . . then who are we?"[13]

Part of the difficulties Elizondo and other *mestizos* face is the tension of living in two worlds and two cultures: "To be an outsider-insider, as the mestizo is, is to have both intimacy and objective distance at one and the same time, for, insofar as we are in Mexico, we are outside the United States; but, insofar as we are in the United States, we are distant from Mexico."[14] However, this tension would provide the

13. Elizondo, "Mexican American Mestizo Christology," 99.
14. Ibid., 102.

insight necessary to dignify not only his own life but also the lives of all those living on the fringes and in between the boundaries of differing worlds. "We are the 'between' people, for our very existence includes portions of both while not being fully either! As such we can see and appreciate the aspects of both which neither see of themselves or each other. In this 'between' existence lie the chromosomes of both so as to create a new one!"[15]

Historical Developments of Mexican American Mestizaje

Mestizos initially came into existence in the region of what is now known as Latin America, when two worlds, initially unknown to one another, came into contact in the sixteenth century. The colliding of Europeans with the native inhabitants of the Americas left an indelible scar on the territory, resulting in a region and people that would never be the same again. This encounter, the first conquest by the Spaniards of the indigenous population, gave birth to modern day *mestizos* in Latin America.

A second *mestizaje* occurred in the Southwestern United States during the nineteenth century. Originating with the migration of U.S. citizens to territories that would eventually become the United States and through the westward movement and dominance reflected in the doctrine of *Manifest Destiny*,[16] the Hispanic and Indian inhabitants of the Southwestern United States experienced a second conquering, a second *mestizaje*, when Euro American immigrants settled in their region. "The Southwest of the United States was the great "frontera" [frontier] between the worlds of Catholic Mestizo Latin America and Protestant White Nordic America, between Mexico and the United States, and the Mexican American people lived in this great "in-between." The same region had been home to great native populations; then it had become New Spain, then Mexico, and is now the United States."[17] Although *mestizaje* has existed since the first encountering of different groups on earth, the *mestizo* person Elizondo speaks of directly refers to his own heritage.[18]

15. Elizondo, "Mestizaje," 49.

16. The term—*Manifest Destiny*—was coined by John L. O'Sullivan (1813–1895), a lawyer and journalist, around 1845; *Manifest Destiny* signified the expectation that the United States was providentially destined to extend from the Atlantic to the Pacific.

17. Elizondo, "Jesus the Galilean Jew," 263–64.

18. Elizondo often prefaces his use of *mestizo* with his own experience of *mestizaje*,

Without having any sense of the existence of the Americas, Europeans from the Iberian Peninsula stumbled on the New World while searching for easier trade routes to India. The possibility of encountering another continent, let alone a new group of people, was completely unanticipated. Similarly, the natives dwelling in the Americas could not have envisioned any such encounter, for they had no prior knowledge of the people whom they encountered. The indigenous people considered the arrival of Europeans as the gods they worshipped in their religious cosmology; in particular, the gods who would arrive at the end of the world in their belief system. The foreign animals and weapons accompanying Spaniards were interpreted as symbols of their indigenous deity. Thus, the encounter of the two worlds—of the Iberians and of the indigenous—would from the beginning be an unhealthy and unequal encounter, benefiting the European foreigners to the disadvantage of those originally inhabiting the Americas. "In the process they [the Europeans] stumbled upon a plot of land that they thought was India. They named the natives Indians without stopping to ask them who they were or listening to what they called themselves. That mistake is symbolic of the encounter between two worlds that had not suspected the existence of each other."[19]

The *mestizaje* of two worlds began with the discovery of the New World in 1492; however, the crucial beginnings of *mestizo* history on the American continent came on Good Friday in 1519, when Hernán Cortez landed at what would later be called Vera Cruz in Mexico. Ironically, the cross would be symbolic not just of the pain and struggles of Christ in the past, but perhaps more significantly, of the pain and struggles of the native inhabitants caused by the clashing of two worlds, "[t]hat started the prolonged Good Friday that is still being lived today by much of Latin America and by the native Americans."[20]

---

even though the term has been used frequently in other contexts; for example: "In this article, I do not attempt to write about mestizaje in general but reflect on the reality of mestizaje from my own personal experience and that of my Latin American people. We are a product of the massive mestizaje initiated by the conquest of 1492 and continuing through the migrations to our day. We are a biological, cultural, linguistic and religious combination of native America, Latin Europe, and African and Anglo-Saxon America (which, of course, is the United States)." Elizondo, "Mestizaje," 53.

19. Elizondo, "Mary and Evangelization," 147.

20. Ibid.

Driven by greed—first in the search for gold and later in the abuse of slave labor—the Spanish occupation proved to be devastating to the native population. The behavior of the Spanish conquistadors, influenced by the European view of the Indians as inferior people needing guidance to better their lives as well as to save their souls, was rarely in question as military superiority along with dominating attitudes dictated the conditions of life in the New World.[21] In addition, the Spanish government, which oversaw the operations of the Americas, also supported the greedy behavior of the explorers and the mistreatment of the natives as long as Spain continued to receive financial benefits from the activities in the New World. What initially justified and reinforced the mentality of the Spanish—the freedom to do as they pleased—was the recent victory over the Moors in southern Spain in 1492.[22] Believing that God was truly on their side in the cleansing of foreign unbelievers from both their physical and spiritual domain, the Spanish conquerors approached the New World with much vigor to establish, or rather to extend, the God-given earthly domain of the Spanish Crown. Religiously, the Church exploited the situation and sought to establish a new Christendom. In every circumstance, the moment seemed ripe for both the Crown and the Church, of desiring to create a new reality; they soon carried their vision out in the Americas forcing native inhabitants to become servants of both the Crown and the Church.

The Church accompanying the Spanish crown was received with mixed reactions. With the discovery of new territories and new peoples, the Catholic missioners hoped for a new beginning for the Church by forming the indigenous population into faithful believers without the political and religious distractions found on the European continent. However, the native people were not a cultural, political, or religious *tabula rasa*. In fact, the reality was just the opposite; the native population believed in an intricate network of relationships between the physical and spiritual worlds, while simultaneously respecting the creation surrounding them. They were both a spiritually and culturally rich people who were conscious daily of the need to maintain order in the visible world in order to maintain balance within the spiritual realm.[23] Many deities filled their cosmology and the need to appease them was a pri-

21. Elizondo, "Our Lady of Guadalupe," 118.

22. Ibid.

23. Elizondo, "María de Guadalupe," 358.

ority the people considered necessary for their livelihood.[24] Thus, the initial assumption of some missioners that the native population was a blank slate ripe for conversion was false.

As much good as the missioners accomplished in bringing the Gospel to the Americas, both the Crown and the Church were also responsible for the destruction of many native people.[25] Greed became the motive for the mistreatment of the indigenous population by the conquerors, and this greed was devastating to the original inhabitants as well as to the land.[26] Through warfare and the diseases brought by the Spaniards, the native population was repeatedly decimated. "The invasion brought about the biggest genocide in human history affecting around 90% of the population. Of the 22 million Aztecs in 1519, when Hernán Cortéz entered Mexico, there were only a million left in 1600. The survivors are crucified peoples, enduring worse abuses than the Jews in Egypt and Babylon and the Christians under the Roman emperors, as was said many times by bishops who defended the Indians."[27] Thus, the elimination of a whole race and culture came quickly and easily for the foreign invaders. What material greed did not destroy physically, many of the missioners destroyed spiritually.

Although in some instances the missioners did protect the indigenous population from those exploiting the riches of the land and even went to the Spanish Crown on behalf of the indigenous people in order to defend their dignity, their efforts encountered mixed results. Missioners such as Bartolomé de las Casas tirelessly worked to defend both the spiritual and physical attributes of the native population.[28] The overwhelming success in evangelization came when the indigenous notions of the divine were utilized in portraying the Christian God. The clearest example of this practice came in the appearance of Our Lady of Guadalupe, signifying the unity of the two worlds where the European belief in the Mother of God was also understood as the indigenous female diety, *Tonantzin*.[29] Events such as these highlight the coming

24. Elizondo, "Guadalupe," 301–3.

25. Elizondo, *Future is Mestizo*, 60.

26. Elizondo, "*Mestizaje* as a Locus," 160–63.

27. Elizondo, "Unmasking the Idols," 217. A comparable genocide was not seen again until the twentieth century, especially during World War II.

28. Muskus, *Origins and Early Development*, 25–33.

29. The Nahuatl title, *Tonantzin*, is translated as "Our Reverend Mother" and is ap-

together of two vastly different worlds—not a relinquishing of the one world, but a union to enrich the missionary activities of the Spanish. The results can still be seen, as the evangelization activities of the sixteenth century have produced a legacy where the majority of those living in the Americas today are still influenced by this Catholic heritage.

Not all evangelizing activities were so positively received by the indigenous people. Rejecting the worship of indigenous gods and labeling their form of spirituality as pagan, many European missionaries saw little value in the native religions. Instead of seeking bridges from indigenous religious forms to Christianity, some missioners simply dismissed what they encountered and considered the religious practices of the natives aberrations of true worship. "One of the greatest tragedies was the fact that the Franciscan missionaries were obsessed with the devil and saw every religious icon, practice, or ritual of the natives as diabolical."[30] The result was the dismantling of the native religious institutions and practices. "For them, the "other" was an infidel who had only one choice: convert or be destroyed. In their efforts to destroy that which they could not understand, they became the agents of the ultimate violence of the conquest: the destruction of the soul of the people, of the very sacred ground of their existence."[31] Inevitably, the inability to maintain the spiritual order of their ancient cosmology through the worship of their gods deeply affected the native people. Their reason for living and the future of an entire race were eliminated as the indigenous population was displaced physically, culturally, and then spiritually.

The comparatively few natives who survived in spite of the tremendous odds against them—battling lethal foreign illnesses, brutal physical treatment, and degrading cultural attitudes—professed a Catholic faith under the pressures of the Spanish powers. The choice was simply presented: either accept death or accept the religion of the conquerors. The acceptance of Christianity by the indigenous people was partially due to their practice of accepting the "gods" of their conquerors. Not until 1531, through the Marian apparition at the holy mountain of Tepeyac, would the native inhabitants come to see the Catholic faith as their own.

Through the encounter of Juan Diego with Our Lady of Guadalupe, a whole new purpose and hope for living was communicated by "one of

---

plied to various feminine deities such as Mother Earth.

30. Elizondo, "Guadalupe," 303.

31. Ibid.

their own." "One of their own" meant that the *mestiza morena* truly represented her children all the way down to their skin tone, encompassing all that was unique to the native people. Guadalupe, as she is fondly called by her children, was brown-skinned like the natives and did not resemble the Iberians. She embraced the important aspects of the natives, *flor y canto*—flower and song—in her revelation to a simple native, Juan Diego. The Marian apparition came to one of their own as one of their own, and she brought hope to those who were devastated by the new political and religious hierarchies. With the apparition of *Nuestra Señora de Guadalupe*, the people could find a home in the Church and more importantly, find a reason for their continued existence. This new-found hope was evidenced in the numerous conversions that took place soon after the apparition. During the following ten years approximately eight million baptisms were recorded.[32] No longer were the natives forced to believe; now they had a reason to do so through the appearance of their *mestiza* mother.

The significance of Our Lady of Guadalupe's appearance to Juan Diego cannot be comprehended without first understanding the impact the Spanish colonizers had on the people: "A proper appreciation of these two key events: the conquest of 1521 and the beginning of the spiritual reconquest in 1531 is indispensable to an understanding of the Mexican personality of today."[33] "Thus, in her apparition, the indigenous world saw the resurrection of their ancient world—it was not simply a return to the old, for the old was finished. Yet, out of the ashes of the old, a new would arise. There would be continuity, yet transcendence of meaning. She had not come with the conquistador, but had arisen out of the native soil. She was the pure, holy and unviolated mother of the new Church, in the new world, of a new people."[34]

Elizondo approaches *mestizaje*—both the encounter itself and the period where the two worlds encountered each other—in a two-fold manner. On the one hand, the clashing of two worlds—the Iberian of Europe and the indigenous of the Americas—was a brutal encounter. The loss of human life was only the beginning of the devastation of a people. Warfare between the two worlds often resulted in the savage raping of native women and the castration of native men. The indigenous

32. Elizondo, "Mary and Evangelization," 154.

33. Elizondo, "Challenge to Theology," 170.

34. Ibid.

men, who were the primary protectors of the community, were left help-less as they watched their women being taken by the Spanish conquer-ors. The result of this violence upon native women was threefold. First, the women taken forcefully felt disdain for the indigenous men who were impotent to defend them. Second, the indigenous men suffered psychologically from witnessing the transgressions upon their women. Finally, the *mestizo* children, the result of this violent encounter, inher-ited negative attitudes from all those involved. *Mestizos* carry the shame of the women who were violated and the men who were impotent, and the rejection of the dominant transgressors who abandoned them. "[T]he most devastating insults of the conquest had been the rape of the na-tive women, the abandonment of the mestizo children who were the off-spring of the rapes, and the castrating effect this had on the Indian men who were forced to witness the rape of their own beloved and respected women but were not able to do anything about it."[35] The result of this forced union was the creation of the Mexican people, a people generated by the cruel clashing of two worlds with long-lasting consequences.

Elizondo, through his gentle and humble manner evident in his writings and in person, sheds light on commonly overlooked aspects of our humanity, overlooked but vital for an understanding of ourselves. Elizondo depicts the effects on the Mexican people as a result of *mes-tizaje* not just in negative portrayals but also as a way of helping to un-derstand his people today and to address the developmental needs of his community. Often, through the raping of the indigenous women by the Spaniards, the original *mestizo* encounter is seen in a negative light. The children of such a forceful interaction are likewise considered to be shameful because of the demeaning act of their creation, even though these offspring, like all children, deserve dignity, acceptance, and praise. Thus, *mestizaje* was originally a pejorative term referring back to a hu-miliating and demeaning encounter with results that were unwanted as often were the children.

For Elizondo, there is more to understanding *mestizaje* than this initial savage encounter involving native women. Often overlooked in this scenario is the psychological effect on the male population of the indigenous people and their offspring. The men, who were the primary protectors of the people and their way of life, stood by helplessly and witnessed such brutality inflicted upon their own family members and

35. Elizondo, *Guadalupe, Mother of New Creation*, 66.

their people. The inability to protect their own seems to have produced the overly excessive masculinity known more commonly today as the *machismo* attitude found in many Mexican men. This extreme attitude results directly from the helpless state of their forefathers. The mental damage suffered by these men as a result of their castration was the male counterpart to the physical rape of the women. This damaged psyche along with the unwanted physical contact has been a legacy for *mestizo* children. It is an inheritance not only physical, but also psychological. It is an inheritance with lasting effects that centuries later still linger in full force today. It is an inheritance that has created a whole race of people who feel inferior.

On the other hand, however, as primarily a pastor of a wounded people who have evolved from this lineage, Elizondo preaches and exemplifies the blessings arising out of the *mestizo* encounter—the new child, a new humanity. Recalling the events of history as a way of finding enlightenment and without denying the horrors and transgressions of such interactions, Elizondo highlights the beauty that emerged through this violent process. In true Christian fashion, Elizondo illustrates the good that God is able to bring about in the messiness of our human encounters. Refusing to see only inferiority, disgrace, and a defeat in his people, Elizondo reveals that our true humanity is in need of an evolution of *mestizaje*—not in the violent ways of the past but in a natural human progression that unites us as one family, the biologically human family. In short, the occasions of races, cultures, and individuals coming into contact with one another constitute a natural process in our human evolution. It is a gradual process often resisted, looked down upon, and shunned by most groups throughout the world. In the past, the encounter between different groups was often violent as civilizations clashed with one another. Out of this struggle and violence was born the *mestizo*. Today, humanity embraces the worldwide technological and economic advancement bringing about a global society in which racial and ethnic encounters are becoming ever more common.[36]

In order to reframe the *mestizo* person in a positive light, Elizondo does not forget the past or deny certain aspects of the shame

---

36. In regard to global *mestizaje*, Jacques Audinet, Elizondo's dissertation director, wrote in the preface of *Galilean Journey*: "Every modern human culture that we know of is a composite . . . It is *mestizo*, made up of disparate elements, which nonetheless form an integrated whole" (in Elizondo, *Galilean Journey*, 9).

perpetuated against his people throughout the centuries. Instead, Elizondo sifts through history to come to an appreciation of sixteenth century Latin America, examining the healthy aspects of the encounter that have often been overshadowed by popular readings or narrow perspectives in viewing the past. While acknowledging the brutality and destruction of a people committed by the Spanish crown and the Church, Elizondo and others point out that there were churchmen who spoke out against the atrocities perpetuated against the indigenous population and defended the dignity of the human person. There were missionaries who saw beauty and goodness in the indigenous rituals and attempted to incorporate them into the Catholic liturgy.

> The common opinion of the ordinary North American thinking about the conquest and conversion of Latin America is that the conversions were forced by the crown. The conquest and rape of Latin America was supported by the missionaries. It was a tragic example of the Church and the State conspiring to plot and execute the robbery of a people and their land. For too long, we have looked superficially at the history of Latin America through the eyes of Northern Europeans and North Americans. They wrote, consciously or unconsciously, from the tradition of an anti-Latin and anti-Catholic mentality of the Reformation. The end result is that even the Latin Americans in this country developed the sense that the colonization of Latin America had been a tragic failure, while that of North America had been a tremendous success.[37]

Reviewing history from the perspective of the native inhabitants whose voices during the centuries have certainly gone unheeded, Elizondo is able to witness how the *mestizo* encounter of two groups produced not a race of shameful or defeated people but a people who are the offspring of two great cultures of their times. What was born from the painful encounter of the dominant Europeans and the suppressed indigenous peoples was a future that potentially comprised the best attributes of both parent groups. Rather than settling for the popular opinion that the clash of two worlds brings about an inferior people, pastoral leaders such as Elizondo have decided to focus on the positive attributes of the past. Instead of succumbing to the widespread perception of the

---

37. Elizondo, "Theological Interpretation," 16.

Mexican people as a despised group, Elizondo led the reassessment of the situation.

Mestizaje is no longer something of which to be ashamed, it is now something to highlight as a proud heritage. First, the pride comes from looking at the past as equipping the Mexican people with the benefits of two great cultures and gene pools. The natives who controlled and maintained the governance of the Americas were groups who were victorious in the power struggles of their time. Similarly, the Spaniards were the dominant group on the European continent and in the New World through their political and religious institutions. Thus, the parents of the *mestizo* people of the New World were powerful people possessing the richness of their respective society and culture. Their offspring, the Mexican people, would be the beneficiaries of two of the most powerful groups in the world at that time. However, instead of the men and women birthed from such painful circumstances being esteemed, the *mestizo* race in the New World was initially seen as an inferior race of people.

Through the efforts of historians and theologians such as Virgilio Elizondo, a reappraisal of this history is starting to occur. In response to those resisting or refusing to acknowledge the beauty and potential in the *mestizo* person, Elizondo prophetically calls for the recognition of the beauty of the Mexican people. He points out that our societal health depends on our acceptance of the emerging *mestizo* situation today. In other words, if we entrench ourselves in the misconceptions of what it means to be pure by isolating ourselves racially, culturally, and socially, then we fail to acknowledge the birthing of new cultures and peoples, and thus we hinder the values and truths manifested through these encounters. Gently and prophetically, Elizondo constantly reminds us that our failure to recognize and accept the *mestizo* person and culture is our own downfall. When we realize that the natural progression of the world requires such painful births of people and cultures through non-violent means, we are able not only to participate in the development of the world but also to enjoy fully the changes that have occurred in the past and that are still occurring today.

The process of *mestizaje* was not a one-time occurrence in the history of the Mexican American people. Often considered a people twice conquered, twice oppressed, and twice *mestized*, Mexican Americans have endured another *mestizaje* here in the United States through the westward expansion of Euro American settlers. Once again motivated by greed, white-skinned migrants in North America flexed their dominance militarily, culturally, and religiously against the native inhabitants. Mexican people living in the Southwestern region of what is today the United States experienced another painful rebirth, another instance of *mestizaje*. Much of what the natives endured from the arrival of the Spanish in the sixteenth century repeated itself with the westward migration of Euro Americans in the nineteenth century. "To the Protestant, racially 'pure' Anglo-Americans, the Mexicans appeared as degenerate and damned! . . . The Mexican was the very opposite of everything the United States considered as normative for humanity and basic for divine election. The Mexican appeared as the absolute contradiction of the WASP model of human existence."[38]

Militarily, the second conquest took a physical and psychological toll on the Mexican people—not only in the countless lives lost in the battles between the two nations but also in the psychological impact evident still today as Mexican Americans are caught in between two realities in conflict. Tensions rise because Mexican Americans must live with the identities of both the victors and the losers as "subconsciously the oppressed will strive to become like the oppressor, since they have already assimilated many of the characteristics of the dominant group."[39]

> In the first stages of the struggle to belong, the first generations of mestizos will try desperately to become like the dominant group, for only they appear to be fully civilized and human. This will be especially difficult for the mestizo children and young people, for it will produce a tension between wanting to identify and belong to one of the parent groups while feeling they are betraying the other. They will even feel that there is something wrong with them, a sort of contamination! This the result of the superior-inferior/beautiful-ugly image which has been projected and somewhat interiorized.[40]

Military aggression and conquest is so fierce and long lasting that it delineates clear winners and losers throughout generations. In contrast, the process of *mestizaje* does not operate on this zero sum level. Instead of clear losers and winners of conflict, *mestizos* represent the wealth

38. Elizondo, "Report on Racism," 62.

39. Elizondo, "Mestizaje," 51.

40. Ibid.

arising out of the ashes of chaos. However, the aggressive nature and attitude of military superiority represent a failure to view the vanquished "other" as a positive contribution to their existence; rather, the other is seen as inferior and one who must be dismissed, by force if necessary. "Yet, in spite of the difficult situation of inequality, the very seeds for the destruction of this dichotomy of 'superior/beautiful' versus 'inferior/ugly' are physically implanted through the process of mestizaje. Through bodily intercourse and intermarriage, a new biological-cultural race is born who will be both conqueror and conquered, immigrant and native, superior and inferior at one and the same time: he or she will be a real blood sister/brother of both, without being exclusively either."[41]

Biologically, the westward expansion provided another opportunity for further amalgamation of races. As European immigrants wandered farther and farther from their original homelands they began to take on the characteristics of the land, particularly by interracial marriages with the indigenous population they encountered. The war between Mexico and the United States provided another venue for Mexican women to be taken forcefully by foreigners as prizes and possessions. Once again, though valiant in the battles against their invaders, the defeated males eventually could only watch the raping of their women and stand by helplessly. Through both the westward expansion and the battles to secure land, this brutal process gave birth to another generation of *mestizo* children; the offspring would have to endure the pain and humiliation of being *mestizos*, the children of two parent groups. However, the the nineteenth century version of *mestizaje* by comparison with the sixteenth century would be even more intensified with bias, shame, and inferiority.

Culturally, the southwestern region of the United States was in a state of chaos as two worlds collided once more. The combined lineage of the indigenous natives with that of the Spanish heritage produced a unique *mestizo* race of Mexican Americans foreign to the Euro American settlers in the United States. Not only was communication difficult because of the differences in the Spanish and English languages, but traditions and manners were also vastly different. The original Puritans who settled on the eastern seaboard of the United States came with a strict religious view and a work ethic needed for survival. Being a new cultural group on foreign soil required isolation

41. Ibid., 50.

for protection and survival. This isolationist mentality not only en-grained a sense of superiority over other cultures, but also a fear of the others as being different. The "other" was not to be invited in, but by their God-given decree in the New World, the settlers had the right and obligation to secure and create an order according to their beliefs. This way of thinking, necessary for survival as the initial generation in a new region, would clash with the Mexican culture that had survived and evolved down through the centuries. The Mexican people had rec-onciled their indigenous cosmology, especially their religious belief, with their previous Spanish conquerors. What emerged was a culture based on tolerance and hospitality, which would eventually come into conflict with the culture of those moving westward.

In addition, the Protestant faith of the Anglo-Saxon migrants clashed with the Roman Catholic faith of the Mexican people. Originally, escaping the hierarchical institutions of England, Protestants in this new land desired freedom by avoiding institutionalism, especially the forms found in Catholicism. Since the settlers not only saw the people as un-derdeveloped but opposed to their religious faith as well, a clash between Mexican Catholics and Euro American Protestants was only a matter of time. "The native religions were eliminated and totally supplanted by a new type of religion: Puritan moralism, Presbyterian righteousness, and Methodist social consciousness coupled with deism and the spirit of rugged individualism to provide a sound basis for the new nationalism which would function as the core religion of the land."[42]

To compound the religious dynamics, European Catholic leaders also saw the Mexican Catholic faith as more underdeveloped than that found in Europe. Mexican Catholics battled on two fronts. First, they had to deal with the discrimination of the Euro American Protestants with whom they came into contact through the westward expansion of the United States. Second, they had to deal with those Catholic leaders who saw the Mexican people as unfit to lead themselves and for centu-ries sent over missionaries from Europe to lead them spiritually. Socially, the original inhabitants of the region lost their identities as Mexicans, when they went from being citizens of Mexico to becoming foreigners in their own land. Almost overnight, Mexicans went from being natives in the northern most regions of Mexico to becoming foreigners in the southwestern United States.

42. Elizondo, "Popular Religion," 127.

The most devastating effects of *Manifest Destiny* and the westward expansion of the United States were felt by the offspring born during this period, especially in the southwestern regions. As always, the birth of a *mestizo* people, this time the birth of Mexican Americans, had a painful beginning. More painful than the physical defeats and deaths suffered during the clash of the Euro American world and the Mexican world, was the further reinforcing of the inferiority of the defeated people.

> The independence of Texas in the 1830's, the American-Mexican war of the 1840's and the treaty of Guadalupe-Hidalgo of 1848 marked the birth and beginning of a new world—the Mexican American. The birth and beginnings are similar to those of Spanish-Mexico: violence, clash, misunderstanding of the native people by the dominant power group of in-coming migrants, overpowering of the natives by the newcomers with the subsequent embitterment and loss of dignity of the native inhabitants of the land. On the other hand, the new conquistadores possessed the feeling of superiority, of righteousness and of divine predilection which prevailed over their whole way of life. Anything non-Anglo was considered backward, uncivilized and stupid. Laws were quickly passed so that no one would do unto them what they had done unto others.[43]

The new race of people—*la raza*—resulting from the sixteenth and nineteenth century encounters would begin its history as an inferior people and continued to be so seen for centuries until the hope shed upon their situation through the work of churchmen such as Virgilio Elizondo. "Even though the process started in the 1500's, however, it was not until mid-1900's that Mexico was able to say with great pride that its glory was in the fact that it was a Mestizo country—not European, not Indian, not African, but a rich blend with an unbelievable variety of shades of color and stock of the great lines of its ancestry."[44] If Mexico has taken so long to recognize and acknowledge its dignity as a *mestizo* people, a people who experienced only the *mestizaje* of the sixteenth century, then Mexican Americans—a people twice conquered, twice oppressed, and twice *mestized*—will need an even longer period of healing and reconciliation to recognize and acknowledge their own dignity as a *mestizo* people.

43. Elizondo, "Challenge to Theology," 171.
44. Elizondo, "A Theological Interpretation," 18.

Another difficulty in finding a *mestizo* identity among Mexican Americans is the lack of an "American" identity within the United States as a whole. Without the dominant culture being able to self-identify, *mestizos* will not be able to self-identify fully either. There is an important and necessary interplay in the United States where the development of the *mestizo* group allows and motivates the rest of those residing in the country to discover their own true identities. It is a slow and sometimes painful process, but a necessary one, if we are to progress as a human race in terms of reconciling differences. "Theologically speaking, the consequence of the United States experience is that since a personality has not yet emerged, no distinctive United States theological thought has yet emerged. Our theologians are not reflecting out of the faith experience of the United States people, but they are, for the most part, echoing and translating the theological thought of Europe. Because the United States is not a people, it does not yet have a name and neither does it have a theological reflection which has arisen out of the faith reflection based upon the United States experience."[45]

Theological Developments of Mexican American Mestizaje

Mestizaje—the result of different ethnic and cultural groups coming together willingly or unwillingly, consciously or unconsciously—became a theological theme through the works of Virgilio Elizondo. His epic, *Galilean Journey: The Mexican-American Promise*, made the theology of *mestizaje* available to readers outside the Mexican American experience. Prior to the publication of this foundational work, *mestizaje* was a hermeneutical key and theological method in Elizondo's endeavors, even outside of his formal theology as a student and an academic. Because of his social, cultural, and biological background, theological *mestizaje* has always been present in Elizondo's approach to God and in his community of worship. The theological formation Elizondo received in San Antonio, in the Philippines, and in France became venues to formulate and verbalize his life struggle within a religious context. In these academic institutions, Elizondo's awareness of what he had already experienced as a Mexican American in the Southwestern United States developed into a theology—a personal language about God—particular to his own people and their circumstances. In short, theological *mestizaje*

45. Ibid., 21.

was already personally present to Elizondo; his different venues of studies assisted him in presenting it in biblical and theological categories others could comprehend.

In order to formulate a *mestizo* theology, Elizondo had to make several connections within his worlds, especially in religious terminology. First, in the liturgical and ecclesial sense, Elizondo had to validate Hispanic/Latino worship as an authentic expression of Catholicism. "The Latin American church could not simply continue to imitate. She had reached the moment in history when she was to break through her multi-cultural inheritance and emerge as a Church with her own identity, characteristics, and symbolic expressions of her belief in God."[46] This task of not simply imitating, but truly embracing a unique way of prayer was doubly necessary due to historical circumstances, an ecclesial development to reflect the lives of a twice *mestized* people. Just as the Mexican American people came into being through a double *mestizaje*; first, through the conquest of the Spanish, and second, through the expansion of the United States, so too would the Mexican American Church need to undergo a two-fold development. Simply imitating the heritage of the Mexican Church was not enough nor would it address the needs of the people who evolved from the original situation in a different manner. Neither did the blind acceptance of Euro American religion address the situation of displaced Mexican Americans. The Church needed to address the social, cultural, and biological identity of the twice *mestized* people, by developing along similar *mestizo* lines in order to dignify the popular practices of the Mexican American faithful.

As a hybrid worship that includes Mexican traditions as well as European influences that came through the United States, the Mexican American way of prayer is often misunderstood. "By popular expressions of the faith I do not refer to the private or individual devotions of a few people but to the *ensemble of beliefs, rituals, ceremonies, devotions, and prayers which are commonly practiced by the people at large*."[47] Thus, one of Elizondo's highest priorities arising from his pastoral work has been to authenticate the *mestizo* worship of his people as being both appropriate and rich.

In the past, Mexican American religious expressions were often seen as inferior ways of worship in comparison to the traditions of their

46. Ibid., 18.

47. Elizondo and Matovina, *Mestizo Worship*, 24.

parent groups. *Mestizo* worship is neither the Mexican expression nor the Euro American expression of prayer and has been discounted in a similar fashion by *mestizo* people themselves. However, Elizondo is quick to point out the error of this view, especially when the richness of the *mestizo* person is recognized and acknowledged. If *mestizaje* is truly a hermeneutic key and theological method that allows a human conception of the divine, then *mestizo* worship rising out of the joyful and painful cries of the *mestizo* people is equally valuable. Instead of seeing *mestizos* and their liturgical expressions as inferior, churchmen like Elizondo see a beautiful richness that is an expression of the deep faith of the people. Thus, rather than being inferior, *mestizaje* in its liturgical form becomes a natural progression both in life and in our encounter with God. "Foundational faith expressions are those religious traditions which the majority of a people celebrate voluntarily, transmit from generation to generation, and persist in celebrating with the clergy, without them, or even in spite of them. The foundational faith expressions of a people are a ritual, symbolic response to their history and contemporary situation. These expressions embody the deepest identity of the people, their collective soul. They are the people's means of encountering the God who accompanies them during times of mourning and joy, tears and laughter, rejection and welcome, hope and despair, death and life."[48]

The ancient expression, *lex orandi, lex credendi*—the rule of praying is the rule of believing—is a reminder that our prayer is a real reflection of our faith for we pray what we believe. Belief and prayer are intimately connected, and thus, authentic prayer expressions which incorporate the whole person are always needed. By appealing to the *mestizo* aspect of his people, Elizondo is able to affirm the authentic communal prayer that respects the traditions and peoples of the past while incorporating the situation of today. It is a reminder not only for Mexican Americans, but for all those searching for a way of expressing themselves before the divine that a unique expression must arise from one's own life situations. The prayers of the Mexican American people are real; Elizondo reminds us that the theological beliefs behind the people's prayers are real as well.

After validating Hispanic/Latino worship as an authentic expression of Catholicism, Elizondo needed scriptural connections to validate a theological *mestizaje*. His examination of biblical narratives led him to investigate the cultural background of the historical Jesus. The questions

48. Ibid., 1.

Elizondo raised revolved around Jesus' upbringing in the Galilean region and the influences this area of the world had on him. Through his investigation of the Galilean region, Elizondo recognized a world similar to his own in San Antonio. This comparison spurred him to depict Jesus as a Galilean whose regional characteristics influenced his earthly ministry. Jesus was born into a *mestizo*-world resulting from the commercial encounter of the Jewish world with the Romans as well as other type of ethnic and religious diversity.

Because of the diversity of this region, there were rumors surrounding Jesus' birth, especially since Joseph wanted to divorce Mary secretly because of her pregnancy. Scandals overshadowed the Holy Family and continued to do so throughout Jesus' life since only in hindsight, after the resurrection, were the Evangelists able to communicate the infancy narrative as found today in the Gospels. One of these scandals was the rumor that Jesus was conceived from relations between a Roman soldier and a young Jewish girl: "Rumors even circulated that the name of the child's father was Pantera."[49] Scandalous rumors do not deter Elizondo's orthodox belief in both Mary's own Immaculate Conception and Jesus being conceived by the Holy Spirit; however, since the people during the time of the Holy Family did not know this, there must have been some gossiping about Mary and Joseph and eventually about the child Jesus. Elizondo uses this speculation to highlight Jesus as a marginalized person from the very beginning of the incarnation.[50]

Galilee was a region particularly unique in the Jewish world because it was a region where many cultures and peoples met. Being a major trade center, Galileans had social and cultural contacts with foreign people, eventually leading to biological intermingling as well.[51]

49. Elizondo, *Future is Mestizo*, 79. Although Pantera is the name of the Roman soldier in this particular rumor; the name can simply mean "Roman," thereby signifying the diverse environment of Jesus' birth. In his classical work on the birth of the messiah, Raymond Brown described this allegation as an "uncomplimentary explanation adopted by opponents" to the Gospel accounts: "The real question that we must ask about this Jewish charge of illegitimacy, attested from the second century in both Jewish and Christian sources, is whether it represents a tradition independent of the Gospels . . . or a polemic in response to and stimulated by the Gospels . . . there is no way to know with certainty whether the post-NT Jewish charge of illegitimacy is an authentic recollection of Jewish charges that were circulating before Matthew composed his narrative" (Brown, "The Charge of Illegitimacy," 534–37).

50. Elizondo, *Future is Mestizo*, 79.

51. Elizondo, "Mexican American Mestizo Christology," 105.

These encounters created a culture as well as a people that would be different from those in Jerusalem, and therefore despised by those in the center of liturgical and political power who possessed so-called purity and superiority over those in the northern region. The Galilean reality, created by the coming together of different worlds, allowed Elizondo and others who have benefitted from his work to make critical connections between the people of Galilee and those living in the Southwestern United States—a people also marginalized because of the mingling of many differences.[52]

This unusual upbringing of Jesus and the type of ministry he undertook contains a unique revelation of God. Through the person of Jesus, an individual living in a marginalized *mestizo*-world, God's message comes to light: those who are initially despised by the world as being impure are later understood as the cornerstone in building the Kingdom of God. Jesus' own ministry reveals his desire to reach out to those outcast because of their heritage and position in life and more importantly to challenge the institutions that believed in the superiority of those who remained unaffected by foreign influences. Jerusalem was considered the correct place of worship for Jews because of its insistence on maintaining purity. Galilee was a place economically necessary for life and any impure encounters with foreigners were to be kept to this region. "According to human standards, [Jesus] was of doubtful origins, and thus by reason of his very birth he entered into solidarity with the masses whose origins are questioned by those in power. As a human being, he did not have to enter into solidarity with the destitute and rejected of the world—because he was born one of them. The world might consider him illegitimate, but God would proclaim him God's own beloved son[.]"[53]

Originally the result of violence, weakness, and shame, the *mestizo* people, resulting from the mixing of indigenous inhabitants with foreign occupation, have become privileged ones in understanding the Gospel accounts of Jesus and our humanity.[54] The second letter to the

52. Lee, "Galilean Journey Revisited," 383–86.

53. Elizondo, *Future is Mestizo*, 78.

54. "Privileged ones" is not an exclusive term for *mestizos*, who are only one among many who have been wounded by society. The hermeneutical privilege of the poor, as Elizondo defines it, includes the oppressed, the exploited, the marginalized, the rejected, etc. The privileged position is not based on superiority, but simply because of a shared experience and out of this common experience they are able to better appreciate

Corithians speaks about a new creation coming into being and being reconciled in Christ (2 Cor 5:17–18). What is the process the scriptures speak of with this new creation? Reflecting on this concept, Elizondo describes the new creation of his people: "Biologically a new man was evolving who shared in his very bloodstream, in varying degrees, the genetic characteristics of three great human stocks: Indian, European, and African. Spiritually, as this new man was growing and developing, so was the faith into which he was baptized. Thus in every aspect of the word truly a new man was being formed."[55] Being a new creation, biologically and spiritually, today creates an avenue to the historical Jesus. By living in a similar environment as New Testament Galilee, *mestizos* occupy a unique position in life with the ability to recognize the Galilean Jesus in his true humanity—a *mestizo*-type figure born of a diverse social and cultural environment. Religiously, keen insights are available through the lives of *mestizos* through their identification with the Galilean Jesus, who is one like them because of the marginalization and exclusion found in the region of Galilee. The *mestizo* culture prophetically guides us to Jesus and to one another in our Christian duty. "It is precisely at this point of history that the Mexican American stands as a human bridge between the two great cultural traditions of North America and of Latin America. Both were conceived and born in some amount of grace and of sin, and the development of these two great American traditions has had a mixture of virtue and of vice."[56]

In a theological sense, *mestizaje* is the hermeneutic key in verbalizing our experience of God. According to St. Anselm, theology is expressed as *faith seeking understanding* where our comprehension arises from our personal encounter with God. Similarly, theologians such as Gustavo Gutiérrez describe theology as the second step in following Jesus. The first step is prayer, which includes both contemplation of God and Christian praxis towards our neighbor. Elizondo speaks of *mestizo* theology in a similar vein, insofar as it cannot be realized without considering the concrete person living in real world situations influenced by social, cultural, and biological conditioning. Without a concrete encounter of God, which requires specific human conditions and actions in the world—a world consisting of a person's biological and

---

the depths of the Gospel message.

55. Ibid., 18.

56. Ibid., 21.

mental makeup—then a proper reflection, the process of doing theology, is impossible. In other words, our personal experience of God requires expressions found only within real life categories.

Mestizaje is the expression of theology not only for the Mexican American people in the United States, but also for the whole of Christianity. Throughout salvation history, revelation has taken root in specific cultures and people. In many ways, Elizondo emphasizes the interaction of revelation, God's self-communication, and the human person—those who are addressed by the self-communication—in a specific historical term, *mestizaje*. From the beginnings of the Church, this *mestizo* encounter is evident especially during the patristic period. With Hellenistic influences in the Jewish world, new expressions were formulated by utilizing categories from both worlds to express human inquiries about the Divine.[57] An example of this expression was evident in the Christological controversies leading to the dogmatic statements at Chalcedon that utilized Greek terminology for a Jewish experience to produce a *mestizo*-type definition of the divinity and humanity of Christ.

In addition, *mestizo* expressions of faith were present during the scholastic period of the Church and in great medieval theologians such as St. Thomas Aquinas. The shift of theology into the scientific realm as a result of encounters with other disciplines produced a foundation for doing theology that is still revered today. With the dawn of the Enlightenment, the scholastic mentality encountered the modern mind and continental philosophies. Theological expressions since this period have sought to address non-believers and those who rely on reason and not simply on revelation. Throughout salvation history, revelation has taken root in human circumstances and through this interaction the Church has grown and developed by incorporating two worlds—the religious and the secular. Accordingly, both are needed in order to comprehend revelation, since the encounter between the religious and the secular results in the *mestizo* offspring of theology, our comprehension of God's self-communication. Thus, Elizondo points to the natural progression of salvation history when referencing his own history, both culturally and religiously.[58]

What is unique in Elizondo's theological approach is the perspective he highlights, a perspective which the Gospel indicates when it

57. Elizondo, "Mary and the Poor," 64; "Mary and Evangelization," 160.
58. Lee, "Galilean Journey Revisited," 383–84.

refers to the lowly ones. While few would deny the connection between revelation and humanity in salvation history, Elizondo emphasizes the hermeneutical or epistemological privilege of the excluded and marginalized[59]—those who are the biological and cultural result of a *mestizo* encounter. The addition of biology to the cultural, social, and religious aspects of our lives provides a new challenge in understanding revelation.[60] In this scenario, the human condition is not simply something that a person can comprehend. Only when biology and culture are taken into consideration can the Kingdom of God be fully realized within a particular group of people. It is one thing to accept a *mestizo* mentality, but another to recognize the *mestizo* person as having a privileged position—bridging humanity to one another and to God by reconciling the deep barriers of separation. "Virgil [Elizondo] shows us that cultures are mestizo and that their survival depends on their acceptance of mestizaje . . . the conflict of the future is not between cultures, but within each culture, between those who accept mestizaje and those who reject it in the name of power, tradition, or purity."[61]

The Mestizo Task

The tasks of *mestizo* theology are numerous for it not only affirms the identity of the *mestizo,* but it also opens possibilities for society at large to come to terms with a corporate identity. Once again, the notion of the specific leading to the universal is evident as the individual *mestizo* challenges and expands the images of the human being within a given society. Most importantly, the Mexican American *mestizaje* which Elizondo addresses in his writings is a bodily reminder of the injustices that birthed it: "For me as a Christian, the mestizo is the biblical 'rejected stone which has become the cornerstone'. Mestizaje offers new breakthroughs—initially they might appear as transgressions of even the most sacred, but in reality they are the beginnings of new life."[62] Thus, a major task of *mestizo* theology is to overcome victimization and allow *mestizos* to regain self-confidence through their identity as God's chosen ones for the mission of creating a more inclusive society. "The challenge is

59. Elizondo, "Jesus the Galilean Jew," 262.

60. Elizondo, "*Mestizaje* as a Locus," 160; García-Rivera, "Crossing Theological Borders," 253.

61. Audinet, "*Mestizo* Theology," 149.

62. Elizondo, "Mestizaje," 53.

to blend our two traditions, our two historical processes, in a conscious and critical, creative way so as truly to produce a new body of knowledge and know-how, a new way of life for humanity, new values, new language, new criteria of judgment and acceptability. Yes, and even new expressions of religion, as antagonistic religions find a new common ground for the sake of humanity."[63]

The healthy process of identifying oneself as a *mestizo* requires investigation of both parent groups, not only revealing the injustices caused both in the past and in the current situation, but also denouncing it by upholding the *mestizo* in society: "To know a people today, we must investigate the roots as far back as possible. Only sufficient distance from the present will bring to us the often hidden patterns and connections of where we come from and, also, where we are going."[64] However, this upholding in society, recognizing and acknowledging the *mestizo* as good and proper in our human development, is not simply a reversal of positions. In other words, inversion or the reversal of societal roles as oppressor-oppressed or dominator-dominated is not the solution if *mestizaje* is to be healthily embraced by an individual or society. Rather, the *mestizo* process points to a different hermeneutic and epistemology of humanity. "In liberating himself, the Mexican American does not want simply to exchange places with the oppressing group, for that would mean accepting himself a new kind of oppression: the oppression of the competitive consumer mentality of the impersonal business world which makes up a great part of our society."[65]

Inversion is a central theme in Elizondo's writings because of its temptation and appearance as an easy solution to the problems of *mestizo* identity. Inversion is tempting in two forms. First, externally, *mestizos* as an oppressed group are tempted to rise up and displace their oppressors only to replace them in that particular role. In this scenario, the oppressed simply replace the oppressors and repeat the cycle of evil once again. As Elizondo has observed: "Evil comes through the perversion and inversion of life-giving relationships as intended by the creator."[66]

Second, internally, inversion appears in the disdain for the weaker attributes of the inherited traits and the desire for the attributes of the

63. Ibid., 52–53.
64. Elizondo, "Theological Interpretation," 13.
65. Ibid.
66. Elizondo, "By Their Fruits," 44.

powerful. In a healthy *mestizo* encounter, the attributes of both parent groups are fully embraced rather than seeing one as superior and the other as inferior. As long as this dichotomy exists between the parent groups, then the *mestizo* offspring cannot fully embrace their identity for there will always be a portion of them that is disregarded.

This inverted characteristic that conflicts the *mestizo* person both internally and externally is for Elizondo exemplified in Cain's devastating attitude toward his brother as told in the creation accounts in Genesis: "The difficulty comes when we begin to appreciate ourselves, not in terms of our uniqueness, but rather in terms of someone else. Once we begin to compare ourselves to others, jealousies begin and our imaginations go wild."[67] Such attitudes based on aggression, seek to destroy rather than to understand the other. Internally, this inversion continues the disgrace and shame of *mestizos* for they cannot take away the elements of their being which they consider inferior. To eliminate a portion of what comprises the *mestizo* would mean self-destruction.

Cain's destructive attitude towards his brother is perpetuated today when people in society strive out of sinful emotions to better themselves at the expense of others. "In such a state of existence, "to be" means "to be better than others." It appears that only by becoming superior to others can one come to the fullness of life. One constantly needs lesser others to affirm one's humanity. It is this attitude that is one of the root causes of racism. We need to define metaphysically inferior peoples to allow us to have an existential sense of well-being. The concrete consequences of this mentality are devastating."[68] This type of mentality entraps the *mestizo* person, for the need to be better creates a reality of those who are less. Racism directed against the *mestizo* heritage will always categorize those who are different as the ones who are less. Therefore, *mestizos* become invaluable in this type of society for they serve to affirm those who consider themselves superior by viewing those who are socially, culturally, and biologically mixed as inferior.

The tensions of the internal and external inversions are also evident in the spiritual realm for *mestizos* as well as for those in society who embrace *mestizaje* in solidarity. The religious realm becomes the conscience, further highlighting the difficulties facing the *mestizo* population. In their religious beliefs and ideology, the *mestizo* way of life is embraced as

67. Ibid., 46.
68. Ibid., 47.

part of God's creative plans for humanity. However, conflicts arise when sharp distinctions are made between one's internal quest for justice and the Kingdom of God, while the outer appearance of the person reflects a different isolationist reality. "The point of conflict is that whereas the innermost desires of the human heart continue to be in conformity and in harmony with God's way of life, their concrete sociocultural and even religious formulations are almost exclusively in terms of humanity's way of death."[69] This compromise further complicates the *mestizo* identity and exacerbates the dilemma caused by both the internal and external inversions of our lives. In addition, the structures maintaining inferiority within the *mestizo* population continue to live on in the guise of charity and love. This tragedy, as Elizondo terms it, is twofold: "One is that cultures are built more upon the foundations of Cain than of God. The other is that they become identified with God, and to question them is to question God. To the degree that cultures become absolutized, they no longer allow human growth and development."[70]

Elizondo makes clear that we cannot buy into the temptations of inversion—simply being the oppressor—for it can never be the real solution. The opposite extreme of eliminating all institutions that create inverted attitudes must also be disregarded. True solutions embracing *mestizo* identity can only come in the form of solidarity with others by bringing to the forefront those who are marginalized along with the realization of our own nature as *mestizos*. The Galilean Jesus reveals this path of reconciliation as he began by entering into blood and ethnic solidarity with the marginalized of society. "Why such a beginning? Because in the very moment of becoming human, God reveals the lie of the world and the truth of God concerning the human."[71]

As Christians, we too follow this example as the hope for our full humanity by coming into solidarity with God's chosen ones.

> One chooses poverty so as to enter into solidarity with the poor of the world and, together with them, struggle to forge new ways of life that will eliminate both the curse of poverty and the curse of materialistic wealth. We dispossess ourselves freely from the spirit of possession so that the goods of this world might be more evenly distributed amongst all of God's children. It is this free

69. Ibid., 52.

70. Ibid., 59.

71. Ibid., 57.

and voluntary sharing of the goods of this world and of the fruits of our own labor that will truly contribute to the buildup of a new society, a new culture, and a new world vision that will be truly life-bearing for all people."[72]

In a similar fashion, in his address to The Catholic Theological Society of America, Elizondo called for theologians to enter into solidarity with not only the Mexican American endeavor, but also the entire *mestizo* journey.[73] He made three specific requests. First, Elizondo called upon his peers to join the ranks and not speak down to the *mestizo* population. Prophetically, Elizondo spoke of becoming one with the little ones of today's society: "Join us in our sufferings, and our *movimientos* so that, having become one with those of us at the bottom, you may exercise your ministry by unveiling and denouncing the demonic powers which are present and at work in the invisible structures which are oppressing people in today's world."[74] Second, Elizondo exhorted his audience to uncover sin not only present in the world, but also accepted and dignified in institutional practices. Finally, Elizondo asked for assistance in identifying the Kingdom which is irrupting through the new humanity formed by *mestizaje*.

MESTIZO CHRISTOLOGY: THE GALILEAN JOURNEY

It is difficult to determine the order of progression in Virgilio Elizondo's theological development. To pinpoint precisely whether his full consciousness of *mestizaje* came first or whether his Christological understanding of the Galilean Jesus was developed prior to his consciousness of *mestizaje* is an unrealistic task. What is clear, however, in Elizondo's theological writings is the intricate relationship between the two. In fact, a more precise description of his theology would focus on the mutual development of the two. There is no doubt that the theme of *mestizaje* was present in Elizondo prior to his doctoral studies in France. However, the full impact of *mestizaje* on Mexican Americans, on Christianity, and on all of humanity could not have developed without his investigation of the Galilean Jesus. In addition, without the theme of *mestizaje*,

72. Ibid.

73. Elizondo, "Challenge to Theology," 175.

74. Ibid.

Elizondo's insights about the Galilean Jesus embracing a *mestizo* humanity and ministry would certainly not have been proposed.

Even with the support of the faculty at the Institut Catholique de Paris, Elizondo initially encountered some hesitation in proposing *mestizaje* as a theological category for his dissertation. First, the concept of *mestizo* derived from the Southwestern United States was foreign to most of the faculty in Europe. In addition, given societal trends such as the theme of the "melting pot" where society as a whole is viewed as blending into one, some wondered if the theme of *mestizaje* would be relevant in the future. In the end, the faculty agreed that Elizondo's use of his unique *mestizo* heritage as the hermeneutic lens in the investigation of the Galilean Jesus was not only valid, but also truly necessary.[75]

Utilizing the ethical paradigm—*ver, juzgar, actuar* (*see, judge, act*)[76]—Elizondo presents the initial *Galilean Journey* undertaken by Jesus as a movement from rejection, to election, and to mission. Rather than simply recounting the events of Jesus in a specific region or explaining how Jesus' upbringing might relate to Mexican Americans in the United States, Elizondo's presentation, following the method of *ver, juzgar, actuar*, analyzed the religious, economic, and political encounters of Mexican Americans and analogous accounts of Jesus' own encounters in the New Testament. The similarities between these two experiences give hope to *mestizos* by affirming the positive attributes of *mestizaje* and by challenging the structures maintaining the oppression and alienation of the *mestizo* population: "This is the method used by the Church of Latin America, which has become basic to the work of MACC [Mexican American Cultural Center], and which I have used in hundreds of grassroots Bible reading sessions throughout the Southwest. It has become so ingrained that I did not even think of identifying it."[77] This natural inclination for seeing, judging, and acting with regards to the conditions

75. Those who were apprehensive regarding Elizondo's proposed topic eventually came to accept the importance of *mestizaje* in their own theological writings. Elizondo's dissertation director, Jacques Audinet, was especially influenced by the creativity and insight that *mestizaje* provided in both religious and secular dialogue. Audinet later wrote his own book on *mestizaje*: *The Human Face of Globalization*.

76. Elizondo in "Jesus the Galilean Jew," 269 n. 15 cites Lee's article, "Galilean Journey Revisited," regarding the definitions of the traditional categories of *ver, juzgar, actuar*: *Ver* is to do a critical analysis of reality; *Juzgar* is to scrutinize the inspired word and tradition for guidance; *Actuar* is to discern a Christian response.

77. Ibid.

of the people allowed Elizondo to apply *ver, juzgar, actuar* to the life of Jesus in three important stages of his life: the beginning of his earthly existence in Galilee, his later life in Jerusalem, and the resurrection event following his death. Through the use of three principles based on the different periods of Jesus' life—the *Galilean Principle,* the *Jerusalem Principle,* and the *Resurrection Principle*—Elizondo presented Jesus' identity and ministry as constitutive of one another.[78] Only through knowing the displacement of his humanity (*mestizo*-type existence) did Jesus reach out to those in similar circumstances and work toward bridging humanity with one another and with God.

The *Galilean Principle,* corresponding to the method of *ver,* is the recognition of the current state of *mestizaje* in the *frontera* of a particular region. Whether it was two thousand years ago when Jesus walked the borderlands of Galilee and Jerusalem or today in the footsteps of Mexican Americans walking the borderlands of the Southwest, the *mestizo* experience transcends time and space. What is common in this *frontera* encounter is the disdain and marginalization people experience from the two worlds that gave birth to them. Therefore the *Galilean Principle* is the critical recognition of the *mestizo* conditions when differing worlds border one another.

In Galilee, Jesus entered into our humanity in an environment defined precisely by a social, cultural, and biological encounter due to the political and economic circumstances of the region. As a center of trade and commerce, Galilee was comprised of foreigners whose economic interactions with one another led to contact on every other human level. In support of his claim of diversity in Galilee at the time of Jesus, Elizondo refers to scripture scholars such as Sean Freyne, who academically and personally supports Elizondo's description of the Galilean *mestizo*-type environment.[79] "[E]ach theme takes on a richer and deeper theological significance when it is set back into the concrete, everyday experiences of Galilean life and landscape . . . a historical-theological approach can illustrate the universal meaning

78. Lee, "Galilean Journey Revisited," 385–86.

79. In my conversations with Virgilio Elizondo while writing this book, he has mentioned that he consulted Sean Freyne to refine his work before publishing his last article (Elizondo, "Jesus the Galilean Jew"). It is important to note that Elizondo's reference to Freyne is a recent one; Elizondo did not have the luxury of citing scripture scholars like Freyne when he first began describing the connections between Galilee and *Mestizaje*. See also Appendix A.

disclosed in and through the particularity of Jesus' life. God did not become human as a universal, but in the particularity of Jesus' life and praxis, which began in Galilee. From a Christian theological perspective, therefore, every particular human life can become a Galilean experience of divine disclosure within the world of actual things."[80] However, Freyne also acknowledges the current uncertainty among Biblical historians as to the exact nature of the race of the people in the Galilean region and thus of the *mestizo*-type conditions.[81] "Contrary to popular opinion archaeology does not provide 'hard facts' but data in need of interpretation, just as much in need of *critical* retrieval as are the texts."[82] Therefore, Freyne has affirmed the need for further scholarly investigations of Galilee and the Galilean Jesus:

> [I]t is important to remind ourselves that Jesus was not a free-standing and isolated figure, waiting to be clothed suitably by his followers in images arising from Jewish hopes and expectations. As a Galilean figure, he must have participated in and been affected by the everyday experiences of life as lived in the region. He would have been inspired and challenged by the stories of Israel's life in the north, been keenly aware of the ways his fellow Galileans in the past had responded to threats from within and without to their identity, and been acutely conscious of the dangers confronting him and his community in the immediate present. In other words, we must allow Jesus a fully human history as a Galilean, but one that is also steeped in his own Jewish religious traditions and the hopes emanating from them.[83]

Elizondo's work should be considered as one of several possible presentations of Galilee, given the many unknowns in the current historical data. With the support of scripture scholars such as Freyne, Elizondo describes Galilee as a region where a unique grouping of people was born.

> It [historical-criticism] doesn't always point to it [*mestizo* encounter], but there is very serious scholarship that does speak about it. Even in the Gospel Jesus is constantly crossing borders, constantly going to Decapolis and the cities. And the fact that it's estimated that many of the Jewish people in Galilee worked as day laborers. I think there is enough evidence to think of

80. Freyne, "Galilean Jesus," 297.

81. Freyne, "Geography of Restoration," 297.

82. Freyne, "Galilee," 581.

83. Freyne, "Galilean Jesus," 285.

> Galilee as a region of encounters. There may have been very
> strong Jewish towns; they were commercial crossroads going
> through them. I don't agree with the criticisms . . . But I think
> I'm on firm grounds. I have worked with Sean Freyne, who is
> one of the leading experts on Galilee. I found his comments
> have led me to be more precise, but I don't think he's led me to
> take a different opinion.[84]

However, this uniqueness as a result of different peoples coming together was not held in esteem in Jerusalem. To the contrary, those who considered themselves pure in Jerusalem, symbolizing the established power, considered the Galileans less so due to their contact with foreigners. "By living and growing up in Galilee, one came into contact with the various civilizations, cultures, and religions of the world. These exchanges would be very ordinary in Galilee but would be abhorred by any "purist" as evidence of decay and contamination."[85] Entering this *mestizo*-type world through his birth along with his upbringing surrounded by those like him, Jesus would also define his ministry in the same light. Jesus not only came into solidarity with the rejected ones in society, but also chose to be a reject himself through the incarnation. Simply stated, Jesus' life and ministry would be defined by his *mestizo*-type existence: the reject who rejects rejection.[86]

> He takes a most common, beautiful, and emotional symbol of his
> people, the "Kingdom of God," and proposes an earth-shaking
> new interpretation: everyone will be welcomed, beginning with
> the despised and impure of his society (Mt 21:31). The "rejected
> one" rejects rejection by living and proclaiming a universal wel-
> come and love for all. He invites all to repent of their feelings
> and attitudes of inferiority or superiority, of impurity or purity, of
> belonging or rejection, and to recognize that we are all children
> of God called to share in the common table, the table of the new
> family that goes beyond blood or social status."[87]

Throughout his ministry, Jesus consistently reflected the goodness of *mestizo* existence, the richness brought about by the coming together of people. He did not embrace the Jerusalem outlook of *mestizaje* as

84. See Appendix A.
85. Elizondo, *God of Incredible Surprises*, 48.
86. Elizondo, *Galilean Journey*, 70.
87. Elizondo, "Jesus the Galilean Jew," 274.

inferior. In his interaction with those displaced in society, especially in his table fellowship, Jesus revealed the welcoming nature and universal love that God the Father has for everyone. In addition, the miracle accounts do not simply represent physical healing. Although healing at all levels occurs through the people's interaction with Jesus, what is truly highlighted is the restoration of people back into society. In particular, through societal recognition of the marginalized and excluded as the privileged ones of the Gospel, those who receive God's attention enjoyed the healing that Jesus brings and most of all, the undoing of rejection which Galileans experienced because of their *mestizo*-type identity.

Thus, the *Galilean Principle* simply highlights the favor God has for those rejected by others in society through the critical assessment of the negative societal view of *mestizaje*. Through rejection comes election: "Thus begins the pattern of whom God chooses to bring about redemption: not the wise and powerful, not the wealthy and famous, not the dominant and well-installed but those deprived of their basic humanity by the unjust structures of this world. Those that the world considers insignificant and inferior God redeems by choosing them to be his very own—and God chooses only the best, never trash!"[88] However, with divine favor comes the demand for discipleship. When a *mestizo* recognizes his or her special place in God's economy, then the responsibility to accept God's call is required, a call realized only through the examination of the other two principles.

The *Jerusalem Principle* is to judge correctly the oppressive situation brought about by marginalization and exclusion and to challenge the beliefs and perspectives held by the dominant group in society through the method of *juzgar*. Believing in their superiority over foreigners, the people of Jerusalem viewed other Jews who came into contact with non-Jews, and in particular those residing in the region of Galilee, as inferior as well. This second principle is the challenge to the activities and attitudes of the Jewish elite, since their actions based on elitism create the negative consequences affecting the existence of those marginalized and excluded. The inferiority complex of the *mestizo* mindset, and in particular the desire to rid themselves of their mixed heritage and become like those who have dominated them in the past, is a concrete result of the oppressive nature of racism towards the marginalized and excluded in society. By utilizing the theme of *mestizaje*, it is easy to conceive

88. Ibid.

Galileans as unaccepted by Jerusalem purists and through this exclusion considered inferior because of their mixed heritage.

The consequences of such exclusion are also evident within the Mexican American community today, especially when aspects of its heritage such as language, dress, and skin color are regarded with disdain. Once again, this second principle is more than recognition, for every principle Elizondo describes ultimately leads to action. The *Jerusalem Principle* is a summons to recognize and act on behalf of those rejected by the elites in the center, those holding political or religious power: "God chooses an oppressed people, not to bring them comfort in their oppression, but to enable them to confront, transcend, and transform whatever in the oppressor society diminishes and destroys the fundamental dignity of human nature."[89]

Instead of responding to centers of power in a violent manner, Jesus responded in a non-violent way, challenging sinful structures to conversion. Rejection, according to Elizondo, is violent. Thus, rejection is rejected by the reject and non-violent means are sought by Jesus: "In his Galilean identity, he questioned the official structures. But still, he was a Jew; he questioned the system from within."[90] Understanding the need for religious institutions in the lives of people, Jesus advocated neither a dismantling of oppressive systems such as those in Jerusalem nor a complete reversal where the status of the Galileans and those in Jerusalem would switch positions. Rather, Jesus challenged the views of the powerful elites in Jerusalem by revealing the favored ones in the Kingdom of God. Instead of favoring isolation and catering to the needs of the so-called pure, Jesus called for their attention to be shifted to the lowly ones outside their so-called realm of purity. The *Jerusalem Principle* involves movements undertaken by Galileans challenging the established powers of structural sin; thereby inviting the centralist elites to conversion. "The mission of those on the outskirts of the established order is to *go to the centers* of power and unveil the root causes of the evil that has become engrained in the structures that shape socio-national life and hide the face of the true God who is Father-*Abba* of all."[91]

The *Jerusalem Principle* is Elizondo's prophetic call for all Mexican Americans to embrace their rightful place in God's economy by

89. Elizondo, *Galilean Journey*, 103.

90. Ibid., 107.

91. Ibid.

adopting God's understanding of their *mestizo* existence. God's election, the result of human rejection, must be lived out by Mexican Americans by allowing their *mestizo* lives to become vehicles for unity in religious and secular circles. In understanding the favor that God has bestowed in the past on ethnically marginalized Galileans and today, on Mexican Americans, the *mestizos* of the Southwest must rise up to challenge the centralist tendencies of those in powerful religious and political systems. The Mexican American presence prophetically reminds us where God dwells. Once correctly understood, God's economy requires that we challenge the rest of society who maintain elite positions.

Elizondo offers several such challenges arising through the development of his own *mestizo* consciousness. For one, Elizondo calls our attention to the racism still prevalent in the Church and society. Elizondo addresses the racism in communication: "American monolingualism must be confronted. Bilingualism is not an impoverishment but an enrichment."[92] Besides racism, Elizondo focuses our attention on another structural issue plaguing *mestizo* existence: liberal capitalism. The economic position of the Hispanic world has disadvantaged and continues to disadvantage the possibility of a dignified human life for the masses. Structural injustices found within the Mexican American world, within the *mestizo* reality, reminds us that the *Galilean Journey* which started two thousand years ago is continuing today in the lives of the *mestizos*, the incarnation of Jesus in the world today.

Finally, the third stage of the *Galilean Journey* is the *Resurrection Principle*, which is that only love can triumph over evil, and no human power can prevail against the power of unlimited love.[93] Here, we find the celebration of what is despised and witness the validation of the lowly ones as the true instruments of conversion. In the Easter events of the resurrection and ascension, the rejected Galileans are affirmed. Jesus coming back to life illustrates the rightful place the Galileans and all outcasts like *mestizos* have in God's economy. Not only is the resurrection the sign of true life, but it also signifies the vehicle God has chosen to continue his presence in the world. In addition, the event of Pentecost reveals the true nature of the Church through its *mestizo*-type beginnings.[94] The foundation of the body of Christ as recounted in the Book

92. Ibid., 109.

93. Ibid., 115.

94. Lee, "Galilean Journey Revisited," 111–12.

of Acts announces the Church coming into being through the outpouring of the Holy Spirit upon different races, cultures, and languages. The opposite of the Tower of Babel occurred as differences between human beings now unite rather than divide as previously was the case. Through the coming together of different peoples, the Church's first steps were characterized by a *mestizo*-type presence in the world. How fitting it is that the followers of Christ would be like Christ in all things? In particular, they possess a mixed heritage produced by the coming together of different people, choosing not only to be in solidarity with the lowly marginal ones but also to be truly marginal in their own being.

The Easter resurrection and the Pentecostal experience at the beginning of the Church's existence were joyful celebrations. From this point forward, Galileans and all those who were considered inferior knew their rightful place as Jesus' resurrection validated their marginal existence. The rejected and excluded would not go away in shame but would rise again like their savior to continue the mission on earth—to bring Good News to the poor and outcast, especially those considered inferior because of their mixed heritage.

For prophecy to be truly Christian, it cannot stop at confrontation and denunciation. Confronting social inequalities and denouncing unjust structures also requires the festive, the *Resurrection Principle*, to ensure that we are not just on the road to an earthly Jerusalem, but, more importantly, that we are going beyond to the heavenly Jerusalem.[95] Today, celebrations continue within the Mexican American community. *Mestiza fiesta* reflects the resurrection of new life in spite of being in a world that still discriminates against *mestizos*. Even in the face of racism and structural injustices, the Mexican American people are able to rejoice, laugh and sing because of their being rejected, elected, and missioned, just like their savior. "The prophetic without the festive turns into cynicism and bitterness, or simply fades away . . . On the other hand, the festive without the prophetic can easily turn into empty rituals or even degenerate into drunken brawls. It is the prophetic-festive that keeps the spirit alive and nourishes the life of the group as a group."[96]

Fiestas, the prophetic-festive celebrations of the people, are reflected both inside and outside the walls of the Church as Mexican Americans come together in table-fellowship. Inside the Church,

95. Elizondo, *Galilean Journey*, 119.
96. Ibid., 120.

mestizo worship and celebration center around the Eucharist. Outside the Church, *mestizo* worship and celebration continue around the *fiesta*. "The Christian community was aware of it when it went on celebrating what had been most original in the way of Jesus: radical forgiveness that flowed into the joy of table-fellowship with all persons."[97] Through table-fellowship, the *Galilean Journey* comes full circle as those who were once excluded through their encounter with the other are now not only included, but become the focal point of table-fellowship with one another and the risen Lord. "It was in the joy of this heartfelt forgiveness that reintegrates the outcast into the community, the joy that comes with the awareness that you are accepted and valued simply because you are you, that the Christians celebrated the death and resurrection of Jesus that had brought about this new communitarian life transcending human frontiers and institutions."[98] "Without these celebrations, [the core knowledge] is simply the remembrance of a historical past, but not the appreciation of a past that lives in the present, transforming it into a future that has already begun. In this way, celebrations are not just the effects of what has been; they are likewise the cause of what is yet to come."[99]

MESTIZO MARIOLOGY: *NUESTRA SEÑORA DE GUADALUPE*

Elizondo's inquiry into Jesus' Galilean journey, a type of *mestizaje*, naturally leads to a closer consideration of Mary who was chosen to be His mother. In the incarnation, Jesus' earthly existence had a *mestizo*-type beginning as the divinity of the second person of the Trinity became one with humanity. Mary's biological contribution to her son along with her cooperation with the Holy Spirit allowed this mystery to irrupt into our humanity. The *mestizo*-type existence of Jesus completely embraces all aspects of humanity by encompassing fully the social, cultural, and even the biological aspects of our humanity. Our Christological belief insists that the second person of God became fully human in order to redeem all aspects of our lives. In contrast, in well-defined ethnic groups, the *mestizo* is usually considered a "half-breed" or a "non-person." In

97. Ibid.
98. Ibid.
99. Ibid., 121.

the *mestizo* world, to be fully human means to be fully *mestizo*. One of Mary's gifts to her son in his earthly existence and to the world in her ecclesial existence is the gift of encounters with the other that allowed Jesus to embrace all of humanity. Thus, not only did Mary play an important role in the birth of Jesus in Galilee, but she continues to do so as a *mestiza* mother revealing her *mestizo*-type son. The clearest example of this is found in the *mestizo* beginning of the Mexican people in the sixteenth century.

The appearance of Our Lady of Guadalupe in 1531 at Tepeyac signaled the birth of a new people and also revealed the love a *mestiza* mother has for all her children—Europeans, Indians, and *mestizos*. The Guadalupe event is a true *mestizo* expression that overcomes human degradation and expresses the dignity God bestows on all of us. The Guadalupe narrative recounting the events between the *mestiza* Madonna and Juan Diego is a complex retelling accentuating the *mestizo* qualities of that encounter. "It is a highly complex mestizo (Nahuatl-European) form of communication in various ways: the image and the narrative are mutually interpretative; there are elements of both Nahuatl and Iberian worldviews in the narrative and the image, and together they say new things that neither alone could have expressed; the image is poetry that is seen while the poem is imagery that is heard, and together they constitute a coherent communication."[100]

As Elizondo has pointed out, "The Nican Mopohua is a careful and serious attempt to put in writing the memory of the prodigious events of 1531."[101] Because the narrative is highly complex, interweaving the beauty of both cultures, the message that is communicated is far from being realized by those who listened to Juan Diego's accounts of his encounters. "Nevertheless, like the Gospels, the force of this text lies not in its exact historical origins but in the fact that it has been consistently re-created in its faithful retelling by those for whom it has ultimate meaning."[102] The *mestizaje* aspect of the retelling resonates with the audience for it utilizes media to which they are accustomed. For example, the visual appearance of the *mestiza* Madonna is accompanied by the elements

---

100. Elizondo, *Guadalupe, Mother of New Creation*, xviii.

101. Ibid., 3. The *Nican Mopohua* ("Here is told") is a Náhuatl account of the apparitions of Our Lady of Guadalupe that was originally published by Luis Lasso de la Vega in Mexico City in 1649.

102. Ibid.

of the Náhuatl religious world. Our Lady of Guadalupe is standing on the moon and in front of the sun with the rays encompassing her. The visual connection for the Nahua would be immediate as these elements signified a religious encounter. The image on the *tilma*[103] of Juan Diego illustrates not the end of the Náhuatl world but a new beginning with the Gospel brought by the Europeans. The sun and the moon signifying the divine elements of the Náhuatl religion are now incorporated into Our Lady. In addition, the *flor y canto* accompaniment found in Juan Diego's *tilma* and the music he hears on Tepeyac utilizes a medium that is very familiar to the customs of the Náhuatl people. To the Nahua, *flor y canto* meant divine revelation since human discourse was always insufficient and needed poetic communication and the beauty of the human heart to dialogue with the divine individually and collectively.[104] "According to the Guadalupan vision, truth exists in the relational, the interconnected, the beautiful, and the melodic; it cannot be reduced to a single, essential element, for it is only in its totality, in its wholeness, that this truth can be perceived and appreciated. Ultimate truth cannot be corralled by definition; it can only be approximated through *flor y canto*."[105] Most of all, the encounter with Guadalupe did not destroy or alienate Juan Diego and his people. Rather, Juan Diego is lifted up as Mary once was and with like obedience carries out God's plan for the lowly ones. "Guadalupe retrieved the original ways of evangelization through personal invitation, respect, patient dialogue between persons and cultures, and liberating and empowering conversion and communion in the new fellowship of the unconditional equality of God's children."[106]

Mary, revealed to us in the Guadalupe event, indicates humanity's ability to undergo the *Galilean Journey*. No one, not even Mary herself, could have imagined that a simple Galilean woman who, through the annunciation by the angel Gabriel, would become mother of the first born of a new creation, and would go on to welcome all the peoples of the world, beginning in Galilee and then in the New World. By her

103. The *tilma* is a traditional cloak worn by indigenous Mesoamericans. Juan Diego was unaware of the image of *Nuestra Señora* on his *tilma* until he opened his cloak. He had used his *tilma* to hold the flowers he picked after encountering Guadalupe; flowers were not in season but appeared as a sign requested by the bishop in his first meeting with Juan Diego.

104. Elizondo, *Guadalupe, Mother of New Creation*, 34–35.

105. Ibid., 116.

106. Ibid., 108.

faithfulness to the journey laid out by her son, she has become both the Mother of God and ethnically much more than a Galilean; she has become mother to all. By imitating her son, Jesus, in all things, in particular, the "Galilean Journey" where she fully comprehended the *Galilean, Jerusalem*, and *Resurrection Principles*, Mary demonstrated how the first disciple, as well as all future disciples, must travel this same road to comprehend fully the Kingdom of God.

Through the acceptance of her marginal existence derived from the region of Galilee (*Galilean Principle*), to the challenges of Jerusalem by following her son to the cross (*Jerusalem Principle*), and finally through her presence at Pentecost (*Resurrection Principle*), Mary traveled the path of her son and came to understand her dignity as the mother of God as well as the mother of all people, especially the marginalized, rejected, and excluded. This new beginning, which included everyone without exception, then would replicate itself again in the encounter between the Spaniards and the natives in the sixteenth century in the Americas. With her appearance in 1531, Our Lady of Guadalupe signaled to the Church and to all humanity the dignity of the *mestizos* of the world (*Galilean Principle*), the need to reform the minds and hearts of the dominant in both Church and society so as to be more unitive and inclusive (*Jerusalem Principle*), and the ways of rejoicing in our being by her unique revelation of *flor y canto* (*Resurrection Principle*). Thus, contained within the narrative of Our Lady of Guadalupe's appearance to Juan Diego in 1531 is the way to understand the *mestizo* path described in Elizondo's *Galilean Journey*. Through the central figures of the apparition, Our Lady of Guadalupe, Juan Diego, his uncle Juan Bernardino, and Bishop Juan Zumárraga, the conversion needed along the "Galilean Journey" is recounted.

First, the appearance of *Nuestra Señora de Guadalupe* signals the fulfillment of Mary's participation in the journey of her son. In *la Morenita* ("the beloved brown one") we encounter the vision of who we are and how we are to embrace our *mestizo* being. By appearing to Juan Diego as one like him, Guadalupe reveals the dignity of the indigenous people as their world collided with the dominant Europeans. In Náhuatl cosmology, darkness is seen as the *kairos* moment, the hour of birth of something new. For Elizondo, this darkness "was not just the physical darkness before dawn. It was the darkness of one who has been made

ashamed of one's very being."[107] The darkness that loomed over a defeated people became the *kairos* for a new *mestizo* beginning as "Juan
Diego leaves his home "when it was night" but arrives at Tepeyac while
"it was already beginning to dawn.""[108]

Through her indigenous appearance, Guadalupe reveals a *mestizo*
aspect of God's plan and allows the people caught in between two worlds
to realize their true potential simply by their being. *La Virgen* further
highlights the encounter and coming together of different worlds as the
future of Christianity and also of our humanity. Our worship of God is
not only the lifting of our praise, but, as Guadalupe reveals to us, it is the
lifting up of our whole being to the Lord. Thus, Guadalupe, the *mestiza*
Madonna, signifies the fulfillment of the *Magnificat*: "My soul proclaims
the greatness of the Lord; my spirit rejoices in God my savior. For he has
looked upon his handmaid's lowliness; behold, from now on will all ages
call me blessed. The Mighty One has done great things for me, and holy
is his name" (Luke 1:47–49 NAB).

Moreover, Our Lady of Guadalupe appears to a simple native, Juan
Diego. All accounts of the current situation of his days indicate that
Juan Diego was a man beaten down psychologically, emotionally, and
spiritually by the Spanish conquest. Similar to other indigenous people
overrun by the Spaniards, Juan Diego had little hope for his existence on
earth, in particular due to the destruction of his native religious world.
For Elizondo, "the low class Indian [Juan Diego] who sees himself as
ignorant, unworthy, even as non-human, is now converted to a confident messenger of the Mother of God."[109] In the figure of Juan Diego,
one realizes for whom the message of Guadalupe is intended. It is for
those living on the "Galilean" borders of life, those who are considered
inferior and simply forgotten like Juan Diego. However, the apparition
at Tepeyac was not only the self-realization of Juan Diego's lowly state,
but more importantly, the conversion of his identity and of that of all
those in similar straits, to an identity similar to Our Lady of Guadalupe.
God's economy utilizes the weak and the humble to bring about God's
will. "He [Juan Diego] is converted from the pain of social non-being to
becoming a full, confident, and joyful human person. He is transformed
from his debasement and shame to a new, confident self-image . . . He is

107. Ibid., 33.
108. Ibid.
109. Elizondo, "Guadalupe," 307.

converted from seeing himself and thinking of himself as the oppressors saw him, to appreciating himself as God knows and appreciates him . . . The converted, and thus rehabilitated, victimized of the new world will now become the cornerstone of the new creation."[110]

In addition to his own conversion, Juan Diego's interactions with his uncle, Juan Bernardino, reveal another conversion necessary to the situation of the Americas. The ill uncle was restored to health by Our Lady's promise as she instructed Juan Diego to go to the bishop of Mexico City to give witness regarding the occurrences of Tepeyac. Initially, Juan Diego's heart and mind were focused on his uncle: first, his uncle was very ill; second, during their first meeting, the bishop wanted nothing to do with Juan Diego or the apparition. However, with the urging of *Guadalupe*, Juan Diego obediently listened and trusted that what she said about his uncle would come true. Miraculously, Juan Bernardino regained full health. Thus, in the person of his uncle, the second and necessary conversion was realized.

In Juan Bernardino's recovery more than an individual is restored. According to Elizondo, the uncle in the Náhuatl-speaking world assumed the responsibility for passing on the traditions and culture of their society: "The rehabilitation of Juan Bernardino is the rehabilitation of the native culture and its religious expressions—it would not die, but rather be rehabilitated and survive through the mediation of Our Lady, the mother and giver of life."[111] Consequently, the conversion of Juan Diego and then the healing of Juan Bernardino meant that God desired the conversion, but not the destruction, of the native cultural and sacred traditions.

Finally, full restoration would require one more conversion, the conversion of the bishop and his household, the Church. It would be a task like no other; Elizondo describes this situation as "the deeper and more difficult conversion," one that would involve "the Bishop and his household of pastors, theologians, catechists, liturgists, canonists and others."[112] The initial visit of Juan Diego, under the instructions of Our Lady of Guadalupe, to Bishop Juan Zumárraga asking for a temple to be built at the location of the apparition at Tepeyac was far from successful. Juan Diego's initial encounter left him so discouraged he avoided even

110. Ibid.
111. Ibid., 307–8.
112. Ibid., 308.

Guadalupe in the hope of not being asked to complete this assign-
ment. However, when confronted by Guadalupe a second time at another part of Tepeyac, the humble Nahua native listened and obeyed her
instructions.

The following meeting was much more successful as Juan Diego
opened his *tilma* and revealed the image of Our Lady of Guadalupe.
Along with the image were fresh flowers that fell to the floor—flowers that were not in season. The senses ignited through the image and
the flowers left no doubt by the bishop and his household that *Nuestra
Señora* had really visited Juan Diego at Tepeyac. Immediately, the bishop
and his household reverenced the image on the *tilma* signifying the final
conversion necessary for the New World. This final conversion would
allow the two worlds, the Spanish and the indigenous population in
the Americas, to come together both spiritually and biologically in the
creation of the new humanity of the Americas. "The conversion of the
bishop completes the good news—the *evangelium*—of the Guadalupe
events. This represents the ongoing call to conversion, especially of those
who use their positions to oppress, dominate, and exploit the weaker
ones of society."[113]

Part of truly embracing *mestizo* existence is the responsibility to
the rest of society and not just ourselves. The newfound *mestizo* identity
requires the uplifting of not just those who have been oppressed in a
similar manner, but the lifting up of the oppressors themselves. In the
case of Juan Diego and the Nahua people, "[t]hey were invited into a
new common enterprise with the Indians but it was no longer totally
under their control."[114] However, under the guidance and care of Our
Lady of Guadalupe, the lowly ones, the Nahua themselves were able to
bring about the conversion necessary for God's plan started through
Jesus' *mestizo* existence and now continued through the *mestizo* existence of the Americas. "This conversion from arrogance to humility is
necessary for the Church to continue its pilgrimage into the realization
of God's reign upon earth . . . This marks the beginning of the on-going
conversion of the Church that is often tempted by the idols of ethnocentrism, power, wealth and social status."[115] Along with this conversion,
the Church embraced a new outlook. "In the conversion of the Bishop,

113. Elizondo, *Guadalupe, Mother of New Creation*, 108.

114. Elizondo, "Guadalupe," 308.

115. Ibid.

the Church joins the struggles of the poor, the marginalized, the despised of the land and the rejected in their quest for dignity, belonging
and inclusion."[116]

Elizondo has devoted much of his theological work to uncovering
the richness of Our Lady of Guadalupe. In fact, it could be said he has
devoted his whole life to relaying the message of Guadalupe not only
to Mexicans and their descendants, but to the whole world as well. He
addresses the first audience—Mexicans and Mexican Americans—not
because they do not believe in the *mestiza* Madonna, but precisely because the belief of Guadalupe as a loving mother is so ingrained in the
lives and consciousness of the people that certain aspects of her message
have simply been taken for granted without much expounding.[117]

The second audience addressed in Elizondo's Guadalupan writings
is the rest of the Church and humanity. It is important for others, those
standing outside the Guadalupan *mestizo* experience, to understand the
events of the sixteenth century and how the message of *Nuestra Señora
de Guadalupe* is still alive today as the struggle for acceptance by *mestizos* continues. "Hence I beg readers conditioned by Western thought
to put aside their very legitimate presuppositions and to take a fresh
look at a theological reality that is totally different from anything in the
Western tradition."[118] Devotion to Our Lady of Guadalupe reveals our
hunger for a unifying symbol that will allow us to break through the
multiple barriers of separation so as to become a people open to the
various ethnic differences that tend to separate us.[119] The amount of love
we have for *la Morenita* reflects the love and care for Mexican Americans
and all minorities today. Our failure to embrace *la Virgen de Guadalupe*
reveals the structures of racism that keep us from embracing God's plan
for humanity—a plan that is unitive rather than divisive. "Jesus suffered
as a man, and Mary suffered as a woman what no man could have suffered. Thus, together they rehabilitate humanity; together they are the
coredeemers of humanity."[120] The closer we adhere to *Nuestra Señora
de Guadalupe*, the closer we arrive at the realization that our Church

116. Ibid.

117. Elizondo, *Mary, The Compassionate Mother*, 1–2.

118. Elizondo, "Mary and the Poor," 59.

119. Elizondo, *God of Incredible Surprises*, 113.

120. Ibid., 117.

and the world is comprised of social, cultural, and biological encounters revealing the loving care of God to all peoples.

SUMMARY: *MESTIZO* THEOLOGY

For seventy-five years, the theme of *mestizaje* has been evolving in Virgilio Elizondo. His life and experience in the Southwestern United States have given the Church and the world a unique perspective of our past, present, and future. Expanding the local into the universal is an ongoing event that will continue until the fullness of revelation is realized. "After 30 years I am still fascinated by the Galilee of Jesus, and continue to investigate and develop its significance as new evidence emerges, and the responses of so many people, especially the poor, excluded, and marginalized, encourage me with new insights. Drawing from the experience of victimization, the poor sometimes have insights into Scripture that even the best of scholars might miss. This pattern, which has come to be known as the hermeneutical or epistemological privilege of the poor and excluded, is proclaimed by Jesus in the earliest collections of his sayings[.]"[121] It is an endeavor that began with Jesus of Nazareth in Galilee, who utilized every aspect of his humanity to reveal God's love for all especially to the marginalized and excluded. The early followers of Jesus meditated on his earthly existence and proclaimed the implications of his existence to other Jews and Gentiles of various regions, thereby making the local events of his humanity into universal principles. Ever since, our Christian vocation has been the same: to discover our humanity in all its particular circumstances and to see how it relates to the earthly existence of our savior. Through the local we arrive at the universal; through the familiar we encounter the mystery of God.

According to Elizondo, Jesus, through the incarnation, revealed his earthly ministry as a reject who rejects rejection. By being a reject and rejecting what others thought or said, Jesus was able to embrace His marginal being and reach out to others who were marginalized and excluded, in particular, those who were marginalized and excluded in Galilee because of its political and commercial encounters with other cultures and peoples. Those in Jerusalem maintained their isolation by deferring these foreign encounters to the regions of the north and by

---

121. Elizondo, "Jesus the Galilean Jew," 262.

doing so kept their elitist position through their purity. Entering our humanity in the multicultural Galilean region meant that Jesus began his life being rejected by ethnic purists. Through his special relationship with the Father, Jesus' election emerged as he began his public ministry. His public ministry to the marginalized and excluded revealed that with election comes responsibility for others. This mission was to ensure that subsequent generations will not endure the same suffering as previous generations. Thus, Elizondo characterizes Jesus´ Galilean journey as well as the journey of the Mexican American people as one of rejection, election, and mission.

Elizondo's insights into this Galilean journey are derived from his own *mestizo* heritage. Being a Mexican American in the Southwestern United States has meant that his existence was in many ways a non-existence. Being accepted by neither Mexico nor the United States meant a marginal existence which would allow Elizondo to develop a hermeneutic of the marginalized and excluded in his *mestizo* theology. Through this unique epistemology, Elizondo was able to connect his own existence and that of people of Mexican American descent with the life of Jesus of Nazareth in Galilee. "I realized that authentic evangelization and the development of local churches are impossible without a deep anthropological appreciation of the people's heritage and culture, and without a sound anthropological translation and interpretation of Scripture and Church teaching."[122]

By no means does Elizondo advocate a master *mestizo* race overshadowing other cultures nor does he uphold the Mexican American people as the only beacon of hope stemming from their unique *mestizo* heritage. To do so would create a world of marginalization and exclusion with humanity never progressing into the Kingdom of God. What Elizondo advocates is the unity that *mestizaje* brings to humanity as a bridge to the divine through the person of Jesus.

122. Ibid., 267–68.

3

Gustavo Gutiérrez
and the Preferential
Option for the Poor

B EFORE BECOMING KNOWN AS a mainstay in Catholic social teaching, the preferential option for the poor was evident in the writings
of Gustavo Gutiérrez, and has remained so throughout his theological career. This chapter begins with Gutiérrez's reference to the Good
Samaritan as the reason why the poor take centerstage. Next, a reciprocal relationship emerging between Gutiérrez's theological reflections
and CELAM is discussed. Originating from the definition of poverty by
CELAM at Medellín and the appropriate response to poverty set forth
by Puebla, the preferential option for the poor is a guide to locate God's
reign in history. An in-depth analysis follows of the three areas of poverty identified in the works of Gutiérrez: real poverty in its historical and
theological developments, spiritual poverty to which we are all called,
and the option for the poor to which all must commit. These important
themes which give us insights into the full meaning of the preferential
option for the poor are then traced with regard to Gutiérrez's two heroes: the Old Testament figure of Job as the prefiguration of Christ and
the historical ecclesial figure of Bartolomé de las Casas as the defender
of the poor in Latin America.

GUSTAVO GUTIÉRREZ AND THE OPTION FOR THE POOR

The theme of liberation existed long before Gustavo Gutiérrez and will continue as long as there are people who are poor and oppressed. However, the contribution of Gutiérrez, not only to the theme of liberation but also to theology, has altered the way many people speak of the poor and oppressed today. No longer is liberation a concept distant from the Church; rather, it has become an integral aspect of theology due to the lifework of people like Gutiérrez. The Peruvian theologian has insisted that "the most important contribution to the life and reflection of the Latin American Church" is the preferential option for the poor.[1] Without the preferential option for the poor, the relationship of liberation and theology would certainly be disjointed, even non-existent, in Latin America today. The theology of liberation is truly an interaction between real subjects in need of liberation and those who follow Jesus laboring on behalf of the poor. The subjects in this case are the poor who are actively seeking the full dignity of their humanity. "At the same time—and it is important to remember this—to be poor is a way of life. It is a way of thinking, of loving, of praying, of believing and hoping, of spending free time, of struggling for a livelihood. Being poor today also means being involved in the battle for justice and peace, defending one's life and liberty, seeking a greater democratic participation in the decisions of society, "organizing to live one's faith in an integral way . . . and committing oneself to the liberation of every human person."[2]

The trademark and one of the most important contributions of the Latin American Church to the universal Church,[3] the preferential option for the poor has become a mainstream social teaching of the magisterium, one reiterated by Pope John Paul II throughout his pontificate, beginning cautiously with *Familiaris Consortio*[4] and strongly concluding with *Centesimus Annus*.[5] John Paul II gave the preferential option for the poor a proper place not only within the Church's social doctrine, but also within the ecclesial tradition.[6] Coupled with

---

1. Gutiérrez, "Renewing the Option," 69.
2. Gutiérrez, "Option for the Poor," 236.
3. Elizondo, "Editorial: Theology," ix.
4. John Paul II, "Apostolic Exhortation on the Family," 453 §47.
5. John Paul II, *Centesimus Annus*, §11.
6. Twomey, *Preferential Option for the Poor*, 267.

the CELAM meetings at Medellín (1968) and Puebla (1979) and with the efforts of theologians such as Gustavo Gutiérrez, the preferential option for the poor can be described as the heart of Latin American liberation theology. Proper theological reflection can only be achieved when we place the poor at the center of our spirituality—our commitment for the other because of God's graciousness towards us. It is possible to reflect, the second step, and theologize about liberation because the first step, the prayer-in-worship before God, is actualized in our prayer-in-commitment for the poor.

Although Gutiérrez mentions this preferential option for the poor as the most important contribution, this option is not only a result or end product of the work accomplished in the life of the Latin American Church, but also the catalyst of events in that Church—thereby making the preferential option for the poor a hermeneutic key to understanding a theology of liberation. Two critical factors led to the irruption of the poor into the consciousness of Gutiérrez and others like him. First, the massive number of wasted lives led him to believe that poverty could no longer be tolerated. Second, he came to believe that the cruel and oppressive conditions created and maintained by structural sin need to be addressed by the Church. Too many Latin Americans are dying before their time due to these two horrific aspects of poverty. The martyrdom of the masses and theological reflection on the situation that created such cruel and oppressive conditions was later deemed as a significant contribution to the universal Church and is also seen as the vehicle that has allowed the whole continent to become aware of a reality which was in direct opposition to the will of God.

"The irruption of the poor" is a term coined by Latin Americans to express the awareness of the massive number of people living in poverty who suddenly exploded onto the scene.[7] No longer could the poor be silenced and ignored, but the sheer number of those living in poverty throughout Latin America forced both Church and society to take account of them. By rising to be heard from their desperate situations, the poor have gradually become "active agents of their own destiny."[8] Becoming active agents also meant that they would take up certain rights for themselves, especially in the Church through the right to "think their

7. Gutiérrez, "Search for Identity," 66; *Theology of Liberation*, xx; *Confrontations*, 8.

8. Gutiérrez, "Renewing the Option," 236.

faith."[9] The irruption of the poor allows those who were previously absent in society and in the Church to be noticed and to take control of their lives in a world where the majority live in poverty. This irruption is invaluable, for, without it, the reality of the poor requiring liberation in all aspects of life (e.g. social, political, and economic) would have been overlooked, as was previously the case. The irruption of the poor forces the Church to reexamine the distinction between the Church and the world in which she lives. The true gift in regards to the irruption of the poor is not that we have an opportunity to assist our impoverished brothers and sisters to live in dignity, but rather that this irruption "represents an irruption of God into our lives."[10] It is a gift of the poor to the Church and to the rest of the world.

Who is My Neighbor?:
The Starting Point of the Preferential Option for the Poor

To illustrate the Scriptural aspect of the preferential option for the poor, Gutiérrez appeals to the Gospel parable of the Good Samaritan (Luke 10:25–37).[11]

> A man fell victim to robbers as he went down from Jerusalem to Jericho. They stripped and beat him and went off leaving him half-dead. A priest happened to be going down that road, but when he saw him, he passed by on the opposite side. Likewise a Levite came to the place, and when he saw him, he passed by on the opposite side. But a Samaritan traveler who came upon him was moved with compassion at the sight. He approached the victim, poured oil and wine over his wounds and bandaged them. Then he lifted him up on his own animal, took him to an inn and cared for him. The next day he took out two silver coins and gave them to the innkeeper with the instruction, 'Take care of him. If you spend more than what I have given you, I shall repay you on my way back.' Which of these three, in your opinion, was neighbor to the robbers' victim? (v. 30–36, NAB).

Through his pastoral approach, that includes a re-reading of scripture, Gutiérrez emphasizes the importance of the passage's shift from the initial question of the scholar of the law to Jesus' concluding question

9. Ibid.

10. Ibid.

11. Gutiérrez, *Power of the Poor*, 44.

in reply. The question "who is my neighbor?" is transformed into the question "Which of these three, in your opinion, was neighbor to the robbers' victim?" Instead of seeing the neighbor in terms of oneself, a question that centers around one's own understanding of the world, Jesus shifts the focus of the question to that of the victim. The question now centers on the other and the situation in which he or she is located. The neighbor is no longer thought of as the person next to me but rather as the one who encounters and addresses the person in need. The neighbor is the one next to the victim and not next to us. Gutiérrez calls this movement the point where we go out of our way to find the neighbor.[12]

Jesus transforms the paradigm of being a neighbor from a passive state to an active movement. If we consider the question of the scholar of the law in the parable, his question is passive; the neighbor, in his perspective, is the one who is in proximity. In contrast, the true neighbor Jesus spoke of is the one who is discovered when we go out of our way to encounter a person in need. It is a movement that actively seeks out the vulnerable person who reminds us we are constantly in the process of becoming, and making ourselves a neighbor. Thus, being a neighbor is the result of one's action rather than a notion of physicality.

The evangelist describes the Good Samaritan as being moved by compassion. The Samaritan, as well as the others who passed by without assisting the wounded man, has a title and a role in society. However, the man who fell into the hands of the robbers is nameless. It is not because of his position in society that he warrants help from the people passing by but because of the simple fact that the man is in a vulnerable fallen state. What motivates the Samaritan man is not revealed by the evangelist and the silence on this matter leaves the reader only capable of rendering the conclusion that his actions were the results of seeing the man in a state of suffering. What is created by the actions of the Samaritan reaching out to the fallen man is solidarity—a solidarity revolving around the other and not us.

The parable of the Good Samaritan shows the combination of the Old Testament laws found in Deut 6:5, "you shall love the LORD, your God, with all your heart, and with all your soul, and with all your strength" and Lev 19:18, "you shall love your neighbor as yourself." These two commandments found in the Jewish tradition become one, as the greatest commandment in the New Testament (Matt 22:37–39). The

12. Ibid.

love of God and love of neighbor become a unity. This unity is constitutive in answering the scholar's question of inheriting eternal life to Jesus at the beginning of their encounter. Through the telling of the parable, Jesus enlarges the understanding of who the neighbor is and of the love needed for solidarity. This epiphany is only possible when the other receives priority over the self as Gutiérrez often states: "If I am hungry, it is a material problem. But if another is hungry, it is a spiritual problem."[13]

Placing the nameless poor in the center of our world as our neighbor has led the Church to formulate her social teaching of the preferential option for the poor. In reality, the preferential option for the poor existed within the Christian tradition prior to its modern conception. In July 1967, Gutiérrez verbalized this reality by describing three kinds of poverty: *real* poverty, *spiritual* poverty, and poverty as a *commitment*.[14] The three notions of poverty later served as portals for understanding the preferential option for the poor, which germinated at Medellín, reached maturation at Puebla, and received further refinement from Vatican critique.

Similarly, the theme of liberation was distinguished into three corresponding categories: political and social liberation, human liberation, and liberation from selfishness and sin.[15] "Although the term liberation exists also in the social and political spheres, it comes from a very ancient biblical and theological tradition" says Gutiérrez—a fact which allows him as a theologian, to make the necessary connections between liberation and poverty.[16] These two realities, poverty and liberation, do not have different or opposing histories but the same lineage and relationship throughout the life of the Church; thus, for Gutiérrez and other Latin American theologians, to speak about poverty without liberation would be incomplete and a further injustice. "Divergent, but at the same time linked, these three dimensions of liberation portray a radical and integral reality, a broad process whose meaning is ultimately to be found in the salvation of Christ. This provides the concept of liberation with its permanent relevance and the demanding appeal, as well as the context for dealing with the issue of poverty."[17]

13. Gutiérrez, "Voice of the Poor," 33.
14. Gutiérrez, "Task and Content," 25.
15. Ibid., 26.
16. Ibid.
17. Ibid., 26–27.

In 1968, the CELAM meeting at Medellín committed the Latin American Church to John XXIII's vision of a Church of the poor. Medellín not only proposed this commitment by the Church on behalf of the poor, but also clarified this commitment by laying the groundwork for the preferential option.[18] Although not definitively stated in the documents of Medellín, the episcopal commitment to the poor gave rise later to the definition at the CELAM meeting at Puebla in 1979, which spelled out the preferential option for the poor and reaffirmed the commitment made previously at Medellín.[19] No one will know the precise role Gutiérrez had in the development of this social doctrine. However, it cannot be denied that his writings before, during, and after Medellín influenced the final understanding of it. In addition, his presence in Medellín and Puebla also indicates his involvement and influence at these CELAM gatherings. By considering Medellín's commitment and Puebla's later refinement, Gutiérrez formulates his own understanding of the doctrine as follows: he speaks of the "preferential (spiritual poverty) option (solidarity and protest) for the poor (real poverty)"[20] as the way for the Church to be the Church of the poor. These three aspects, addressed in-depth in the next section, represent the reality of the poor, our call to common brother- and sisterhood, and the commitment we must make daily on behalf of the other.

In brief, one must remember that tackling real poverty, a lack of material goods, which is considered an evil, comes before addressing anything else. Preference refers to the universal love of God but realized in a particular, preferential manner, where God's love first comes to those who are "last." The option on behalf of others is a daily commitment that even the poor themselves must make to one another.

In many ways, the preferential option for the poor represents the culmination of Gustavo Gutiérrez's lifework as well as the maturation of the Latin American Church. The Preferential option for the poor emerged as a result of the acknowledgement of poverty in Latin America.

18. Some of the statements made at Medellín are found in the first chapter. Of particular note are the statements made on poverty by the episcopal conference identifying poverty in three forms; real, spiritual, and in solidarity.

19. Some of the statements made at Puebla are also found in the first chapter. Note the early tensions over defining poverty in specific terms in the preparatory draft and how the final statement of Puebla affirmed and furthered the commitment established at Medellín.

20. Gutiérrez, "From Exclusion to Discipleship," 88.

Initially through Gutiérrez's first article in 1968 and then in the Medellín statements, poverty was defined as being primarily real or material; all were required to embrace spiritual poverty in order to enter into solidarity with the poor and to labor on their behalf. Once poverty came to be seen in this manner, Gutiérrez and the Latin American Church at Puebla spoke about our calling as Christians, as brothers and sisters, and about the manner in which we must address each aspect of poverty. In summary, the impoverished world was recognized at Medellín; over a decade later, at Puebla, one learned how God responds to the poor and how we are also called to imitate that response.

Real or Material Poverty: Historical Developments

Gustavo Gutiérrez argues adamantly that liberation theology, born in the poorest of the poor in the barrios of Lima, Peru, is not an adaptation or an offshoot of European theology. "The interlocutors of [European models of] theology question faith; the interlocutors of liberation theology "share" the same faith as their oppressors, but they do not share the same economic, social, or political life."[21] Neither is this theology a retrieval of something lost in the history of the Church nor an aberration in theological studies. Rather, the theology of liberation was born out of the tradition of the Church lived out by the poor responding to the Gospel message while being confronted by the injustices of today's world.

Gutiérrez and other liberation theologians in Latin America reject the proposal that liberation theology is simply an offshoot of European theology based on forms of political or progressive and revolutionary theologies. The primary reason for rejecting any such similarities is that liberation theology is a completely different way of doing theology; for example, liberation theology addresses the non-person. In contrast, Gutiérrez maintains that the primary emphasis of Eurpoean theology addresses the non-believer. Although theology is always done by believers, the treatment of circumstances surrounding the person is what separates Latin Americans from their European counterparts. In other words, the topic of discussion for Latin American theologians is dehumanization, whereas European theologians have been preoccupied with the topic of non-belief.

---

21. Gutiérrez, "Two Theological Perspectives," 214.

Political theology, for example, does not propose the creation of a new theological discipline but seeks to analyze critically the theology already being done, by addressing questions that have arisen from the Enlightenment and from nonbelievers. "It did not propose the creation of a new theological discipline . . . It took up a profoundly critical position rooted in the views of the Enlightenment on the political field as the arena of freedom."[22] What concern these theologians are the disjointed relationships between theory and practice, and between the understanding of faith and social practice. They also question whether theological reasoning could be done in the modern world.[23] Another theology that has tried to bridge the gap between theory and practice is the theology of revolution, which attempts to enter into the political realm of social and class struggles through revolutionary commitment.[24] Although the theology of revolution has sought to address unjust social situations by appealing to the involvement of Christians in the revolutionary process, it has become more ideological than practical. In contrast to the leftist theologies in Europe, theologies of liberation seek a new way of doing theology by addressing the people on a continent where the majority are Christians who live surrounded by inhuman poverty and oppression.

Although liberation theology was aided by social theories focusing on development and dependency, it grew separately from these theories and revealed their weaknesses and limitations. Specifically, these social theories were unable to address the aspirations of the entire human person in a particular context and to identify the causes of the oppressive social situation. Gutiérrez and other liberation theologians have never shied away from acknowledging the use of social theory in their theology. In fact, instead of appealing to philosophy as do their European counterparts, liberation theologians prefer to appeal to social theory. The reason for their appeal to and use of social theory is to understand better the social conditions of a continent filled with poverty and oppression. What is needed on a Christian continent suffering from an inhumane situation is a grasp of the causes of poverty and not simply a description of the conditions of the poor. This requirement has been one of Gutiérrez's theological mantras: go to the causes of poverty so that unjust social situations can be addressed. It is only through the assistance

22. Gutiérrez, "Liberation Movements," 136.

23. Gutiérrez "Two Theological Perspectives," 234–35.

24. Ibid., 245–56.

of social theory in theology that Gutiérrez and others feel that such efforts can be made. Without such assistance, theology could not speak to
the social situation of the poor and to sinful social structures.

Regarding the use of Marxist analysis, a social science tool utilized
by liberation theologians to identify poverty and its causes, there are
some who feel that any use of Marxist analysis in a Christian setting is
unacceptable.[25] However, the experience of Marxist analysis in Europe
has not been the same as in Latin America. In the latter experience,
Marxist analysis has been useful in revealing the class struggles that
create situations of poverty. Gutiérrez and others utilize this tool while
maintaining the magisterial understanding that any regime which creates a totalitarian system or condition that is against Christianity ought to
be rejected.[26] In contrast, Europeans have difficulties separating Marxist
analysis as a social tool from Marxist ideology. While this concept is not
a difficulty for theologians in Latin America, the tension still remains.

In 1955, representatives from Third World nations gathered for a
conference at Bandung (Indonesia) to reflect on the common reality
found in underdeveloped countries and to denounce this unjust situation.[27] What grew from this meeting was a theology of development
that addressed human aspirations for a fuller life socially, politically, and
economically. Initially, the theology of development was hailed enthusiastically as the breakthrough needed for human fulfillment. However,
the stress on progress in purely economic terms proved inadequate for
the situation of Latin America. Other difficulties with the theology of
development arose as well, especially with regard to its starting point.
The theme of development perpetuated a belief that people in the Third
World were "less human" and needed to be moved into a condition
of being "more human." However, this movement did not address the
causes of impoverishment nor did it challenge the established order to
create a new reality based on justice and love.

Soon the inadequacies of developmentalism—which tended to
view underdeveloped countries as simply primitive versions of developed ones—gave way to the theory of dependence which looked at the

25. *Liberatatis nuntius* and *Libertatis conscientia* are two examples of CDF notifications on the incompatibility of Marxism and Christian thought. See biographical
introduction on Gustavo Gutiérrez in the first chapter.

26. Gutiérrez "Two Theological Perspectives, 234–35.

27. Gutiérrez, "Task and Content," 21.

causes of poverty. Dependency theory considered the impoverished conditions of the underdeveloped countries as the result of gains made in the developed world.[28] The solution to this "unhealthy" relationship would be to move away from being economically dependent on the dominant countries. Peaking in the 1960s and 1970s, dependency theory was a vital tool for comprehending the Latin American reality: "It made possible a structural analysis of the evils present in this reality, and suggested courses for remedying them . . . Its contribution was significant during the first few years of the development of the theology of liberation in Latin America."[29]

However, like most social theories located in a particular time and place, dependency theory served its purpose but could not respond completely to the complex reality evolving in Latin America. "While it would be a serious error not to acknowledge the contribution of this theory, it would be worse to remain tied to a tool which clearly no longer responds adequately to the diversity of the present situation, and which pays no heed to new aspects. Many such changes are the product of important changes on the international scene. They also arise from different perceptions of elements which, while they may have long formed part of the social framework in Latin America, now help provide a better picture of its contours."[30] Consequently, the theology of liberation came to the forefront of the consciousness of the Latin American Church in order to address the inadequacies of social theories. Thus, in order to grasp the origin and circumstances that gave birth to liberation theology, one must understand its spirituality, a spirituality experienced in the lives of the poor within a specific historical context.

Real or Material Poverty: Theological Developments

For Gutiérrez, early Christianity related theology to the spiritual life: "Primarily it dealt with a meditation on the bible, geared toward spiritual progress."[31] Only in the twelfth century did theology take a different direction. Primarily through the works of St. Thomas Aquinas, theology began to be considered a science. With this heritage, theology would

28. Ibid., 22.
29. Ibid.
30. Ibid., 23.
31. Gutiérrez, "Latin American Perception," 58.

be rational in its core. With the challenges of the Enlightenment in the eighteenth century, theology began to address the mind of nonbelievers. The German theologian, Dietrich Bonhoeffer (1906–1945), who was executed by the Nazi regime, raised questions about how to talk about God in a world come of age and how to speak about God in an adult world— questions that describe the transformation that was needed of theology in modern society. However, these theological shifts by European theologians aware of the people living within an Enlightenment context, could not pose questions that would speak to the conditions of Latin America. For Latin American theologians, questions, not answers, were the real solutions for they opened up another possibility, another way of being in the world. "Some may well complain that the positions expressed in [the Commission for Social Action] do not offer any responses or solutions. But we must not forget that those who change the course of history are usually these who pose a new set of questions rather than those who offer solutions."[32]

Gutiérrez maintains that present day theologizing has inherited all these different approaches. It is an oversimplification to say there is only one way of doing theology, because of the various approaches and questions being raised. At the same time it would be presumptuous to say that European theology is the correct way of theologizing. Theology on the European continent continues its attempt to address the reason-based questions of unbelievers and has been kept in a private spiritual domain. According to Gutiérrez, the direction theology has taken in Europe is inadequate for addressing the modern world, especially in Latin America. The nature of theologizing done in Europe is inadequate for this side of the Atlantic; however, Gutiérrez did clarify the different theological positions needed for Latin America through his dialogue with his European counterparts. From encounters with his European counterparts, Gutiérrez formulated his own questions that reflect the situations of his people: "How are we to talk about a God who is revealed as love in a situation characterized by poverty and oppression? How are we to proclaim the God of life to men and women who die prematurely and unjustly? How are we to acknowledge that God makes us a free gift of love and justice when we have before us the suffering of the innocent?

---

32. Gutiérrez, "Introduction," xxiii.

What words are we to use in telling those who are not even regarded as persons that they are the daughters and sons of God?"[33]

Concluding that the course that European theology has taken is irrelevant to address the lives of the poor in Peru, Gutiérrez re-reads the Gospel in light of the reality of his pastoral situation. Instead of the non-believer, the non-person becomes his focus: he who is "not recognized as such by the existing social order: the poor, the exploited, one who is systematically deprived of being a person, one who scarcely knows that he or she is a person."[34] By posing simple questions to himself and to those in the Church, Gutiérrez arrives at a new starting point in theology: "How are we to proclaim God as a Father in a nonhuman world? What is implied when we tell nonpersons that they are sons and daughters of God?"[35] Thus, liberation theology is not simply an extreme or leftist version of theology, but a completely new way of doing theology because of the questions it poses on behalf of the poor and oppressed.

Gustavo Gutiérrez's Understanding of Real Poverty, Spiritual Poverty, and Poverty as Commitment

Real Poverty and the Material Poor

After Vatican II, historical developments in Latin America and theological developments in the Church came together in theologians such as Gustavo Gutiérrez and helped highlight the world of the poor, the world of real poverty where the poor live in an inhuman state that is contrary to the will of God: "Poverty is certainly a social and economic issue, but it has much more than a social and economic dimension. In the final analysis, poverty means death: unjust death; early death; death due to illness, hunger, repression; physical death; and cultural death."[36] Gutiérrez is always quick to balance the notion of poverty so that it does not slip solely into the economic realm or solely into the social arena. "In our context, we say poverty is not only an economic issue, poverty is also to be insignificant for several reasons; one is economic, or the color of the

---

33. Gutiérrez, "But Why Lord," 18.
34. Gutiérrez, "Faith as Freedom," 43.
35. Gutiérrez *Confrontations*, 7.
36. Gutiérrez, "Church of the Poor," 14.

skin is another reason, or to speak badly—the dominant language of our country is another reason, to be a woman is another reason."[37]

In biblical terms, poverty is the result of injustice and sin; when translated into the Latin American reality, poverty is an evil situation that cannot be tolerated because it denies the life given by God. This situation has prompted Gutiérrez not only to express the reality of the poor in Latin America, but prophetically to denounce the hijacking of theology to defend the creation of a capitalistic system which supports the actions and social structures of the rich and powerful in their exploitation of the most vulnerable. In other words, Gutiérrez sees the capitalist system domesticating theology and concurrently taming the Church to support its economic agenda. In contrast, a proper theological reflection prophetically condemns the structural injustices caused by capitalistic economic practices.

A quick scan of Latin America shows a continent that has been dominated by Europeans throughout much of its recorded history. Originally conquered by Spain after the discovery of the New World in the sixteenth century, Latin America afforded opportunities both for a new Christendom for the Church and for new wealth for Europeans. Without autonomy, the indigenous inhabitants soon were subjugated under a cruel and oppressive European system. As Spain dwindled in influence, England thrust Latin America into another state of colonization, this time in the form of neo-colonialism. Instead of benefiting from a free market economy like their European counterparts, Latin Americans were shackled in neo-colonialism and forced to serve their rich European masters once again.[38]

Capitalism, in the form of neo-colonialism, did not afford the indigenous peoples freedom and liberty. Rather, neo-colonialism made life worse in some cases and became more oppressive because of the false hope created by capitalist ideology. Reflecting on what Latin America inherited through this transition, Gutiérrez states this whole process "has been and is carried out under conditions that are specifically designed to keep us in a subordinate and limited place in the international division of labor within the capitalist system."[39] In both the Spanish and English domination of Latin America, the Church was used to support

37. See Appendix B.

38. Gutiérrez, "Two Theological Perspectives," 235.

39. Gutiérrez, "'Preparatory Document' for Puebla," 212.

practices that allowed Europeans to grow richer at the expense of the poor and indigenous people of Latin America. Simultaneously, theology was distorted to support the exploitation of human beings and natural resources in Latin America.

There is no doubt that discussion about material poverty causes tension in the Church and in theological reflection. Tensions arise when reviewing the history of Latin America, especially in examining the role of the Church. For example, discussions about Latin American theologians accused of identifying or collapsing the Kingdom of God with purely earthly practices naturally cause rifts within the ecclesial community.[40] Considering poverty in a strictly spiritual realm eases this strain somewhat for those uncomfortable with political activity in the name of the Kingdom of God. However, Gutiérrez argues that those who "escape" this tension practice their own form of reductionism and do not truly comprehend the notion of poverty in its spiritual sense.[41]

This situation is further highlighted by the Gospel accounts of the Beatitudes. In Luke 6:20, the Evangelist calls the "poor" blessed in the Kingdom of God, while Matt. 5:3 claims the "poor in spirit" are the blessed ones. There is an obvious distinction between the economic poor and the poor in spirit. However, for Gutiérrez this distinction is not problematic but simply serves to highlight the materially poor.[42] The materially poor are dependent people just as the spiritually poor are dependent on God. Their dependence is different but not totally unassociated. The materially poor are dependent on certain things, material goods, while "poor in spirit" reflects dependence in all areas of the human person including the material. Thus, the poor in spirit must also include the materially poor in the form of solidarity; otherwise spiritual poverty cannot be realized for Gutiérrez.[43]

Along with the ongoing description of the poor in Latin America, the theme of where the poor live is important in the writings of Gutiérrez.

40. The dialogue regarding "the distinction of planes" between then Cardinal Joseph Ratzinger, now Pope Benedict XVI, and Gustavo Gutiérrez can be found in the fourth chapter. How to keep the kingdom of earth and the kingdom of heaven distinct without separation is a difficult matter.

41. More will be said regarding this reduction in the next section; for present purposes, what is important is the awareness of the temptation to reduce Christianity to either purely practical activities or to some ephemeral state.

42. Gutiérrez, *Confrontations*, 160–64.

43. Ibid.

Exploration of the places where the poor reside uncovers their world, which includes a culture of its own. Instead of viewing the poor in some vague subhuman grouping that needs elevation into the dominant class, Gutiérrez highlights the humanity of the poor. Those in poverty have a way and reason for crying, but they also have a way and reason for celebrating: "To be poor is to survive rather than live; it is to be subject to exploitation and injustice; it is also, however, to possess a special way of feeling, thinking, loving, believing, suffering, and praying."[44] There is a whole culture where the poor live and it is one that must be continually penetrated if we are to embrace the preferential option: "Anthropologists love to say that culture is life. When one culture is not respected, we are killing the persons who belong to that culture. When a race is despised, we are killing people belonging to this race; when we do not recognise women and give them full rights we are killing them. It is another kind of death from physical death, but it is death."[45]

On the one hand, we are called to enter the world of the poor in order to know them as subjects of their own destiny and to preserve their culture. On the other hand, our entrance and presence in the world of the poor has its limitations. Gutiérrez reflects on his own limitations by recalling his ordination to the priesthood and how he was no longer insignificant because of his education and position in society and the Church. From this point forward, Gutiérrez would work like everyone else, even though he was born a *mestizo*[46] (part Hispanic and part Quechuan Indian) in the barrios of Peru, to be in solidarity with the poor and to remain in the world of the poor. "I cannot say that here or in my country a priest is an insignificant person—it is not true. I could be poor economically maybe, but I am not insignificant, my family background is poor in the global view, but I was studying, being a priest doing theology—I am not insignificant."[47] Thus, the world of the poor is accessible but with limits. "It will be necessary, therefore, to undertake this commitment although knowing in advance that the situation of the poor will almost certainly overstrain the human capacity for solidarity.

44. Ibid., 148.

45. Gutiérrez, "Joy in the Midst of Suffering," 82.

46. Although Gutiérrez sees *mestizaje* as a "planetary reality," he is quick to point out that *mestizos* in Latin America are not the same as those in the United States because of a different set of circumstances facing those of mixed race. See Appendix B.

47. See Appendix B.

The will to live in the world of the poor can therefore only follow an asymptotic curve: a constantly closer approach that can, however, never reach the point of real identification with the life of the poor."[48]

To acknowledge and still navigate within the world of the poor is possible, when one becomes a friend of the poor. Most people who are not poor encounter those in need strictly in the workplace. People go out of their homes to help others, but unless we encounter the poor in our own homes and in our everyday social venues, we cannot truly be friends of the poor. Friends are people we encounter anywhere at any time and unless we have these encounters with the poor, we will not know who they are or the world in which they live. "This is very important—the question is not only to fight for the rights of the poor, but personal friendship. As Jesus [says] in the Gospel of John, chapter 15—I don't call you servants, but friends—because friendship supposes a kind of equality. We share our lives with friends, this is the point."[49]

Spiritual Poverty: Our Method is Our Spirituality (Preferential)

I recall sitting across the table from Gustavo Gutiérrez, the humble, but world-renowned theologian, who reminded me that his theological method is secondary. What is primary—the first step—what is needed even before discussion can occur regarding the theological method is a spirituality of liberation: "In liberation theology, we often say theology is 'the second moment'—a *logos*, a word, a reflection about the first moment."[50] Thus, theology is the second step, a reflection on prayer. For Gutiérrez, prayer is only prayer when it includes both contemplation and action: "*Spirituality* is a relatively new word, originating in the seventeenth century. But it denotes a very old reality: following Jesus."[51] This point is key in Gutiérrez's thought, and it reminds us that spirituality is not to be kept in the private domain. Rather, spirituality is an active way of following Christ—a way of following Christ based on one's own reality.[52]

An illustration given by Gutiérrez regarding his understanding of spirituality is derived from the lives of great saints of the past. For

48. Gutiérrez, *We Drink from our own Wells*, 126.

49. See Appendix B.

50. Gutiérrez, "Spirituality for Liberation," 41.

51. Ibid.

52. Ibid., 43.

example, in order to understand the life and work of St. Bonaventure, Gutiérrez insists we need first to understand St. Francis of Assisi.[53] Only through the Franciscan way of following Christ developed by St. Francis can we understand the theological reflection of St. Bonaventure. Another example is St. Thomas Aquinas: if we want to understand St. Thomas, we must first understand St. Dominic. The Dominican way of following Christ is what St. Thomas first lived out. Before St. Bonaventure or St. Thomas engaged their theological method, they first engaged their spirituality, the prayer of contemplation and action of their respective founders. Thus, to uncover one's theological method, one must first discover the spirituality of the theologian, his or her way of following Christ.

For Gutiérrez, it is important to understand that theology is a language of God developed in prayer. Once again, prayer is twofold including both the mystical and prophetic dimensions. Mystical language reveals grace, the gratuitous love of God, while prophetic language expresses the demands of God's gratuity. The former allows us to understand why the poor are preferred because of God's discretion and not our moral character. The latter requires those who experience this grace to denounce the injustice and exploitation of those who are preferred by God. "Without prophecy, the language of contemplation runs the risk of detachment from the history in which God is acting and in which we encounter God. Without the mystical dimension, the language of prophecy can narrow its vision and weaken its perception of that which makes all things new."[54] The two can never be separated, rather they complement one another: "Both languages are necessary and therefore inseparable; they also feed and correct each other. And both languages arise, among the poor of Latin America . . . out of the suffering and hopes of the innocent."[55]

This twofold prayer which Gutiérrez describes is characterized by silence. It is within this silence that Gutiérrez differs from other theologians, especially Europeans. Although few would disagree that following Christ requires contemplation, Gutiérrez insists upon this praxis of silence. Silence is described as the moment of worship and praxis, gratuitousness and justice, and the silence of contemplation and

---

53. From a lecture at the University of Notre Dame, Fall 2008.

54. Gutiérrez, *Confrontations*, 16.

55. Gutiérrez, "But Why Lord," 22.

commitment.[56] Regardless of terminology, what is clear in his spirituality of liberation is the necessity of listening to God and to the needs of
others. Thus, in order to understand the theology of liberation, a specific
language is needed. This language is developed in prayer and is the first
moment. Theology, a reflection on that prayer, is the second moment.
Only in contemplation of the divine and praxis towards our neighbor are we able to reach the second stage, the ability to reflect on our
worship and commitment and thus elaborate a theology of liberation.
"Liberation theology's second central intuition is that God is a liberating
God, revealed only in the concrete historical context of liberation of the
poor and oppressed. This point is inseparable from the first: if theology
is reflection on and from within concrete praxis, the concrete praxis in
question is the liberation praxis of the oppressed . . . It is not enough to
know that praxis must precede reflection; we must also realize that the
historical subject of that praxis is the poor—the people who have been
excluded from the pages of history."[57]

Often, people looking in from the outside mistakenly critique the
theology of liberation for its overwhelming focus on praxis. For example,
the charge of reductionism is leveled against theologians who advocate
political activity in response to poverty and oppression.[58] In other words,
it seems that faith is set aside until material needs are met.[59] Gutiérrez
argues against this charge of reductionism and sees his critics falling into
their own trap of reductionism where political activity is non-existent.[60]
In addition, Gutiérrez counters this criticism by leveling one of his own.
Acknowledging that reductionism is always a danger, Gutiérrez feels
that "denying it would be [dis]ingenuous and dishonest."[61] However,
another danger of reductionism for Latin American theologians is especially evident when the Gospel is used in the service of dominant groups
to secure and reinforce their positions in society. This type of reductionism looks like "a discarnate spiritualism that emphasizes the religious
side of a people without attending to the material conditions in which

56. Gutiérrez, *Confrontations*, 3.

57. Gutiérrez, "Two Theological Perspectives," 247.

58. Gutiérrez, "'Preparatory Document' for Puebla," 213.

59. Gutiérrez, *Confrontations*, 8.

60. Gutiérrez, "Faith as Freedom," 8; *Praxis de Liberacion*, 55; also see Brown, "After
Ten Years," xiii.

61. Gutiérrez, "Faith as Freedom," 56.

they live."[62] Gutiérrez points out the dangers of reductionism when theologians move to the extremes and fail to locate theology within the context of a specific people. "These two kinds of reductionism ignore both the fullness of the Christian message and the concrete life of the Latin American people."[63]

To overcome the dangers of reductionism, especially the temptation of Latin American theologians to reduce Christianity to sociological, political, or economic matters, Gutiérrez emphasizes the theme of God's gratuity. God's gift of salvation includes liberation from all areas of injustice and is not just a religious condition removed from concrete lived experiences in the world. Thus, God's gratuitous gift to humanity requires a response, a response in the form of commitment to others. Citing St. Thomas' twofold understanding of salvation—"freedom from" and "freedom for"—Gutiérrez applies the same criteria in terms of God's gratuity.[64] We receive freely from God so that in freedom we may commit ourselves to others. Furthermore, reductionism is avoided by placing ourselves in solidarity with the dispossessed of the continent. Once again, liberation is not reduced to one area affecting the poor, rather it encompasses both the historical and political conditions in which the poor find themselves.

In response to critics fearing reductionism in liberation theology, Gutiérrez indicates an equal danger when the human condition is removed from salvation.[65] In addition, when liberation theology is seen within the framework of God's gratuitous gift and our response to that gift is reflected in our solidarity with the poor, then all forms of reductionism are avoided. Liberation is not simply freedom in the religious realm; it encapsulates every realm of humanity. The beginning stage is the gratuity of God; however, the end stage is commitment to the other. Thus, the encounter with the Other needs also the encounter with the other.

Preference is a difficult concept to embrace especially when one is not standing on the side of poverty and death. In essence, one feels like an outsider when questioning why the poor would receive preferential treatment when God is the Father of all creation. However, this is a

62. Gutiérrez, *Confrontations*, 8.

63. Ibid.

64. Ibid., 15.

65. Gutiérrez, "Faith as Freedom," 56–57.

crucial revelation of God. We must know how God's economy operates if we are to enter fully into solidarity with the poor. Throughout his pontificate, Pope John Paul II referred to the preferential option, but revised the formulation in a homily given at the Basilica of Guadalupe: "preferential but not exclusive love for the poor".[66] The rephrased preferential option for the poor, with its non-exclusive aspect, did not alter what was said by Latin American bishops—who did not speak of this preferential option in exclusive terms. It was always presented in a universal aspect because God truly loves all his children. However, the statement of Puebla, reinforcing the message of Medellín, stressed the priority of God's love and did not exclude its universality. The preferential option for the poor reminds the Church that God's love is prioritized, first to the poor—the economic poor—simply for who they are. Thus, John Paul II's addition to the statement rephrased it but did not change its original meaning. In fact, the attention given to the question of universality and exclusivity gave theologians like Gutiérrez another opportunity to clarify the message of poverty.

One of the clarifications made by Gutiérrez in defending the preferential notion regards the gratuity of God. For Gutiérrez, the poor, the materially deprived, receive preference simply by the fact of their economic situation: "the preference for the simple is not due to their moral and spiritual dispositions but to their human weakness and to the scorn of which they are the object."[67] Therefore, preference reflects a pure gift of God and Gutiérrez goes as far as to say that this is in the nature of God.[68] While we cannot merit God's love, we only receive it as a gift. Therefore, it is the gratuitous act of God that gives us the notion: "The word *preference* itself rejects all exclusivity and underlines those who should be the first—not the only ones—in our solidarity."[69] Thus, the notion of preference is constitutive of the notion of universality and vice versa. We cannot have one without the other and the former allows us to grasp the latter: "In this tension between preference and universality resides the richness and originality of the Christian message."[70]

66. John Paul II, "Homily at the Basilica of Guadalupe," 74.

67. Gutiérrez, *God of Life*, 114.

68. Gutiérrez, "Opting for the Poor," 11.

69. Gutiérrez , "Liberation Theology and the Future," 102.

70. Gutiérrez, *Confrontations*, 156.

We are called to go to all nations to proclaim the love of God, but this proclamation must begin in a concrete place and time and be directed to concrete human beings. Throughout God's self-communication, the message of God's love has come to the poor where the truth of the Gospel resides, "the last shall be first" (Matt. 20:16). More importantly, preference allows all to enter the Kingdom of God through our solidarity with those first to hear the Good News, the poor in our midst. Our commitment in response to the gratuitous gift of God would be incomplete without this preference, a priority for our living out the Christian vocation. Here the first step comes together, prayer in the form of worship and commitment, contemplation and praxis, is realized often living in the midst of conflict.[71] "To deny [conflict] would be to deny our own selves as human beings who are bound in solidarity to our fellows and as Christians who must live out both the universality of God's love and God's preference for the poor."[72]

Gutiérrez also appeals to scripture to support this claim of preference. From the beginning, God's preference is revealed through sibling rivalry. In the telling of the story of Cain and Abel, God's preference for Abel's sacrifice cannot be rationalized: "In the course of time Cain brought an offering to the LORD from the fruit of the soil, while Abel, for his part, brought one of the best firstlings of his flock. The LORD looked with favor on Abel and his offering, but on Cain and his offering he did not (Gen. 4:2 NAB). Often this passage is explained away by emphasizing Abel's "best firstling" versus Cain's mediocre offering; however, the preference God shows Abel is not because Abel's offering was better; according to Gutiérrez, this would only lead us back to the theme that we somehow merit God's love. Rather, Abel was the younger of the two, the more vulnerable of the brothers; thus, God chose Abel's offering over Cain's because of his status in life. "God preferred the sacrifices of Abel, the more fragile one, over the sacrifice of Cain . . . Cain's sin was not to accept God's preference for Abel . . . The rejection of preference consists of not understanding that one must combine the universality of God's love with His preference for the poor."[73]

Consequently, spiritual poverty calls us to live out our vocations in spiritual childhood where detachment from material goods is necessary

71. Ibid., 68.

72. Ibid.

73. Gutiérrez, "Renewing the Option," 74.

as an acknowledgement that we understand who receives preference in God's economy. Without preference, we cannot complete the spiritual life of following Jesus. Without the poor, the favored ones, we cannot receive freely from God as Jesus did, for we would not understand to whom this gift is then directed. Jesus, in his earthly life, embraced orphans, widows, foreigners, and all who were poor and vulnerable in the society of his day in order to illustrate that the grace received from the Father must be related to those around us who are suffering.

Without a commitment to the poor, following Jesus would strictly fall into the mystical dimension of our faith life and lose its complement, the prophetic.[74] The mystical and the prophetic are necessary and can only be realized if we understand and embrace the preference God has for the poor. Preference allows us to see those to whom the Good News is addressed. Thus, we are able to say once again that the poor become a gift to the Church and to the rest of the world, and not necessarily vice-versa. In preference, we do not approach the poor thinking ourselves as gifts alleviating the pains of the impoverished, but rather, we receive the gift of the poor who allow us to fulfill our spirituality by giving us access to both the prophetic and mystical, both worship and praxis, both contemplation and action—all, dimensions of our faith. Without the gift of the poor, there would be no way for us to follow Jesus as he lived on earth two thousand years ago.

In *We Drink from Our Own Wells*, spiritual childhood plays an important role in Gutiérrez's understanding of the spirituality of liberation where this option must be engaged in freedom. Gutiérrez gleans from the Gospel one of the most important concepts in his theology: a reminder to all, even the poor, of the obligation as disciples to follow Jesus. Spiritual childhood stems from the opening up of our lives to the gratuitous gift of God as we realize our sonship or daughtership. In turn, being sons or daughters of God makes us brothers and sisters to one another. It is only through this reception and realization of the first that brings us to the reality of the second and to see the other in need. "The gift of filiation brings with it the obligation to create brotherly and sisterly relations among human beings."[75] Thus, "[s]piritual poverty is obligatory for every Christian and for the Church as a whole"; indeed,

---

74. Gutiérrez, *Confrontations*, 8.

75. Ibid., 39.

"those who renounce their possessions gain a new realization of the Lord's fidelity."[76] Only when we embrace spiritual poverty, the denunciation of the unjust situation caused by the lack of material goods, can we speak about commitment, the third sense of poverty.

Poverty as a Commitment

In *A Theology of Liberation*, Gustavo Gutiérrez describes the "distinction of planes" between the Church and the world, to illustrate the proper relation that liberation theology seeks to establish. This issue is not new but rather "essentially traditional" for it is a "classic question of the relation between faith and human existence, between faith and social reality, between faith and political action, or in other words, between the Kingdom of God and the building up of the world."[77] In the view favoring the separation of "the planes," social praxis does not necessarily involve political activity, since action is sought only for the building of God's Kingdom (praxis of heaven) and not the worldly one (praxis of earth). For this reason, Gutiérrez and others reject the model of "distinction and separation" and seek a "distinction but not separation," since separation of the Kingdom and the world is inconceivable. "Stress was placed on private life and the cultivation of private values; things political were relegated to a lower plane, to the elusive and undemanding area of misunderstood "common good" . . . Hence there developed the complacency with a very general and "humanizing" vision of reality, to the detriment of a scientific and structural knowledge of socio-economic mechanisms and historical dynamics. Hence also there came the insistence on the personal and conciliatory aspects of the Gospel message rather than on its political and conflictual dimensions."[78]

By maintaining the "distinction of planes," but also their unity Gutiérrez is able to consider "history as one."[79] We do not live in a world with two histories: one of salvation and the other of the world. Rather, Gutiérrez maintains there is only one history which includes both the world and salvation.[80] In his reading of scripture, Gutiérrez traces this one history from the beginning to the end: from the Old Testament's

---

76. Gutiérrez, *We Drink from our own Wells*, 123.

77. Gutiérrez, *Theology of Liberation*, 29.

78. Ibid., 32.

79. Gutiérrez, *Confrontations*, 18.

80. Ibid.

Creation and Exodus accounts to the New Testament's Gospel accounts of Christ.

According to Gutiérrez, one should not forget the link between creation and salvation that is highlighted by the liberating experience of the Exodus.[81] Gutiérrez proposes an understanding in which there is a single act of God, where creation and salvation are included, and not a twofold act where creation comes first and then salvation after the fall of humanity. In the act of creation, the act of salvation is also present, for the creation of the world is not only an act of creation, but also an act maintaining creation. Thus, creation and salvation are synonymous and cannot be separated when history is viewed as one. By portraying God as Creator and as Redeemer, salvation is then the very act of God as Creator and creation is a salvific act which continues to the end of time, reaching its pinnacle in Christ. However, creation-salvation is still the one act of God. What closely knits the Exodus event with the Creation event as the one saving act of God is found in the technical Hebrew term *bara* (to create). In the Genesis account, this term is originally associated with the creation of and covenant with the world; i.e., God created heaven and earth, created sea creatures and birds, created man, etc. (Genesis 1). The second instance of this term is used in conjunction with the creation of Israel through the crossing of the Red Sea and the covenant made with the people who will come to be known as God's own as told by Isaiah (43:1, 15).[82] Thus, Gutiérrez equates the Creator of the world with the Creator and Liberator of Israel based on the similar characteristics of creation and covenant found in both passages: "Yahweh will be remembered throughout the history of Israel by this act which inaugurates its history, a history which is a re-creation. The God who makes the cosmos from chaos is the same God who leads Israel from alienation to liberation."[83]

Gutiérrez sees the Exodus event as salvific liberation, not completed as one step but as an ongoing process represented by the Israelites wandering in the desert. God's loving gesture not only leads the oppressed out of the oppressive situation in Egypt, but also teaches the people how to be in relationship with one another and with their Liberator. The desert experience thus reflects the lessons the Israelites

81. Gutiérrez, *Theology of Liberation*, 86.

82. Ibid., 88.

83. Ibid., 89.

had to learn in order to be called God's people. "The realization of the liberating love of Yahweh had been present from the beginning of the process. At the same time, when this festival of liberation and life was celebrated outside the land of enslavement and death, it served as a means of learning freedom during the crossing of the wilderness and its solitude. The full experience of that freedom was to come in the communion of the promised land."[84]

Gutiérrez calls the experience after the liberation from the Egyptians a "two-fold apprenticeship." It is two-fold because it is a time when God, through the testing of the people in the desert, reveals the contents of their hearts while at the same time they witness the revelation of God's love in their midst. "Growth in this reciprocal knowledge included growth in mutual love, for, as we know, the biblical word 'know' has the connotation of intimacy and affectivity."[85]

The Exodus is a political event when viewed as a whole—an experience of liberation from slavery and destruction, whereby the Israelites now are destined for the Promised Land and for a new construction as God's people. The political act (liberation from captivity) as witnessed in the Exodus narrative requires human beings to be both the recipients and agents of liberation. It is true that God's free will begins the process of liberation; however, it must also include a response, a free and conscious consent, from those guided by God's grace. Because of the intimate connection between creation and liberation, Gutiérrez asserts that active human participation is necessary in the building up of any society. Consequently, Gutiérrez claims that Exodus has placed together or "desacralized" both creation and social praxis as part of the one history. No longer is salvation thought of as otherworldly, but the Exodus event provides a framework of salvation that begins in this world and includes our participation. "Secularization is, above all, the result of a transformation of human self-understanding."[86] This transformation affects all areas of our being (nature, society, psychology, and history) and brings about a fundamentally new way of conceiving our relationship with God.[87] Rather than awaiting relief in the next life, liberation as a constitutive part of salvation is part of God's gratuitous gift in the

---

84. Gutiérrez, *We Drink from our own Wells*, 74.

85. Ibid., 75.

86. Gutiérrez, *Theology of Liberation*, 42.

87. Ibid.

present life. However, this gift of salvation does not imply that the world is now "profane" but that the liberating transforming experience has brought this world into the reach of human praxis.

This new creation brought about by the Exodus event also reveals the movement of desacralization for Gutiérrez. If faith "desacralizes" creation, making it an area proper for human work, the Exodus from Egypt, the home of a sacred monarchy, reinforces this idea: as a result of the "desacralization," social praxis from that time on will be the work of humankind.[88] In other words, God's will in liberating the people from Egyptian slavery reflects a movement where God's people are now called to become agents of change by participating in the divine plan. For Gutiérrez, liberation from Egypt is crucial since the oppressed are barred from a relationship with God, with each other, and with creation purely by the type of work they must undergo as slaves.[89] This alienation is what Egypt represents, while the exit from slavery restores the true relationships of God's people as witnessed in their journey through the desert, which reached its heights in the Promised Land. Once again, creation and salvation are linked by the restored relationship described in both Creation and the Exodus: the people now have relationships with the Creator, with one another, and with creation as free people. If the Exodus event represents desacralization, as Gutiérrez claims, then what was once alien to the people, communion with God and one another in this life, is now realized. The divine will is still recognized as the initial cause, but now participation is equally important.

The Exodus experience propelled God's people to seek their own destiny by working for liberation and, by their efforts, to transform their environment. Gutiérrez sees this heritage as being passed on to successive generations in the bible and to the people of Latin America today. Understanding "the Exodus experience as paradigmatic," Gutiérrez asserts that this narrative remains "vital and contemporary due to similar historical experiences which the People of God undergo."[90]

Consequently, when we assert that humanity fulfills itself by continuing the work of creation by means of its labor, we are saying that it places itself, by this very fact, within an all-embracing salvific process. To work for the transformation of this world is to become human and

---

88. Ibid., 90.

89. Gutiérrez, *Power of the Poor*, 5.

90. Ibid.

to be part and parcel of the human community; it is to build, but also to save. Likewise, to struggle against misery and exploitation and to build a just society is already to be part of the saving action, which is moving towards its complete fulfillment. Hence, building the temporal city is not simply a stage of "humanization" or "pre-evangelization"; rather it is participating in a saving process which embraces the whole of humanity and all human history.[91]

Explicit in the Exodus account is the formation of the people of God who will be eventually delivered into the Promised Land. Implicit in this reading is that this event is also the formation of the Kingdom which is to come. Jesus, in the New Testament, taught that the Kingdom belongs to the poor. Theologians will note that the economic disenfranchisement and spiritual poverty can be found in both the poor and the people fleeing Egypt. If this analogy exists, then the Kingdom formed in the Exodus event implies a similar utopian formation among the poor today.[92]

When theologians such as Gutiérrez speak about utopia, they mean that the in-breaking of God's reign is here and now although not fully realized. However, liberation theology presents a broader picture of utopia with one eye on the present while another eye focuses on the future. In order to envision a future utopia, some connection with the present reality is required. "Three elements characterize the notion of utopia . . . its relationship to historical reality, its verification in praxis, and its rational nature."[93] The reason for seeking a better world while holding on to this world is that they are intrinsically tied to one another, since without the present, there could be no future to anticipate with joy. Gutiérrez describes this relationship as consisting of a denunciation of the current world because of the deficiencies present in it. These deficiencies are seen as the cause of oppression, which in turn creates a desire for a better situation. Therefore, in the denunciation of deficiencies, an annunciation occurs (the prophetic with the mystical) as the voices of unrest prophesy a new society with a just ordering of reality to come. In short, "if utopia does not lead to action in the present, it is an evasion of reality."[94]

91. Ibid., 91.

92. Ibid., 81; Gutiérrez, God of Life, 143; Theology of Liberation, 135–39.

93. Gutiérrez, Theology of Liberation, 135.

94. Ibid., 136.

The concept of utopia follows Gutiérrez's understanding of the eschatological promises revealed in the Exodus account. Eschatology is the promise, much like utopia, for it includes the present to inaugurate the future. In the present, the promise is accepted in faith for the realization of the promise yet to come. The future element means that the promise made must unfold over time. Not only does it unfold in the Exodus where God's people are liberated to wander out in the desert, but the promise is also revealed in other concrete manifestations throughout Israel's history.[95] Gutiérrez presents the eschatological promise, the utopia for God's people not as a reality already complete here. However, the future promise depends on the present as the Exodus reading illustrates. Therefore, what we do here and now matters in the Kingdom to come.

In addition, the notion of sin must be addressed in order to understand true liberation. Sin in Egypt took the form of alienation. The people in captivity were alienated from God, from one another, and from creation. What the Exodus reveals in abolishing alienation is the forming of a people who are liberated and saved from sin in the present moment: "From this point of view the notion of salvation appears in a different light. Salvation is not something otherworldly, in regard to which the present life is merely a test."[96] Salvation becomes a historical-political reality because sin is also a historical-political reality as witnessed in the Egyptian captivity. "Sin demands a radical liberation, which in turn necessarily implies a political liberation."[97] Gutiérrez maintains that this radical liberation illustrated by the Exodus can only be accomplished as a gift, which only Christ offers us.

As previously stated, Gutiérrez's notion of liberation is found on three levels: political liberation, human liberation, and liberation from sin correlating with the three notions of poverty: "These three levels mutually affect each other, but they are not the same. One is not present without the others, but they are distinct: they are all part of a single, all-encompassing salvific process, but they are to be found at different levels."[98] In the preface to his 1988 revision of *A Theology of Liberation*, Gutiérrez again mentions liberation on three levels that highlight the correlation with the three definitions of poverty. The first level of lib-

95. Ibid., 92.
96. Ibid., 85.
97. Ibid., 103.
98. Ibid.

eration concerns "the social situation of oppression and marginalization that forces many (and indeed in one way or another way) to live in conditions contrary to God's will for their life."[99] The second level is personal transformation; here, liberation results in personal growth. The third level is liberation from sin itself; on this level is the proper restoration of our relationship with God and one another: "Theological analysis . . . leads to the position that only liberation from sin gets to the very source of social injustice and other forms of human oppression and reconciles us with God and our fellow human beings."[100] However, in order for liberation to be realized on this third level, liberation on the first two must also be achieved. Thus, Gutiérrez's understanding of liberation follows the Exodus narrative where all three levels are achieved and thus, all three notions of poverty are addressed as well. The flight from captivity in Egypt illustrates liberation from oppressive social structures. The wandering in the desert reflects the personal transformation through the interior disposition of God's people. Finally, the Promised Land, the new creation, highlights the liberation of God's people from sin for proper relationships with God and each other.

Finally, to encapsulate Gutiérrez's reading of Exodus, one may return to the distinction of planes. Because Gutiérrez emphasizes "distinction but not separation," between salvation history and world history, he also views liberation as affecting temporal progress. Liberation from sin on all three levels implies that salvation is occurring here and now and through our participation with the divine will. The distinction is maintained when the historical liberating events are not equated directly to the Kingdom in a one-to-one equation. In other words, Gutiérrez would never say directly that one act of liberation in history directly corresponds to an act in building up the Kingdom. Rather, it is in a general sense that the correlation is made, for Gutiérrez maintains there would be no growth of the Kingdom without liberating historical events. "Temporal progress—or, to avoid this aseptic term, human liberation— and the growth of the Kingdom both are directed toward complete communion of human beings with God and among themselves. They have the same goals, but they do not follow parallel roads, not even convergent ones. The growth of the Kingdom is a progress which occurs historically in liberation, insofar as liberation means a greater human

99. Ibid., xxxviii.
100. Ibid.

fulfillment. Liberation is a precondition for the new society[.]"[101] Thus, Gutiérrez's interpretation of the Exodus encompasses a unified view of the world, one which includes distinctions but also heavily stresses unity. The present is always connected with the future, while this world is connected with the Kingdom.

"It is because of this comprehensiveness that the event of the exodus can be called paradigmatic for biblical faith."[102] Since the Exodus is not a separate event of salvation but part of the one great act of salvation starting with the Creation event and reaching its pinnacle in Christ, the cross also becomes paradigmatic. Thus, any discussion of liberation and salvation must be conducted in reference to the salvific act of Christ. According to Gutiérrez, the great hermeneutic of faith is found in Jesus Christ for he is the foundation of all theological discourse.[103] By the incarnation, Jesus establishes the hermeneutic circle of faith, a movement of the divine to humanity and vice versa. By embracing our human nature, Jesus, like us in all things but sin, is able to reveal the path of union with God and communion with one another. "[This is the] basic circle of all hermeneutics: from the human being to God and from God to the human being, from history to faith and from faith to history, from love of our brothers and sisters to the love of the Father and from the love of the Father to the love of our brothers and sisters, from human justice to God's holiness and from God's holiness to human justice, from the poor person to God and from God to the poor person."[104] Thus, while maintaining the distinction between nature and grace, God's self-communication and our capacity to respond, Gutiérrez also maintains the unity of this relationship by locating it in "Christo-finalized" history,[105] that is, the one history which Gutiérrez has stressed from the beginning of God's Creation. This one history enables us to see all things in the one salvific act of Christ.

Poverty gives rise to commitment, expressing our option, our solidarity with the poor, precisely because history is one. Solidarity is another crucial concept in relating to the poor; as previously mentioned, it entails entering the world of the poor and becoming friends of the poor.

101. Ibid., 104.

102. Gutiérrez, *Confrontations*, 117.

103. Gutiérrez, *Praxis de Liberacion*, 43.

104. Gutiérrez, *Power of the Poor*, 15.

105. Gutiérrez, *Theology of Liberation*, 86.

Solidarity is our entrance into the world of the poor and an opportunity to see them as Jesus saw them, as equals. The healing accounts of the Gospels show interactions between Jesus and those who were healed. These encounters involve bringing the poor to a fuller life where Jesus reveals them as equals and as active participants in the healing process through their act of faith.[106] What is at times overlooked is the holistic healing Jesus brings to the poor. In addition to the physical healing, Jesus allows those he encounters to come out of anonymity. The poor who are nameless even in the Gospels are brought to their rightful place in society as children of God. Part of the miracle of Jesus is to bring a non-person to the status of a person in his or her community.

The encounters with the poor in their world also reveal another important characteristic of liberation theology: the goal of allowing the poor to become subjects of their own destiny. Often Gutiérrez has written about the "underside of history," the "losers" of history forgotten in the pages of the history books because history is written by the "winners."[107] One of the goals and proofs of true liberation is the rewriting of history from the perspective of those on its underside. In other words, history must be told from the perspective of the poor, since a majority of those in Latin America live this reality. This is one of the reasons why it is vital that the Latin American Church adopt a perspective of the poor in its outlook. For without such a perspective, the Church would not be able to address poverty and liberation in all three of its aspects. Thus, liberation is not something handed from "us" to "them" especially since faith is something held in common; rather liberation is our solidarity with the poorest of the poor; joining the poor in this process of liberation is what God desires for the most vulnerable in society. "All our works must try to contribute to helping the poor take their history and their destiny into their own hands. The question is not only to establish a more just society but also to ensure that this is the task of the poor themselves."[108] For Gutiérrez, even the poor need to make this option, an option for the poor and not an option for the rich.

The preferential option for the poor is certainly a useful theological perspective in seeing the activities of the Church in Latin America

---

106. Gutiérrez, *Power of the Poor*, 12–16.

107. Gutiérrez, "Reflections from a Latin American Perspective," 223; *Confrontations*, 110.

108. Gutiérrez, "Opting for the Poor," 10.

and the contributions made by this Church to the universal Church. Without the poor, the spirituality of liberation would be incomplete and proper theological reflection on liberation would be impossible. With reference to the poor, however, theological reflection has powerfully and forcefully announced liberation on three levels: in relation to the social situation, personal transformation, and sin. In regard to the poor, the theology of liberation has denounced poverty at all three levels—which correlate with the three levels of liberation: real or material poverty, spiritual poverty, and poverty as commitment. Thus the preferential (spiritual poverty) option (poverty as commitment) for the poor (real or material poverty) is truly the hermeneutic lens for viewing the Latin American reality.

With this definition, Gustavo Gutiérrez turns to scripture and to a missionary figure of Latin America to deepen his understanding of the Church's social teaching. In the Book of Job, Gutiérrez discovers that the innocent suffering of Job allows the preferential option for the poor to manifest itself in the theology of the Old Testament. In the person of Bartolomé de Las Casas, Gutiérrez discovers that the missionary activities of the sixteenth century reveal theological principles for the preferential option for the poor.

PREFERENTIAL OPTION FOR THE POOR: THE BOOK OF JOB

Gustavo Gutiérrez appeals to the Word of God throughout his writings, especially in order to consider the images of the poor in scripture; in their anonymity, in their poverty, in their vulnerability, and in their social status or lack thereof. Gutiérrez is especially fond of the Book of Job, where he finds a situation of unjust suffering similar to what Latin Americans and all those who suffer endure. Job does not sin against God throughout his entire ordeal; even when suffering unjustly, he finds hope and consolation in a situation that cannot be justified. The answer to what he is experiencing is not simply the alleviation of his suffering or a return to his prior condition. Rather, Job finds hope in his understanding of the world as one in which others are suffering unjustly as well, through his bitter condition, and through interactions with his so-called friends, who insist that victims of tragedy, like Job himself, must have sinned, and therefore are in need of repentance.

Maintaining his innocence throughout the verbal onslaught from those standing in judgment around him, Job comes to understand that he is not alone in his condition, but is one of the many victims who suffer unjustly. His prayers, his cries of anguish, are thus transformed from his own situation to encompass all those around him. In the end, his true reward is not the prosperity of his own life with all his earthly possessions, but his understanding of a God who identifies with those who suffer. "It is important that we be clear from the outset that the theme of the Book of Job is not precisely suffering—that impenetrable human mystery—but rather how to speak of God in the midst of suffering. The question that concerns the author is the possibility of disinterested religion, of believing "for nothing"; in his view only a faith and behavior of this kind can be offered to a God who loves freely and gratuitously. But is it possible?"[109]

The possibility of a disinterested religion or rather, the impossibility of worship without reward, is what causes the devil to approach God and propose a wager involving Job, a wager that "has to do with speaking of God in the light of the unjust suffering that seems, in human experience, to deny love on God's part."[110] As one who strives to live as an upright and just man, Job does not sin against God either in his prosperity or in his tragedy. Though he curses the day he was born and insistently complains to God, he does not transgress by sinning against God. In the end, Job is found faithful in all his ways before God, thus allowing the possibility for a disinterested religion, where belief and worship of God is purely because of who God is and not because of any benefit from it. This idea is especially evident in the dialogue between Job and his three friends, Eliphaz of Teman, Bildad of Shuah and Zophar of Naamath, who, in line with their theological notion of temporal retribution, insist that Job must have sinned, thus meriting punishment from God. "The friends of Job follow the prevailing theology of the age: a doctrine of temporal retribution, which says that the upright are rewarded with prosperity and health, while sinners are punished with poverty and sickness."[111] Although there is some semblance of value in the doctrine

---

109. Gutiérrez, *On Job*, 13.

110. Ibid., 5.

111. Gutiérrez, *God of Life*, 146–47.

of retribution in terms of ethical requirements, temporal retribution becomes distorted within the framework of rewards and punishments.[112]

The lesson of Job is twofold. From God's perspective, the lesson to be learned is the concept of gratuity from which God's economy flows. Our theological reflections and concepts of God should not hinder God from being God. In other words, the Book of Job is defending God's freedom and debunking the limitations we place on the divine because of our misconceptions.[113] From the perspective of human beings, the lesson to be learned is the suffering of the unjust.[114] Simple rationales, such as temporal retribution, cannot be used to explain one's status in life. Rather, the Book of Job states succinctly that people suffer for no good reason at all and that their plight should not be seen as resulting from a misdeed or sin on their part. Consolation for those suffering is found in solidarity, in particular, the solidarity that God reveals to his creation through Job and ultimately through the suffering servant, Jesus. Job, through his innocent suffering, is the prefiguration of Jesus and thus the example *par excellence* of what it means to be in the position of those who suffer and to see the God who suffers with the people.[115] Suffering is not justified by Christ's identification as the suffering servant. On the contrary, Christ's identification reveals that unjust situations are opposed to the God of life and must be dealt with by gaining a new perspective—through the eyes of the suffering poor—by entering into solidarity with those living under such conditions.

Accordingly, Gutiérrez's analysis of the Book of Job is easily relatable to his understanding of the preferential option for the poor. In his reading of Job, Gutiérrez finds the three elements of poverty located in the figure of Job and thus, ultimately, in the figure of Christ since the former is a prefiguration of the latter. In Job, one sees the real or material poverty of those who are stripped of every resource for a dignified life by losing their wealth, social status, and even their families. In Job, one sees the spiritual poverty of those who have nowhere else to turn and freely open themselves to receiving the grace of God, thus, understanding the preference God has for those who are suffering. And finally, one sees poverty as commitment through the actions of solidarity. Job

112. Gutiérrez, "But Why Lord," 22.

113. Gutiérrez, *On Job*, 31.

114. Ibid.

115. Ibid., 97.

transforms his prayers to God from being prayers on his own behalf to being prayers on behalf of all those in a similar plight.

The Real or Material Poor in the Book of Job

At first glance, the sufferings of Job and the poor of today seem unrelated. Job's sufferings occurred through personal tragedies, while those of today's poor result from political, economic, and social conditions. The former is a private matter while the latter is a societal or public matter. The suffering that Job endures appears to be outside the scope of his control, while the poor in Latin America appear to have some, but very limited avenues of betterment in the poverty they face. At first glance then, the two worlds, that of the Old Testament and that of Latin America, appear to have only vague connections to each other and to describe subjects that are addressed in opposing manners. However, a closer examination by Gutiérrez reveals two worlds that are not totally unrelated to one another, but rather, two worlds which allow us to penetrate and understand both the reality of scripture and the reality of Latin America.

In essence, Gutiérrez reads scripture through his personal experience of his homeland and permits scripture "to read" the events of the poor in his midst. Thus, the preferential option of the poor becomes a reciprocal hermeneutical lens for reading the Book of Job and vice versa: "I believe that we approach scripture in the context of our present situation; it is with the questions in mind that come to us from this situation that we read the scriptures. But the word of the Lord is not a repertory of answers to our questions; it addresses us and often changes our questions or raises others. That is what I wanted to say when I claimed that "it reads us." The phrase is a symbolic way of saying that between us and the scriptures there is not a one-way street but a circular relationship."[116] Thus, an interesting interplay between the current world of the poor and the world of scripture comes to light. For Gutiérrez, scripture expounds the situation of injustice that the poor live in, a world contrary to the will of God, while the situation in Latin America itself clarifies our understanding of God and of the relationships to which we are called, as in the case of Job. In the end, his re-reading of the Book of Job, as well as the way the Book of Job reads Gutiérrez, comes to the conclusion that a

---

116. Gutiérrez, *Confrontations*, 47.

disinterested religion is possible only in solidarity, when the sufferings of those who suffer unjustly do not go unheeded by both the Creator and God's creatures.

Through the use of this hermeneutical circle, a reciprocal relationship between the sufferings of the past and the poverty of the present day, Gutiérrez discovers that the position Job finds himself in has an intimate link to the suffering of those today in Latin America. As an Old Testament figure, Job is an archetype, making him *"the spokesman not of his personal experience alone but of the experience of all humankind."*[117] "The innocence of Job makes it historically possible that there may be other innocent human beings. The injustice of his suffering points to the possibility that other human beings may also suffer unjustly, and his disinterested outlook points to the possibility that others too may practice a disinterested religion."[118] Because of this historical connection, we are able to say that the real or material poor and Job have several attributes in common. First of all, the locations in which Job is situated and in which the Latin American poor live have significant commonalities in our hermeneutical reading. The "garbage heap" of the city found in the Book of Job becomes the location in which to look for a suitable language for our dealings with God. "Situated as we are on the underside of history here in Latin America, it is the second wager that is ours: to speak of God from the standpoint of the poor in the earth."[119] In addition, the reality of unjust suffering in the world of the Old Testament reaffirms that Job did not sin and did not deserve such a situation in life. In much the same way, the poor who are in the forefront of Gutiérrez's thought also do not deserve their lot in life. Both Job and the poor in Latin America exist in a state of suffering, poverty, and undignified living not because they deserve such conditions, as is maintained in the doctrine of temporal retribution; rather, both Job of the past and the poor of today suffer such poverty and injustice for no good reason. Instead of being able to explain their lot in life as a result of their sinfulness, carelessness, or laziness, Gutiérrez is adamant that in both situations the ones suffering are doing so unjustly. In short, the world of Job and the world of today's poor are neither easily comprehensible nor explainable.

---

117. Gutiérrez, *On Job*, 1 (italics in original).

118. Ibid., 3.

119. Ibid., 16.

Another commonality between Job and the poor is their ostracism by every strata of society. Being shunned also includes a feeling of abandonment by God: "Job's suffering causes him to see the universe as chaotic, as lacking the presence of God . . . Job's response is so radical as to be baffling; it can have sprung only from a very deep and unbearable misery.[120] In Job's case, his wealthy friends, including those who theologize about God, along with his wife, chastise him for his current state in life. Even with their original intent of consoling Job, their words never console the suffering man. Rather, their words further aggravate and add to the misery Job must endure. Job's condition is not rational and depicts how an innocent man can be caught in an unexplainable reality. Therefore, Job is seen as an outcast, who, until he repents of his ways, remains on the outskirts of society. The irony is that there are no solutions in this particular scenario since there is nothing for which to repent. In effect, there is truly no way for Job to re-enter the world of his past since there is no truth in the path laid out by his friends. Part of Job's realization is that he initially thought he traveled this path alone. However, in the end he realizes that he is never really alone for God is always with him and that there are many who suffer unjustly like himself.[121]

The poor in Latin America continually relive Job's scenario. They are labeled as subversive, thereby undermining their own future, along with the stability of society. They are labeled as outsiders, unwanted and disruptive, while at the same time not having any way of engaging society because its oppressive structures keep the poor at bay. Like Job, they cannot follow the ideology of those who sit on top and preach to the bottom. The loneliness felt by the poor is a result of false hopes and promises of the dominating rich in society. The work of theologians such as Gutiérrez sheds positive light on their situation. Hope is restored by an awareness of God's preference and their loneliness is shattered through the solidarity of others like themselves as well as of those who wish to engage their impoverished world.

Spiritual Poverty in the Book of Job

Gustavo Gutiérrez's commentary on the Book of Job reflects his own spirituality of liberation, comprising both the language of prophecy and

120. Ibid., 8–9.
121. Ibid., 31.

the language of contemplation. In addition, by utilizing the fluid relationship whereby scripture reads us while we read scripture, Gutiérrez naturally connects the Old Testament understanding with the Church's social teaching through his understanding of the preferential option for the poor. "[E]mphasis on the practice of justice and on solidarity with the poor must never become an obsession and prevent our seeing that this commitment reveals its value and ultimate meaning only within the vast and mysterious horizon of God's gratuitous love."[122] Those who believe in God must therefore try to lighten the burden of the poor by helping them and practicing solidarity with them. The speeches of God occasion the second shift: Job now understands that the world of justice must be located within the broad but demanding horizon of freedom that is formed by the gratuitousness of God's love.[123] For believers like Job, rejection and acknowledgement are needed. In relation to God, we reject misconceptions such as temporal retribution and acknowledge a God who is not bound by our conditions. In relation to the poor in our midst, we reject misconceptions about their poverty and acknowledge that their suffering becomes a common bond for humanity in relation to one another and to God. "Our task today is like Job's: to find the words with which to talk about God in the midst of the starvation of millions, the humiliation of races regarded as inferior, discrimination against women (especially women who are poor), systematic social injustice, terrorism of every kind . . . What we must deal with now is not past tragedies but, unfortunately, a cruel present and a dark tunnel with no apparent end.[124]

Just as the Church's social teaching on the preferential option for the poor reflects God's gratuitous favor for the poor based on the simple fact of their lowly economic status, the Book of Job similarly reflects God's gratuity by maintaining the freedom of God's actions on behalf of those who suffer unjustly. In opposition to the theology of his three friends, Job realizes through conversations with them, that their theologizing, as good or as poor as it may be, does not reflect his reality. Instead of being consoled by the words of Eliphaz, Bildad, and Zophar, Job realizes that these theologians are working from the perspective of temporal

---

122. Gutiérrez,"But Why Lord," 22–23.

123. Gutiérrez, *On Job,* 16.

124. Gutiérrez, "But Why Lord," 23.

retribution, a perspective which does not resonate with Job because he is convinced of his innocence.

Rather than giving in to his wife, his friends, and the people around him who pity his current state in life, Job remains steadfast, claiming not only to being innocent but also to being sinless. In order to remain steadfast, he is impatient, stubborn, and rebellious: "His rebellion is against the suffering of the innocent, against a theology that justifies it, and even against the depiction of God that such a theology conveys."[125] His stubbornness and his belief in his own uprightness allow him to continue on a path controversial to his peers but revealing for himself. His stubbornness in not explaining away his situation permits God to win the wager with Satan that human beings are able to worship God simply for who God is and to make sense of their suffering in solidarity. "In this sense, Job the rebel is a witness to peace and to the hunger and thirst for justice . . . he is more than simply patient, he is a peace-loving man, a peacemaker."[126] Instead of suffering leading Job and others like him away from God by cursing God, the Old Testament account shows the wonderful capacity for human beings to embrace suffering, to love God ever more faithfully, and to turn to those around them because they share a common plight. "Job or, more correctly, God has won the wager: Job's religion is disinterested, he practices it 'gratis.'"[127] "*In the end, God wins the wager. The rebellious but upright Job, in all his suffering and complaints, in his dogged commitment to the poor and his acknowledgment of the Lord's love, shows that his religion is indeed disinterested. But what path did he travel in finding the right way to speak of God?*"[128]

"This deeper response on Job's part, this deeper understanding of his faith, will require a passage through the dramatic crisis,"[129] a path taken by Job involving brutally honest dialogues with himself, with his friends, and before God with the conversations progressing in that order. Once convinced of his own innocence, and then verified in his encounter with his friends, Job must now address God about his devastating situation. In order to address God properly, Job realizes he is in need of an arbiter because of his place before the Creator. In essence, this

125. Gutiérrez, *On Job*, 14.

126. Ibid.

127. Ibid., 6.

128. Ibid., 1 (italics in original).

129. Ibid., 6.

encounter regarding his situation in life resembles a lawsuit against God; therefore, Job is seeking a mediator so he may speak freely and without fear. However, Job comes to an ironic conclusion at this point. He realizes that in his need for an arbiter, the only one who can fulfill this role is God. This shift marks an important milestone in Job's understanding of God. Seeing God as the addressee of his complaint gives way to viewing God as his arbiter. In this movement, Job gains further insight that the God who hears his complaint and who mediates on his behalf is also the God who will be his witness in defending his cause and who eventually will be the one who also liberates him from his condition.

> We have witnessed a gradual increase in Job's faith and hope. From a nebulous request for the presence of an *arbiter* he has advanced to the need of a *witness* and thence finally to an expression of confidence in a *liberator* who will come to rescue him. Each affirmation of hope is immediately preceded by a renewed expression of angry complaint and protest. The spiritual struggle with himself, with his friends, and, above all, with God brings him to a conviction that for the time being amounts to no more than a cry of hope: that he will see, and with his own eyes, his liberator, his *goēl*, and be able to look upon him as a friend."[130]

Instead of a God who reacts positively or negatively to something we do, Job comes to know a different God through his suffering, a God who as *goēl* is the defender and vindicator, the liberator and avenger of the poor and oppressed.[131] Thus, God is the *goēl* of the poor, and as *goēl*, God becomes intimately connected with the people as reflected in the intimacy found in the covenant of the Old Testament. "The word *goēl* came out of the Jewish people's experience of solidarity and had the family for its initial setting; subsequently it found a place in the sphere of the covenant and became a term that emphasized a particular aspect of God's justice."[132] It is within this familial situation that the notion of the preferential option for the poor is made concrete. Just as the economic

130. Ibid, 66.

131. Gutiérrez highlights the use of the Hebrew terms in this section since there is an important and intimate connection between the title of God and the action of God in the world. The Hebrew verb, *ga'al*, means to liberate, ransom, redeem, while the Hebrew noun, *goēl*, represents the rescuer as an "avenger of blood." What God does in the world, on behalf of God's people, speaks of how God is known and who God is for Israel.

132. Gutiérrez, *On Job*, 64.

poor of today receive preference, the God of the Old Testament likewise shows preference because of God's familial relationships to Israel. Within this familial relationship, further solidarity is witnessed with those who are the most vulnerable for the *goēl* is not just a defender of the family but more importantly an avenger of the exploited. "The application of the name to Yahweh implies that as a result of the covenant God has become part of the family of the people. God is thus the nearest relative, the one who takes responsibility for the people, the one who rescues them and avenges them if necessary."[133]

Poverty as Commitment in the Book of Job

God's willingness to defend, vindicate, liberate, and avenge the poor and oppressed reveals the Father's heart towards children in need and also our response to those addressed by God. This new found revelation of God in Job brings about conflict between the portrayal of God as a judge in prevailing theology and the God of mercy, whom Job now encounters, who stands on the side of those perceived already to be "judged" in society. Through this dialectical tension, Job is able to comprehend, more faithfully and fruitfully, his suffering in relation to a God who is merciful. "Job acknowledges that God passes judgment on human behavior, but he also detects that God's mercy is greater than God's justice or, more accurately, that God's justice is to be understood only in the context of prior and gratuitous love."[134]

Divine justice is described in God's two speeches to Job. In the first, the plan of God's creative powers is manifested. In the second, God's just governance is stressed. Through these two speeches, God is able to relate to Job that true justice and uprightness are rooted in those who struggle through life's tragedies. Job daily attempts to live a life of innocence in terms of the moral law; however, until he lives the life of suffering that puts him in touch with the context of where justice and righteousness need to be lived out, he is unable to make concrete connections. "Uprightness and judgment cannot be promoted in the abstract but only in relation to the inhuman situation in which orphans, widows, and strangers live ('the orphans, widows, and strangers' is a classical biblical

133. Ibid.
134. Ibid., 66.

synonym for 'the poor')."[135] This connection, the entering into the world of those who suffer unjustly, transforms Job's reality.

Although Job continues to appeal to God, the cries of anguish are no longer for himself, but for all who suffer. Job also realizes that just as he remains innocent in his torment, so too, do the masses who undergo a similar ordeal. In contrast to the view of temporal retribution, Job's view now finds people in distress not guilty of transgressions against God or others. Rather, his own experience replaces the common view in society and prophetically points out the innocence of others. In addition, Job's own experience of personal distress further reminds him of the prophets' call to care for the most vulnerable in society. Precisely because God is not negatively judging those in grief, but positively standing on their side as *gōēl*, Job is reminded that he must now work to better the situations of all those in pain and poverty. God as *gōēl* reveals a further relationship of intimacy, one of friendship. Being a friend of the poor in Job's world or in Latin America concretizes our friendship with God.

> The obligation to care for the poor means that the poor are not persons being punished by God (as the doctrine of temporal retribution implicitly asserts), but rather God's friends. To give to the needy is therefore to give to God . . . The image of a "father" that the Bible uses in this connection brings out the close and affectionate relationship that should characterize this commitment to the poor. But the image also implies determination: defense of the poor requires their liberation . . . and resistance to those who oppress and exploit them . . . Job's life bears witness to his solidarity with the poor and the helpless[.]"[136]

What Job realizes in this new-found relationship with God and other sufferers is that the life of uprightness and justice is not a state of being but an endeavor, the creation of a reality. Only in the concrete efforts to build up a righteous and just society will one live a life pleasing to God. Job's realization is in fact simply a reminder of what has always been part of the covenant between God and Israel. Job is reminded of "the great requirements of the covenant: real belief in God entails solidarity with the poor so as to ease their suffering by establishing 'uprightness and judgment.' This is a major theme in the prophetic tradition

135. Ibid., 40.
136. Ibid.

of Israel."[137] "The point is that commitment to the poor provides firm ground for prophetic talk of God . . . Their language has its historical roots in commitment to the poor, who are the favorites of God . . . God is the ultimate and comprehensive ground of human behavior. This is the central idea in the ethic of the reign of God, the proclamation of which becomes more and more definite as the Bible advances, reaching its full form in Jesus the Messiah."[138]

Summary: The Preferential Option for the Poor in the Book of Job

The wager between God and Satan is played out in concrete human events and in the most vulnerable state of humanity. This choice of venue indicates our need to find God in a human reality where most of the world find themselves, including the subject of the wager, Job—a humanity in an exposed and defenseless condition. "Human suffering is the harsh, demanding ground on which the wager about talk of God is made; it is also that which ensures that the wager has universal applicability."[139] Precisely because the poor find favor with God in their weak condition, simply by their plight in life, and not based on their moral conduct, we can answer the questions posed by the Book of Job: "How are human beings to speak of God in the midst of poverty and suffering?" and "How are human beings to find a language applicable to God in the midst of innocent suffering?"[140]

Through the re-reading of the Book of Job with the hermeneutical lens of the preferential option for the poor, Gutiérrez is able to provide readers with a positive response to these questions. The people of God are called to establish justice and righteousness which look to alleviate all areas of oppression and exploitation. Only in this setting does Job make sense of his suffering and the suffering of others. Today, in Latin America, only a similar outlook on life makes sense to the majority living in poverty and pain. Knowing that the poor are God's friends require our friendship allows us to speak about God in the midst of their anguish. Understanding that they are favored and not punished because of their situation allows us to speak about a religion not based on judgment, but

137. Ibid., 48.
138. Ibid.
139. Ibid., 15.
140. Ibid., 12.

mercy. Equating Job's experience with the lives of those experiencing the same plight in Latin America allows us to be faithful to God and to one another. In the end, only this knowledge will allow us to stand with Job and live out the life of justice and righteousness to which God calls us through his covenant. "Talk about God presupposes and, at the same time, leads to a living encounter with God in specific historical circumstances. It requires, therefore, that we discover the features of Christ in the sometimes disfigured faces of the poor of this world. This discovery will not be made apart from concrete gestures of solidarity with our brothers and sisters who are wretched, abandoned, and deprived."[141]

Gutiérrez presents the preferential (spiritual poverty) option (poverty as commitment) for the poor (material or real poverty) as the reality of Latin America and the Church today. The same reality is also found in Job: preferential (God as *gōēl*, the defender, vindicator, liberator, and avenger of the poor), option (commitment to a world of justice and uprightness by alleviating oppression and exploitation) for the poor (those similar to Job who suffer unjustly). Perhaps the original intention of Job's friends and not their theologizing best describes our preferential option for the poor: "The three friends were so moved by Job's plight that before they spoke they wept; then "they sat there on the ground beside him for seven days and seven nights. To Job they never spoke a word, for they saw how much he was suffering" (2:13). Their attitude was one of respectful compassion that showed how seriously they regarded their friend's situation. The silent sharing of suffering is a manifestation of fellowship."[142]

PREFERENTIAL OPTION FOR THE POOR: BARTOLOMÉ DE LAS CASAS

A Peruvian priest once said that in order to understand the theological method of a theologian, his or her spirituality must first be comprehended. Spirituality—the manner of following Jesus—is often derived from imitating the path laid by a disciple of Christ who has gone before us in the ways of faith.[143] This statement is corroborated by the spiritual-

141. Ibid., 17.

142. Ibid., 7.

143. As mentioned earlier, in order to understand St. Thomas, an understanding

ity of Gustavo Gutiérrez. In order to understand the theological method of Gutiérrez, one must turn to Bartolomé de Las Casas (1474–1566), whose spirituality Gutiérrez has studied and imitated throughout his priestly ministry.[144] For Gutiérrez, questions and not simple answers are the key to understanding our humanity, one which can only be reflected on in relation to God and to one another. "The question we must ask when it comes to Las Casas is this one: How, in his time, under particular conditions and with specific opportunities, was he able to proclaim the Gospel of Jesus?"[145]

There are several reasons why Gutiérrez follows Christ in the manner of Las Casas. Although predating him by approximately 500 years, Las Casas was one of the first defenders of the Indians after the Spanish discovered what is today known as Latin America and the Caribbean. The events that occurred during the lifetime of Bartolomé de Las Casas resonate with those of Gutiérrez's own time. Although the historical persons have changed over the centuries, many characteristics have not. One thing that remains as consistent today as it was five hundred years ago is the oppression and exploitation of the indigenous population of Latin America. The poor are a consistent subject both of the missionary efforts of Las Casas and in the liberative efforts of Gutiérrez. Neither Las Casas nor Gutiérrez sees himself as full-time theologian but simply as a pastor whose writings reflect the plight of the poor in their midst. Theological writings are secondary, simply milestones and manifestations of a concrete solidarity with others.[146] There is little wonder why Gutiérrez finds such solace and consolation in the figure of Las Casas. Gutiérrez is never alone and continues to find allies with his peers and

---

of the spirituality of St. Dominic is necessary; likewise, in order to understand St. Bonaventure, an understanding of the spirituality of St. Francis is necessary.

144. Gutiérrez's monumental work, *En busca de los pobres de Jesucristo: El pensamiento de Bartolomé de Las Casas*, translated by Barr as *Las Casas: In Search of the Poor of Jesus Christ* took him over twenty years to complete. This lengthy period reflects a reciprocal hermeneutical perspective in Gutiérrez's reading the works of Las Casas: on the one hand, Las Casas sheds light on the situation of the poor in Latin America today through his understanding of history, politics, and the Church in this region; through his dialogue with rulers, Church officials and theologians in Europe, Las Casas magnified the complexities of his day, thus revealing the complexities of the world of the poor. On the other hand, Gutiérrez's experience of poverty in Latin America has helped him understand the situation and theology during the time of Las Casas.

145. Gutiérrez, *Las Casas*, 8–9.

146. Ibid., 7.

in the figures of the Church over the centuries, especially in the figure of Bartolomé de Las Casas. In fact, fascination with Las Casas has led Gutiérrez to dedicate much of his priesthood to expounding the life's work of this Dominican missionary as a source of inspiration and motivation for his own life's work with the poor of today.

Las Casas, who later came to be known as the apostle of the Indians primarily for his relentless efforts to protect the native people, crossed the Atlantic thirteen times during his missionary period to advocate on behalf of the oppressed and exploited in the Americas. Beginning in 1502, and continuing on his trans-Atlantic journeys after his ordination in Rome in 1507, the experience of encountering two worlds across a wide ocean reflected the spiritual journey of Las Casas. By 1514, Las Casas understood what it meant to have a vocation not only to the priesthood and religious life as a Dominican, but more importantly, a vocation as a defender of the Indians. Rather than disguising the mistreatment of Indians in Latin America as the will of God, Las Casas sided with the natives by advocating for a peaceful proclamation of the Gospel.[147] Ultimately, he realized that the evil brought upon the natives at the hands of the Spaniards could never be justified by the message of Christianity. Consequently, Las Casas campaigned for the withdrawal of the Spanish from the New World. It would be better, in the view of Las Casas, to leave the natives alone but alive in their ignorance of Christianity, than to make them believers who would eventually lose their lives. Referring to the native Indians as painted corpses, Gutiérrez explains Las Casas' view, one that still echoes in those who work on behalf of the poor in Latin America today: "Here we have a premise for argumentation [on] behalf of the Indian that we often find with Bartolomé de Las Casas, and one frequently invoked by all of those who take their position from the perspective of the oppressed: the *fact* (*hecho*) of the untimely, unjust death of the poor contradicts the *right* (*derecho*) that they have to life."[148]

---

147. Initially, Bartolomé de Las Casas supported the *encomienda* or landgrant system where the Spanish Crown entrusted the care of natives in the hands of Spanish settlers. He also supported the introduction of black slaves to replace the Indian slaves. However, Las Casas experienced a conversion through witnessing the slaughtering of the Indians along with the defiance of other Dominicans defending the native people against the Spaniards. Eventually, Las Casas relinquished his *encomienda*, repented the introduction of black slaves and abandoned everything else in his life that was contradictory to the defense of the Indians.

148. Gutiérrez, *Las Casas*, 38.

Material or Real Poverty according to Bartolomé de Las Casas

The reality of poverty leading to an early death is a central theme in the works of both Bartolomé de Las Casas and Gustavo Gutiérrez. Most people were poor in Las Casas' time as they still are today. Not much has changed over five hundred years in the situation of the majority in Latin America. For Las Casas, the poor were the native Indians who carried their poverty on their backs because of the ruthless greed of the Spanish conquerors. Today, the poor are the masses that bear the burden of maintaining a capitalistic system that caters to a few at the expense of the many. Not only are the resources for living a life of dignity stripped away by the constant displacement of their homeland, culture, and people, but now the poor must serve the greed of the wealthy by literally dying for the causes of others. "The death of the Indian was therefore a necessary consequence of the alienated labour system on which the new order was built, a social system designed to satisfy the interests and greed of the conquerors. The murder of the poor is not really an individual impelled by evil instincts, but an oppressive social system based on the interest and gain of the conqueror, and on the accumulation of wealth in the hands of a few."[149]

It was not only the care of the souls of the Indians, but more importantly, the transgressions of the Spanish that Las Casas had to address. The idolaters were not the "pagan Indians" who, at times, sacrificed human beings to their god. No, the real idolaters were those from Europe who came under the banner of Christianity but whose only concern was the promises of material riches found first in gold, then later in the controversial slave trade. In either situation, the exploitation of the indigenous population became the main resource for the conquerors in fueling their greed. "Las Casas was particularly scandalized by the fact that this real idolatry is disguised as though it were a service of the true God . . . . In this Dominican friar's judgment, the worst idolatry is that of Christians and not that of the Indians."[150]

Given the Spanish conquerors' concern for gold and not God, the missionary activities of the Church were used to support the actions that increased wealth for the Europeans since the Church benefitted from these transactions as well. However, the Dominicans, as well as others

---

149. Gutiérrez, "Violence of a System," 96.
150. Gutiérrez, *God of Life*, 61.

with true concerns for the native Indians, at times denounced Church practices as well as the prevailing European theology. For missioners like Las Casas, the defense of life became the primary concern and any activity opposed to life was considered opposed to the God of life.[151] In contrast to those European theologians whose preoccupation was conversion and baptism, true missioners did not care whether the indigenous were Christian or not; their concern centered on life and death issues. Becoming a Christian was a secondary concern especially when such cruelty accompanied the activities of those claiming to be Christians.

The common characteristics of the poor of Las Casas' time and the poor of Latin America today are the effects of poverty on human life, in particular, the limited lifespan of the poor. Due to inhumane situations which cater to the economically wealthy, the Indians of yesteryear and the poor of today share a cruel reality, an early and unjust death. Death comes early because of oppression and exploitation by one individual of another. In the view of both Las Casas and Gutiérrez, this cruel reality is a humanly created scenario and not a predestined condition. Regardless of the century, poverty takes its toil physically on the human body, and, in a particular way, poverty harshly affects the world of the poor. "A hope for and welcome of the Reign of life must necessarily call in question, and radically, a political reality of oppression and injustice. Las Casas said that the Indians were being "stripped of their lives before their time" and thus despoiled of "space for their conversion" . . . Unfortunately, something of the same must be said of the poor of today in Latin America, who continue to suffer a premature, unjust death."[152]

Spiritual Poverty in Bartolomé de Las Casas

"Las Casas reminds his compatriots that their condition as Christians is not a lifelong guarantee of their salvation—which they will reach only if they practice justice toward the Indians and among the Spaniards themselves."[153] The interlinked themes of mysticism and prophecy are found in Gutiérrez's reading of Las Casas where the announcement of the Good News must coincide with the denouncement of unjust situations. The missionary activities of Las Casas presented a message of life

---

151. Gutiérrez, *Las Casas*, 18.

152. Ibid., 4.

153. Ibid., 13–14.

and a true concern for the indigenous people while at the same time publicizing Spanish atrocities against the Indians. "A continuous inter-action takes place, in Las Casas's work, between reflection and concrete commitment—theory and practice. His is a thinking that not only *refers* to practice, but is developed by someone *engaged* in practice . . . this engagement actually enhances the theoretical quality of his work."[154]

For Las Casas, real concern for the livelihood of the Indians here on earth as well as care for their eternal souls gradually developed through the events in the Indies: "Salvation was Bartolomé de Las Casas's passion and the motive of his missionary work. But in his eyes salvation was so closely associated with social justice that he inverted the usual hierarchy of missionary principles in two respects."[155] Instead of seeing missionar-ies as evangelizers entering a foreign land to announce a way of life for the betterment of the people in all aspects of their lives, the reality of the Indies simply showed the opposite. The proclamation of the Gospel message was mutilated by greed and destruction, thereby, bringing a message which was not good news for the natives, a message of horrific implications. This proclamation was not necessarily contained in the words, but in the action of the Spaniards, especially in their treatment of the Indians as people less then themselves. The way that so-called evangelizers treated the indigenous people was so alarming to Las Casas that he eventually shifted his concern for the salvation of souls from the Indians to the Spaniards. Fearing the impossibility of salvation without the practice of justice, "Las Casas pointed out, the Spaniard's gratuitous or exploitative cruelty toward the Indians was endangering their own salvation."[156] This was the first inversion pointed out by Las Casas: the Spaniards were in need of conversion because of their actions against the poor in Latin America.

The second inversion of evangelization mentioned by Las Casas was the realization that the so-called infidels or pagans were not far re-moved from the world of scripture. In their poverty and oppression, the native people echoed the Gospel cry of the poor. They encountered the Gospels through the experiences of their own lives and not necessarily through the presence of Christians from another land. In a reversal of Las Casas' world, the so-called missioners were seen as idolaters and the

154. Ibid., 4.

155. Gutiérrez, "Two Theological Perspectives," 242.

156. Ibid.

so-called infidels were identified with the Gospel poor. No longer did the presence and activities of the Spaniards make sense in this inverted reality. Instead of bringing about a utopia based on Christian principles by creating a foundation for the Kingdom in the Indies, the Europeans mutilated the message of God's love with one of purely human self-love.

In the faces of the poor, Las Casas saw the weak and vulnerable ones of the Gospel. "The poor come with 'their poverty on their back,' as Bartolomé de las Casas put it, with their suffering, their culture, their odor, their race, their language, and the exploitation they are experiencing."[157] Because of the close connection of the Indians to the poor in scripture, Las Casas was able not only to see the indigenous population receiving God's attention, but just as significantly, to see Christ in their suffering— Christ being scourged and sentenced to death, time and time again. For Las Casas, the natives were not simply ignorant pagans but an intimate revelation of Jesus through their cruel treatment at the hands of those in power. In the poor Indians, Christ was being crucified repeatedly by the Spanish as they decimated the native population and the resources of the land—all in the name of a false god.

The "scourged Christ" became a frequent theme in the presentations of Las Casas, since the faces of the dying revealed the face of Christ. This Christology "from below" focuses on the human activities of the Son of God. "To exhume the truth of the Indies will be Bartolomé's life purpose. The hidden truth, hidden deeper than the mines worked by the Indians, is this: in these abused and despised beings, Christ is present. To oppress and bury the dwellers of the Indies is to oppress and bury Christ himself, who is "truth and life" and also "the way" to take (John 14:6) in order that that truth might resound and breathe: the preferential option for the poor."[158] A direct correlation between the native Indians and Christ was proposed by Las Casas. Differing from many European theologians of the time, Las Casas refused to consider the indigenous people as either Christians or non-Christians. What concerned Las Casas was not the question of whether or not salvation is possible outside of the Church, but rather, how to address a people whose humble lives resonate so clearly with the experiences of those in scripture?[159] More importantly, how should we address a

---

157. Gutiérrez, "Irruption of the Poor in Latin," 108.

158. Gutiérrez, *Las Casas*, 66.

159. Ibid., 64–66.

scourged Christ who stands before us in the faces of those who are being oppressed and destroyed? For Las Casas, these two questions form a unity; for without addressing both, the discovery of the poor and the encounter with Christ would be lost.

The indigenous population of the continent held the hermeneutic key for understanding the faith because in the native population both the mystical and prophetic dimension came together. On the one hand, the mystical dimension—the contemplation and worship of the true God—cannot be realized without the acknowledgment of the scourged Christ in our midst. On the other hand, the prophetic dimension—praxis and commitment—cannot be realized if it is separated from the creation of justice in the dismantled lives of the native poor. "A clearer view of the situation in the Indies leads not to flight or retreat, but to a commitment to alter that situation."[160] Thus Gutiérrez could say: "One reaches this pinnacle of spirituality only if one perceives in the Indian, as did Bartolomé de Las Casas, the poor of the Gospel."[161] It is this perception that allows us to recognize that the poor are favored by God for two reasons: first, they are the poor ones found in scripture and, second, in the poor, Jesus, the Son of God, is revealed. For those who were able to see the truth of what was happening in the New World, God's preference hinged on these two points during the sixteenth century. What makes Las Casas unique from others who worked for justice on behalf of the native poor during this period is the simple fact that he was able to see God's economy, the preferential option for the poor, operating both in scripture and in the poor Indians.

Bartolomé de Las Casas: Poverty as Commitment

Bartolomé de Las Casas provided the world and the Church with another understanding of the Gospel message and the treatment of human beings by insisting on respect for their cultures and customs. "Las Casas believed that if we want to understand what is happening we have to adopt the point of view of the inhabitants of the Indies."[162] The discovery of otherness, as Bartolomé de Las Casas would call it, consisted of both the recognition and correction of the situation at hand. Just as

160. Ibid., 51.
161. Ibid., 65.
162. Gutiérrez, "From Exclusion to Discipleship," 83.

the mystical is incomplete without the prophetic and vice versa, the acknowledgment of the injustices created by the Spaniards against the Indians is also incomplete without proper restitution. Restitution was not a new concept even in the sixteenth century.[163] It is a longstanding principle within moral and sacramental theology and when applied to the specific situation of the exploitation and oppression of the Indies, restitution requires the correction of both the material and spiritual concerns of those who are violated.[164] "According to Las Casas, everything which happened in the Indies was robbery and nothing was justified. As a consequence the Europeans must restore everything that they had taken from the [Indians]."[165] This is one of the reasons why Las Casas eventually decided that it would be better for the Europeans to leave with their Christianity and allow the Indians to live, than for the Europeans to stay and perpetuate death and destruction in the Americas in the name of God. The evils being perpetrated by the Spaniards were such that they would have to leave for restitution to occur.

Restitution—authentic rectification—indicates a rejection of all activities contrary to the will of those violated and not the calculations of what would be best for the victims. Las Casas was faced with replying to the justification of the Spanish presence as being God's will even though the obvious motivating factor was gold. An example of this is found in the *Yucay Opinion*[166] which ideologically disguised the activities of the Spaniards "under the postulate that without gold there would be no Gospel in the Indies."[167] In this case, restitution meant uncovering all false arguments supporting exploitation and removing the perpetrators of such atrocities. Short of this act, restitution could not be realized. Those in favor of this longstanding principle needed to side with the native poor in solidarity. Commitment during Las Casas's time meant saving lives here on earth, in the present, and not just saving souls for the life to come. In fact, the commitment Las Casas envisioned consisted

163. Gutiérrez, "Bartolomé de Las Casas: Defender of the Indians," 268.

164. Ibid.

165. Ibid.

166. The *Yucay Opinion* was a letter written by García de Toledo, a fellow Dominican, who argued against Las Casas and claimed that the mountains were filled with earthly treasures by God to attract Christians to bring natives to Christ. See Dahlen, "Bartolomé de las Casas: Ethics and the Eschaton,", 289–90.

167. Gutiérrez, *Las Casas*, 58.

of three levels of solidarity: with the people, with their culture, and with the resources surrounding them. Solidarity in these three areas was necessary since abuses in these areas were rampant. ""Destruction" here means principally the premature, unjust death of the Indians and the depopulation of entire localities—in a word, the brutal ruin of a people. But it also implies the annihilation of autochthonous cultures and the laying waste of the world of nature. The defense of life, on these three levels—which, as it happens, are interdependent—constitutes one of the great motivations of Bartolomé's struggle."[168]

Summary: The Preferential Option for the Poor in Bartolomé de Las Casas

Gustavo Gutiérrez is insistent that Bartolomé de Las Casas not be made into a figure that he was not by casting modern labels upon the Dominican friar. In other words, Gutiérrez considers it an error to speak of Las Casas as a figure who was ahead of his time because of his theology reflecting the sanctity of human life for the Indians or as a liberation theologian of the sixteenth century. Neither description fits the missioner who chose to act on behalf of the poor simply based on a preferential option for the poor during his time.   "Let us dispel one misconception from the outset. It is frequently said that Bartolomé de Las Casas was "ahead of his time" and that he employs a kind of modern language, one more familiar to us today, when he speaks of the rights of the Indian nations to be different, when he defends what we call civil liberties, or when he manifests his sensitivity to the concrete, historical dimensions of faith."[169] Rather than seeing Las Casas as a figure we can relate to simply because of similar conditions, the real and important lesson we glean from Las Casas is the discovery of the other, especially their viewpoint. Gutiérrez agrees with this lesson for in it he finds "one of the earliest intuitions of liberation theology" where "the perspective of the 'underside of history' is an obligation still in full force."[170]

Memory, the ability to remember honestly, is a key component of this obligation, a requirement in order to rewrite history through the perspective of the native poor. This fact is why Las Casas found it

168. Ibid.
169. Gutiérrez, *Las Casas*, 8.
170. Gutiérrez, "From Exclusion to Discipleship," 83.

necessary to recover the memories of the past if proper restitution was to be made. Memory is synonymous with life, which includes the past, the present, and the future: past treatment of the Indians along with the real reason for such actions are remembered, so that proper restitution can be made in the present, which will allow for the indigenous population, at its minimum, to have a future. Therefore, "memory lives on in elements of our culture, in popular religion, in resistance to ecclesiastical high-handedness."[171] To remember is to assess and to assess means to rectify. "We cannot reinterpret history without being actively engaged in the liberation struggle. To remake history is to subvert it, to channel its course from the standpoint of those on the bottom."[172] Therefore, the preferential option for the poor makes us remember where we stand before God and one another.

> Part of this memory means acknowledging our responsibility in what the poor have always had to suffer. The Christian manner of assuming this responsibility is to beg for humble forgiveness from God and the victims of history for our complicity, explicit or tacit, past and present, as individuals and as a Church. To ask to be forgiven expresses a will to change in our behavior and reasserts the obligation of being an efficacious sign in the history of the Reign of love and justice. It is not a fixation on the past. It is a step toward the future."[173]

Bartolomé de Las Casas was able to stand in this relationship, relinquishing and repenting of his old way of life as an *encomendero* to become one of the most ardent defenders of the Indians as the future prospects for the indigenous people dwindled. Through his unrelenting efforts to defend the Indians, we come to understand more intimately the Church's relationship with poor. "It is necessary to read history, our history, human history, from the point of view of the victims of history. Frequently we have a very wrong understanding of history because our sources, the historical sources, are written by the dominant persons and they have written history from their point of view. It seems to me that Las Casas helps us to take another perspective, to read history from below."[174]

---

171. Gutiérrez, "Two Theological Perspectives," 248.
172. Ibid.
173. Gutiérrez, *Las Casas*, 457.
174. Gutiérrez, "Bartolomé de Las Casas: Defender of the Indians," 265.

Obviously, history in Latin America has not been rewritten "from below," since the situation of poverty and oppression is still evident today. In addition, a sad comment must also be made in regard to the Church's response to the conditions of misery, which has also not changed radically over the centuries. Because of the continuation of poverty, especially the inability of the poor to be recognized, and thus, allowed to become active participants of their own destinies, Gutiérrez writes: [w]hile the poor have always been physically present, they have been absent in terms of the way history is understood. Today they are making themselves felt once again, and I believe that this presents a great challenge.[175] The missionary effort of Las Casas to preserve life is still an unfinished work that today's defenders of the poor such as Gutiérrez have continued in their own ministries. "In view of all of this, Las Casas's witness is particularly important for the self-discovery that the peoples of Latin America must make today. The sixteenth century was decisive in our history. Things happened and options were made then that marked the centuries to come."[176] However, Gutiérrez is also quick to remind us of the dangers of associating too much of the past with the events of today and vice versa. Some autonomy must be maintained in historical events preserving their own locale and time, but in order to understand the poor we must also make strong historical connections for only through these connections can we make real changes that bring about a new history.

> We have no intention of positing facile equations between eras endowed with [their] own coordinates and personality. But neither must we fail to perceive the points of contact between them or the teachings that we can gather from the past. The present acquires density and substance when it is nourished by the memory of a journey, when the courage is found to identify unsolved problems and wounds not yet healed. Here are gaping maws that hunger still and voraciously consume so many energies today. The historical view gains effect and luminosity when maintained from the present. This has its risks, of course, and consequently must be done with great respect for a far-off age so different from our own.[177]

175. Gutiérrez, "Search for Identity," 66.

176. Gutiérrez, *Las Casas*, 456.

177. Ibid., 457.

There is little debate that the theological and political arguments of Las Casas have inspired Gutiérrez's own dialogue with modern political and religious leaders. It is important to note, however, that the real subjects in need of God's attention have not changed; the poor in Latin America continue to experience the racism and exploitation that Europeans introduced into their history. As long as the poor remain the real subjects of concern, then any efforts by Christians on their behalf must follow the paths laid by people like Gutiérrez who imitate followers of Christ within history, especially the path of Bartolomé de Las Casas. Following this path quickly reveals there are no easy answers or simple solutions to a complex problem stemming from the complexity of the world of the poor. "How often we have asked ourselves the same question, in this, the hour of Latin America and Peru! Why indeed does death continue to be so sovereign among us? Ours is a time of drought and tribulation, but also, in terms of the rich Lascasian focus, of calling and mercy . . . When we have transformed the one into the other, we shall have embraced the ultimate meaning of Las Casas's life and work; to be a witness of the God who is "rich in mercy" (Eph. 2:4) in the Indies."[178]

Finally, we cannot make Bartolomé de Las Casas into something that he originally was not (e.g., a liberation theologian). Likewise, we cannot use his words to make a case for our ecclesial understanding today. However, we are able to gain significant insights by the foundation Las Casas has laid for the Church especially in Latin America. Although, Las Casas never specifically spoke the words, "preferential option for the poor," he obviously lived it. Without his approach to God through the sufferings of the native Indians, we could not have reached the understanding we have today. The preferential option for the poor is not simply a modern creation, perspective, or understanding. Rather, the preferential option for the poor is a viewpoint that has been built upon the foundation of Christianity, one which has been built upon the action of those seeing the gift of the poor in their unique circumstances of life. Thus, we gain a unique and deeper perspective of the social teaching of the Church when we incorporate Las Casas's insights into our preferential (spiritual poverty of the Suffering Christ of the Indies and the poor that the Gospel speaks of) option (poverty as commitment as seen in the act of restitution) for the poor (the native Indians).

178. Ibid., 456–57.

SUMMARY: THE PREFERENTIAL OPTION FOR THE POOR

During my conversation with Gustavo Gutiérrez at Notre Dame in December 2009, regarding his theological method, he seemed pleased with the depiction of his life's mission as characterized by the preferential option for the poor.[179] However, he reminded me that before any theological method can be conceptualized, a spirituality of liberation is needed. He emphasized that my presentation of his theology, the second step, needed the first step, prayer consisting of contemplation and praxis, worship and commitment.

In his article, "The Option for the Poor Arises from Faith in Christ" in 2009, Gutiérrez summarized his thoughts regarding the option for the poor in three particular areas: *la sequela Christi*, theological writings, and evangelization.[180] First, Gutiérrez is a theologian working concretely on behalf of the poor rather than attempting to provide abstracts, proofs, or principles to be applied later. The insignificant or the poor ones receive preference; therefore, the fulfillment of a crucial and essential aspect of Christianity comes from solidarity with the poor. This identification with the poor comes from the first act—the spirituality of liberation as Gutiérrez calls it, the act of following Jesus, *la sequela Christi*. "The option for the poor is a key part of a spirituality that refuses to be a kind of oasis or, still less, an escape or a refuge in difficult times. At the same time it involves a walking with Jesus that, without being disconnected from reality and without distancing itself from the narrow paths trod by the poor, helps us keep alive our trust in the Lord and preserve our serenity when the storm gets worse."[181]

Only through practice of our love of God and our love of neighbor can proper theological reflection be engaged. Therefore, Gutiérrez's characterizes his theological writings as "a hermeneutic of hope" as the Good News of following Jesus penetrates every aspect of our lives. "In the end, theology—all theology—is a hermeneutic of hope, an understanding of the reason we have to have hope."[182]

---

179. See Appendix B for a complete transcript of my interview in December 2009 with Gustavo Gutiérrez at the University of Notre Dame.

180. Gutiérrez, "Option for the Poor Arises from Faith," 317–26.

181. Ibid., 321.

182. Ibid., 322.

Faith is a grace; theology is an understanding of this gift. Theology tries to say a word about the mysterious and ineffable reality that we believers call God. It is a *logos* about *theos*. Faith is the ultimate source of theological reflection, giving theology its specificity and delimiting its territory. Its purpose is—or should be—to contribute to making the Gospel present in human history through Christian testimony. A theology that is not nourished by walking Jesus' own path loses its bearings. Those we call Fathers of the Church, for whom all theology was spiritual theology, understood this very well."[183]

Lastly, the reason for this hope in following Jesus is revealed when evangelization consists of a prophetic proclamation which includes an intimate connection between justice and God's gratuitous love.[184] "In addition, solidarity with the poor also sets forth a fundamental demand: the recognition of the full human dignity of the poor and their situation as daughters and sons of God."[185]

These three dimensions of the preferential option for the poor; *la sequela Christi*, theological writings and evangelization, are prioritized by Gustavo Gutiérrez as a theology of liberation. Throughout his pastoral and academic career, Gutiérrez has reflected upon the meaning of God's preference for the poor and the Church's understanding of this preference in solidarity with the poor. Thus, in his theological method, the preferential option for the poor is the constitutive hermeneutic lens. In addition, his reflections on scripture, especially the Book of Job, and figures in Church history, especially Bartolomé de Las Casas, further highlight the preferential option for the poor that is always on the forefront of his mind.

183. Ibid., 321.
184. Ibid., 323.
185. Ibid., 324.

4

Theology of Context as the Theological Method

THIS CHAPTER BEGINS BY considering the theological and pastoral similarities of Virgilio Elizondo and Gustavo Gutiérrez in four areas: their theological method, their dependence on a culture of context, their use of the method *See, Judge, Act*, and their espousal of ecumenism. Next, this chapter examines some of the differences between Elizondo and Gutiérrez in regard to their theologies of context and their understanding of denouncement and announcement, as well as the work of the Spirit in the Church and *comunidades de base*. The third section of this chapter is devoted to considering characteristic topics of Virgilio Elizondo: the conquest of the sixteenth century, the borderland resonance of Galilee and the U.S. Southwest, and Our Lady of Guadalupe. The next section then examines characteristic topics of Gustavo Gutiérrez: his theological differences with Joseph Ratzinger, the example of Bartolomé de Las Casas, and scriptural and theological interpretations in liberation theology. This chapter concludes by examining recent developments in a theology of context, first of all by considering the present status of *mestizo* theology and liberation theology and then by examining the theology of migration and contextual self-identity.

VIRGILIO ELIZONDO AND GUSTAVO GUTIÉRREZ: SIMILARITIES IN THEIR THEOLOGICAL METHOD

Since the Second Vatican Council, non-European theological writings have increased dramatically. Theologians of many different places have provided thoughtful reflection on salvation history in the context of their own personal histories: "Modern theology has broadened the horizons of theological reflection. It has opened its doors wider and admitted a larger group of people, thus making the task of theology more democratic in many ways. Rather than leaving matters of reflection about God to the clergy and a small number of authorized specialists, modern theologians found that everybody shares in an awareness of God."[1] With this increase in theological reflection throughout the world, theologians have found personal inspiration to speak about God in their unique set of circumstances. Many theologians have benefitted, directly or indirectly, from the contributions of Elizondo and Gutiérrez as pioneers not only in their respective fields, but in the overall theological enterprise. Virgilio Elizondo and Gustavo Gutiérrez have been recognized for their contribution to their own communities as well as to the worldwide community in *Festschriften* and other publications.

In 1988, *Beyond Borders: Writings of Virgilio Elizondo and Friends*, a collection of Elizondo's writings with commentaries by those who have benefitted from his theological investigations, was published in his honor. More recently, a selection of Elizondo's spiritual writings reveals the depth of this Mexican American theologian.[2] Two *Festschriften* have been published honoring Gustavo Gutiérrez: the earlier *Festschrift* celebrating his sixtieth birthday, not only focused on his contributions to liberation theology in Latin America, but also his contribution to liberation in other contexts.[3] The latest *Festschrift*, on his eightieth birthday, celebrates the themes of freedom and hope exemplified in Gutiérrez's lifework.[4]

Both Elizondo and Gutiérrez have served on the editorial board of *Concilium*. Speaking about those who have served on the editorial board, David Nichols has commented: "Elizondo, in fact, is one of 43

---

1. Rieger, "Theology and the Power," 179.
2. Matovina, ed., *Virgilio Elizondo: Spiritual Writings*.
3. Ellis and Maduro, eds., *Future of Liberation Theology*.
4. de Prado and Hughes, *Libertad y Esperanza*.

Catholic theologians worldwide who edit *Concilium*, a prestigious international theological journal published in seven languages."[5] Accordingly, the theological endeavors of Elizondo and Gutiérrez have been valued throughout the global theological community.

Through the theological efforts of Elizondo and Gutiérrez, considerable attention has been given to distinguishing and categorizing newly-developed theological approaches, in particular those found in the Americas which often differed from so-called "mainstream" theology.[6] Some critiques, especially from the Vatican, have seriously questioned the direction of some of these theological approaches. While addressing certain individuals, the Vatican critiques seem to have been unfairly applied to the massive amount of theological work being accomplished throughout the Americas.

Other European theologians have also downplayed the relevance of theologies emerging from the Americas either by categorizing them as a novelty or subset of European theology or by criticizing them as immature theology. For example, Hans Urs von Balthasar, while serving on the International Theological Commission, concluded that liberation theology is not a complete theology on its own, but rather a theological reflection within the theology of the Kingdom of God.[7] In a more critical stance, Henri de Lubac in his *Brief Catechism of Nature and Grace* characterized Latin American liberation theology as incomplete and not representative of any theology. "Their only drawback, but it is a fundamental one, is that they pretend to take the place of theology itself. Even if they aimed at something less than this, by claiming to be self-sufficient in their limited areas, they would still lack the only basis which would give them a right to the name "theologies"."[8] Thus, the attitudes of Roman authorities and some European theologians have brought the theological reflection of the Americas under close scrutiny, thereby prompting Elizondo and Gutiérrez to refine their theological methods.

5. Nichols, "Particular Man," 88.

6. Granted that all theologies are local, the theological endeavors undertaken in the Americas focus on the cultural locale of the theologian and/or the audience; thus, "the theologies of the Americas" or "the theologies emerging from the Americas" here refer to the "theologies of context" being developed in various parts of the Americas.

7. de Lubac, *Brief Catechesis*, 115.

8. Ibid., 113.

How does a theology that is rooted in a local context and is so apparently isolated and particular become universal? For Elizondo, it is axiomatic that the more particular the theology, the more universal its application. For both Elizondo and Gutiérrez, universal theological concepts are unique translations from their local context which are applicable to the theological endeavor of the Church. As Letty Russell has commented: "Hope in God's promise of a new creation can be discovered in each context, and in that discovery new hope in the one story can be born and shared."[9] "By beginning with the new we move out of future wholeness of the new Jerusalem and are beyond the dichotomies which are characteristic of fallen creation. We cannot return to the "simple life of Adam and Eve" but we can seek the unity in which all nations will be invited to God's banquet of riotous variety, where all persons come to share and tell their own stories of God's liberation."[10]

Elizondo and Gutiérrez: Two Phases in their Theological Method

In the lifeworks of Virgilio Elizondo and Gustavo Gutiérrez, one can roughly distinguish two stages of their theological development. Their first stage was to separate themselves from their European counterparts. Rather than settling for a borrowed form of trans-Atlantic theology, both Elizondo and Gutiérrez insisted their theology was different insofar as the questions being raised in their starting points differed from those that preoccupied European theologians. Addressing their people, whose origins can be traced back to the 16th Century Spanish conquest, Elizondo and Gutiérrez find believers still living under a continued oppression. Elizondo begins his theological questioning with the border-crossers without any homeland and those rejected in society because of their ethnicity; while Gutiérrez is preoccupied with the poor dying before their time. Both theologians address the oppressed and marginalized who need liberation, in contrast to European theologians who are concerned with non-believers needing redemption.

What allows these two theologians to raise questions on behalf of their people is their own personal identity. More than simply writing about their observations, both Elizondo and Gutiérrez find themselves the subjects of their own theology as well. They identify with those in

---

9. Russell, "Universality and Contextuality," 26.

10. Ibid., 25.

similar situations and so ask and address actual questions in a theological light. For Elizondo, as a *mestizo* himself, the questions stem from deep within his being and reach out to those in similar situations: how are we to identify today with a God who crossed biological, cultural, and social boundaries of the past? For Gutiérrez, being a poor *mestizo* in a country pervaded by poverty, the questions stem from his childhood and throughout his pastoral ministry: how are we to speak about God as Father to those who are considered insignificant to the point of not being recognized as human beings? In short, Elizondo and Gutiérrez are both asking how are we to speak about our faith in God to people who already possess faith living in their current conditions of suffering and injustice.

Without attempting a specific delineation of its timing, the second phase of Elizondo's and Gutiérrez's theological efforts arises as they seek to find similarities with other theological endeavors. As *mestizo* theology and liberation theology mature through fruitful dialogue and further reflection on their own unique situations, a natural development has occurred. No longer are the theologies of the Americas addressing solely those living on this continent; every theological process undergoes a similar methodology. A theology of context is not only the theology of the Americas or a theology of Third World theologians; rather, all theologians engage in theologies of context, for it is impossible to do theology outside a given context. "Every discourse on faith is born at a precise time and place and tries to respond to historical situations and questions amidst which Christians live and proclaim the Gospel. For that reason it is tautological, strictly speaking, to say that a theology is contextual, for all theology is contextual in one way or another. Some theologies, however, take their context seriously and recognize it; others do not."[11] Accordingly, European theology is not the only theology but a theology in a given context that has managed to dominate the current political and theological landscape. The theological method of Elizondo and Gutiérrez reveals the fact that theology cannot escape dialogue with each theologian's context. In other words, theology cannot be done in a vacuum and requires dialogue with the culture of the people to whom it is addressed.

The maturation of Elizondo's and Gutiérrez's theological writings discloses universal understandings of our humanity and our

11. Gutiérrez, "Option for the Poor Arises from Faith," 317.

relationship with God. In the case of Elizondo, the theme of border-crossing that produces the *mestizo* identity is not just the situation of the Mexican American people. Rather, this *mestizo* identity becomes a Christian identity as we are called to be a people bridging cultures in a globalized world and bridging this world with the next. As Christians, we are not called to an isolated identity, but one like the person we follow; our identities come from a mixture of encounters around us. Just as Jesus' earthly identity was formed through the *mestizo*-type process of divinity-humanity and Galilee-Jerusalem, we, as His followers, use our encounters to form a people of God and through this unique *mestizo* identity. Thus, we gain an insight about God that would otherwise not be available through our own perspective.

In the case of Gutiérrez, a similar universal identification is evident. His emphasis on the preferential option for the poor has not only become the mantra of his entire lifework, but it has also become an important social teaching in both Latin America and the universal Church. As part of Catholic social teaching, the preferential option for the poor is a perspective which all theologians must possess. It is not a suggestion but an option that all believers, including the poor themselves, must recognize. Thus, the preferential option for the poor is a hermeneutic lens for all theology, not just for theologies outside of Europe in the Third World. Often Gutiérrez speaks about those who are insignificant—those whose poverty means that they are overlooked and discarded by society. From the perspective of the poor and insignificant, Christians can gain a valuable insight into God's love for the impoverished throughout history.

Culture of Context and Culture of Content

In light of Elizondo's *mestizo* theology and Gutiérrez's liberation theology, scholars have made a distinction between cultures of content and cultures of context. Since all theology is contextual—both in terms of theologian and those to whom theology is addressed—further delineations are needed. Along with acknowledging the content of one's culture, recognizing the context of one's culture became important to the theological endeavors of Elizondo and Gutiérrez. The cultures both of content and context are necessary considerations in the theological process since, for Elizondo and Gutiérrez, the content of their theological reflections can only be understood within the context of their lives. There is a hermeneutical circle, such that content (language, expressions, categories, etc.) can only arise from context (the lived experience of a particular group) and context can only be communicated through content. Therefore, culture becomes key, for only in understanding the culture can a true context be determined, as well as a proper communication of the content.

It is when we separate the two and see the culture of content or the culture of context as independent that proper theological reflection is hindered. John Ford describes the differences between the culture of content and the culture of context and the difficulties when these are not held as a unitive hermeneutic circle, but in isolation, as in the Americas.

> American culture tends to be a culture of *content*: a culture that values logic and deduction, a culture which emphasizes the objective and the quantitative. For example, when Americans want to make a point, defend a decision, or especially when they want to win an argument, they usually present their views in a straight-forward way: "these are my reasons for doing this"; "my decision is based on the following facts"; "just look at the data." In contrast, the Hispanic/Latino culture is one of *context*: a culture that values induction and the symbolic, a culture which emphasizes the personal and the qualitative. For example, when Hispanics/Latinos want to make a point, they often tell a story.[12]

Another example distinguishing the culture of content and the culture of context is language, a classic example of how the world is seen through a particular cultural lens. Full comprehension of a language goes beyond syntax and grammar to engaging persons and their surroundings. In addition, language highlights philosophical differences as a set of cultural values that must be embraced for a language to be fully comprehended. "Unfortunately, many people who learn another language do not really appreciate the cultural views and values undergirding that language. Such people seemingly regard another language as a matter of knowing the correct words and using the correct grammar; such people may fail to grasp the cultural reality behind vocabulary and syntax; in effect, some people treat language-learning as a linguistic game, rather than as a cross-cultural encounter."[13]

The culture of content and the culture of context do not constitute an either/or proposition where one chooses one approach over another.

12. Ford, "Hispanic/Latino Theology," 126–27.

13. Ibid., 126.

Rather, cultures reveal the necessity, for any theological method, of understanding both content and context in a dynamic hermeneutical relationship. This distinction between cultures of content and context is especially important in the case of Hispanic/Latino theology and Latin American liberation theology. To claim that the theologies of the Americas are based on a culture of context while European theologies are based on a culture of content would be to oversimplify the reality. However, the distinction between cultures of context and cultures of content is useful for contrasting the two approaches, and noting that Hispanic/Latino and Latin American liberation theologians appeal to cultural context as their starting point.

Pastorally speaking, Ford illustrates the distinction between cultures of context and cultures of content in Hispanic/Latino ministry by contrasting three areas of life: time/*tiempo*, obligation/*fiesta* and Church/*casa de Dios*.[14] For instance, time or *tiempo* has a differing connotation in Hispanic life and Euro American life: for Hispanics/Latinos, *tiempo* is characterized by "walking" (*el reloj anda*) and not the axiom familiar to most westerners: "the clock is running." Similarly, the theme of obligation/*fiesta* also reveals a divide between cultures: for many English-speakers, Sunday Mass is an "obligation" which must be fulfilled; in contrast, Spanish-speaking communities consider Sunday Mass a time for celebration, a religious *fiesta* joining friends and family: "In many Latin American pueblos—a word that means "village" as well as "people"— Sunday is the day when the people of the village and the surrounding area come to celebrate Mass and to enjoy the companionship of their friends and neighbors. Indeed, in Latin American villages, many people are related not only by blood but also by sponsorship–for Baptism, Confirmation, quinceañeras, weddings. These family-like relationships are respected and reinforced on occasions of religious service."[15] Finally, Church/*casa de Dios* reflects a similar connotation: where Euro Americans might have their own ideals about proper dress and behavior in Church, Hispanics/Latinos consider the *casa de Dios* a place of welcome like one's own home.[16]

Theologically speaking, another way of characterizing the relationship between a culture of context and a culture of content is by

14. Ford, "¡Bienvenidos!," 73.

15. Ibid., 75.

16. Ibid., 76.

examining the contrasting relationship between an inductive method and a deductive method of theological knowledge. Although Elizondo and Gutiérrez do not categorize their works as such, others have done so to distinguish their methodology. "Hispanic/Latino theologies, like other contextual theologies, usually employ an *inductive* method, one that begins in a specific context but then suggests more general findings or universal applications. In contrast, many Euroamerican theologies espouse *deductive* methods that move from general principles to specific applications. For example, deductive theologies frequently rely on some type of syllogistic reasoning: major premise, minor premise, conclusion. Since this type of argumentation is so logical, deductive theologians tend to expect that everyone else will come to the same conclusion."[17] As with any deductive scientific approach, a deductive theological methodology begins with a general principle of faith and moves to its application. From this general and often abstract starting point, the theological task is to apply the abstract principles to concrete situations. Within this approach, logical philosophic argumentation becomes the vehicle in proving the connection between the general principle and its specific application. Because logical arguments are the basis of proof, these arguments are then considered universal—the correct conclusions at which all within a religious tradition must arrive.[18] However, the Achilles' heel in this type of deductive methodology stems from a failure to recognize the cultural influences on so-called "universal" statements.[19] Without throwing the baby out with the bathwater, deductive theological methodology is still valuable, legitimate, and necessary. However, its claims of universality are questionable insofar as each theologian's cultural context truly influences the understanding and communication of the logical arguments. The specific pastoral applications of general theological principles may be appropriate and necessary in some locales, but not applicable to others.

On the other hand, an inductive theological method flows in the opposite direction. An emphasis on the world and its current events can be traced back to the method of John XXIII.[20] "With the advent of the papacy of John XXIII, a new phase emerged in Catholic social

17. Ford, "Hispanic/Latino Theology," 125.

18. Ibid.

19. Ibid.

20. Twomey, *Preferential Option for the Poor*, 7.

teaching. Pope John XXIII moved from the deductive to the inductive method. He took as his point of departure the 'signs of the times' in the historical moment, to be scrutinized under the lens of the Gospel." Rather than beginning with a general or abstract principle of faith, an inductive approach to theology begins with a concrete event, situation, or application. Stemming from a specific context, the theological enterprise is to uncover the more general principles and/or universal applications back-dropping the specific context. Liberation theologians as well as Hispanic/Latino theologians begin their theological enterprise inductively with events, stories, and experiences of their culture and people as manifestations of the universal principles of faith. "This evident strength of contextual theologies is simultaneously an unavoidable and sometimes insurmountable weakness: The very context that "insiders" find so appealing and reassuring, so confirming and comforting, may be alienating or even unintelligible to "outsiders." One and the same context simply does not fit all."[21] However, not every "concrete event" is a source for theological reflection. As previously mentioned, neither Elizondo nor Gutiérrez use the terms inductive or deductive to describe their theological endeavors, but rather, these terms are used to illustrate their theological method. One of the difficulties in this illustration is the discernment of concrete events for theological reflection since not all "concrete events" have theological implications. For Elizondo, the concrete events that hold meaning for him involve *mestizaje*, while for Gutiérrez concrete events involving the poor are what matter most.

In sum, a culture of content stresses the objective, the legal, and the political while a culture of context stresses the subject, the familial, and the communal. On the one hand, a culture of content stresses a deductive theological method, which begins with general principles and/or abstract ideas to obtain a specific application into living out one's faith. On the other hand, a culture of context stresses an inductive theological method, which begins with the concrete events and experiences of our lives and then translates them into overall principles of faith. The two, content and context, deductive and inductive theological methods, should not be seen as completely foreign to each another for both have their utility and validity. "In the Gospel message, universality and contextuality are joined together in a dialectical relationship. To place them in opposition to each other, it seems to me, creates a false dichotomy.

---

21. Ford, "Hispanic/Latino Theology," 125.

The universal proclamation of hope for all humanity is at the same time the concrete, situation-variable proclamation that the blind see, the lame walk, the prisoners are set free."[22] What one finds in the theological method of both Elizondo and Gutiérrez is their starting point based on the culture of context that gives life to the content. By utilizing a culture of context and an inductive theological approach as their starting point, both theologians address their own people through stories, images, and *religiosidad popular* that everyone within a specific context can comprehend. Accordingly, a theological approach of this type is very appealing to the audience it addresses. Correspondingly, the initial limitation of this appeal is quickly revealed as those outside the cultural context speak of their difficulty in relating to and embracing what is foreign to their culture. Nevertheless, the specific theological starting point of Elizondo and Gutiérrez is not limited to themselves nor to their own people as their starting point quickly broadens to universal concepts in theology. The two stages in the theological works of Elizondo and Gutiérrez are the movements of an inductive approach where concrete situations in the Americas have given birth to universal principles that prompt an appreciation of the lifework of these two theologians.

See, Judge, Act

Another historical and theological consideration for analyzing the similarities in the theological works of Virgilio Elizondo and Gustavo Gutiérrez relates to the influence of secular and religious history on the life and work of these two pioneering theologians. Oppression, racism, and other injustices stemming from the 16th Century Spanish conquest to the modern day as well as the initiatives for dialogue with the world fostered by Vatican II became constitutive elements in the theological method of Elizondo and Gutiérrez. Both have subscribed to a theological and ethical tool that is popular today and traces its origins back to the European Church prior to Second Vatican Council. Known simply as the method of *See, Judge, Act*, this process of discerning a response to a specific situation became a useful tool in assisting the Church not just to engage with the world, but more importantly, to respond to the challenges posed within it.

---

22. Russell, "Universality and Contextuality," 23.

The method of *See, Judge, Act,* introduced by the Belgian Cardinal Joseph Cardijn (1882–1967), was utilized by the Young Christian Workers to make relevant the Catholic faith in the world.[23] With the rise in cultural awareness about the injustices perpetuated against them, Christians in the Americas also embraced *See, Judge, Act* as a method to respond to the atrocities of life surrounding them. As recently as 2007 at the CELAM gathering at Aparecida, Brazil, the Latin American Bishops reaffirmed *See, Judge, Act* as a valuable tool for base ecclesial communities.[24]

The method of *See, Judge, Act* does exactly what it states. Those using this method are called upon to *see* the conditions of their surroundings and the injustices within it. After considering the situation at hand, we are asked to *judge* how God, through the scriptures and the Church, is calling us to respond. Finally, after seeing and judging the events around us, we must *act*—deciding on an appropriate action that responds to the moral imperative of this method. The advantages of this method are the ease and accessibility of its use by people all over the world. However, with such conveniences comes limitation. The most evident is the perspective one uses to judge. We are only able to view a certain distance forward and from side to side; thus, our limited view always limits our action in the world.

Elizondo and Gutiérrez utilize the method of *See, Judge, Act* in their spirituality as followers of Christ. In *seeing* who their own are as the *mestizos* and the poor, in *judging* that their conditions in life are at many times a result of the structural sins unjustly created by other human beings, and in *acting* liberatingly on behalf of their own, both Elizondo and Gutiérrez prophetically denounce the current situation while announcing the Good News contained within the poor, insignificant, marginalized, and excluded. The method of *See, Judge, Act* is then a vehicle for their spirituality of denouncing in order to announce; it is a method for the in-breaking of the Kingdom here on earth.

Ecumenism

Both Virgilio Elizondo and Gustavo Gutiérrez address their own people in the Americas. A common characteristic of the populace is that the

23. Gaillardetz, *Church in the Making,* 52.

24. Consejo Episcopal Latinoamericano, *Discípulos y Misioneros de Jesucristo,* 19.

majority are Christians, who formally profess a Catholic faith in their active practice in the Church or culturally in the religious society into which they were born. Thus, a majority of the people on whose behalf Elizondo and Gutiérrez speak—rather than speaking at—are already Christians, in contrast to those whom European theologians constantly address, the non-believers in their culture.

Instead of rallying people around the pole of belief rather than disbelief as is sometimes the case of European theologians, Virgilio Elizondo and Gustavo Gutiérrez gathered people around those living on the borders of life and poverty. Thus, ecumenically, the theological positioning of theologians in the Americas is much more friendly to, and accessible by, people of differing faiths, both inter-denominationally and inter-religiously, insofar as the theological tenets of a person's faith are based on God's preference for the poor and the rejected. As Gutiérrez states, "liberation theology is not Latin American, [it] is biblical."[25] Without abandoning the critical tenets of their faith, many are able to relate with the struggles of poverty on the borders of life. Thus, people of differing faiths can come together to dialogue and address the issues arising from a common ground shared by masses of the people.

A Hispanic/Latino Protestant theologian, José Míguez Bonino, has raised the banner of ecumenism: "unity through freedom, ecumenism through liberation."[26] However, Bonino points out that ecumenism does not always mean "unity" for he sees this term as a further "tool of oppression rather than liberation" in order to maintain the status quo, "for the sake of the economy, the authority, the comfort of the powerful."[27] Accordingly, the ecumenical spirit found in other parts of the Church appears foreign in the Americas, where unity is only achievable as the end result of freedom through liberation: "It is, nevertheless, my conviction that we cannot approach the issue either as an 'internal Christian affair' nor as a confessional question. Such conviction is not primarily the result of theological struggles, sufferings, victories and defeats, of thousands of Christians in our sub-continent. We call it sometimes

25. See Appendix B.

26. Bonino, "Freedom Through Unity," 255. José Míguez Bonino has served as professor of dogmatic theology and ethics in the Facultad Evangélica de Teología de Buenos Aires and as director of postgraduate studies in the Instituto Superior Evangélico de Estudios Teológicos de Buenos Aires, as well as one of the presidents of the World Council of Churches.

27. Ibid.

"a struggle for liberation." In it we are slowly learning to re-define the lines of separation and the bonds of unity. And consequently also to re-articulate the idea of unity and ecumenism as it relates to freedom and liberation."[28] From this struggle for identity, voice, and survival with human dignity against the rampant forces of oppression, Bonino redefines Christian faith: "Empirically, faith can always be described as a particular way of being, understanding and acting in the world. Theologically, according to the Scriptures, it *should* always be so described, because it is a total response to God's being and action. Translated into ecclesiological language, therefore, the issue is that of the 'mission of the Church.'"[29] Thus, for Bonino, the real issue of ecumenism and unity is not based on the tenets of our faith; rather, the real issue for ecumenical unity lies in the way the Church relates with the world in her mission: "The question of unity is, as we see it, the question of the mission of the Church in the world."[30]

Dangers of reductionism exist when social action in the world is separated from the faith of the Church. However, reductionism also exists when we do not extend ourselves into the realities of the poor and oppressed and keep our faith life privatized. Theologians such as Elizondo and Gutiérrez have devoted much of their pastoral efforts and theological thought to avoiding these two extremes of reductionism and to making social justice an integral and constitutive part of the faith. Our response to the poorest of the poor and the marginalized in society coupled with our worship of God makes us true Christians, true followers of Christ. Accordingly, spirituality is the lived out actions of our lives, the communion with others, reflecting our union with God. The visible aspect of our spirituality, our response to others in need, becomes the foundation for ecumenical dialogue and unity with others who are also believers. Challenges to the mission of the Church in oppressive and poverty-stricken environments are what unite people of faith for activities of social justice that are ecumenical by nature.[31]

Another reason why it is so critical for Elizondo and Gutiérrez to address believers rather than non-believers is the voicelessness of the impoverished and marginalized in two areas of life. First, many of the

28. Ibid., 256.

29. Ibid., 258.

30. Ibid.

31. Condolo, "Ecumenism and Human Liberation," 36.

poor and *mestizos* have often been shunned by society at large. It has been too easy for the world to neglect these groups and force them to the fringes of society. By doing so, the political, economical, and social centers of power can rest comfortably in the status quo. What Elizondo and Gutiérrez illustrate through their theological endeavors is that these groups need society's attention and embrace. For Elizondo, *mestizo* identity is not to be shunned, since it is the wave of the future: "Differences are not being destroyed, but they are being transcended and celebrated as together we usher in the beginning of the new race of humanity."[32] In other words, the world's population is currently filled with biological, cultural, and social *mestizaje*. The lack of attention to this reality means that the majority of the world's population is not acknowledged and their gifts are not utilized in society at large. For Gutiérrez, the irruption of the poor indicates the overburdened state of this marginalized portion of society. Irruptions of this magnitude usually occur when the surrounding pressures become unbearable and those being pressured uncontainable. Thus, the masses in poverty can no longer exist in a state of oppression and exploitation; the irruption of the poor signifies an unhealthy and undignified human existence. In order for there to be stability in any and every area of the world, there must be opportunities for life with dignity.

The second area Elizondo and Gutiérrez prophetically address is the neglect and sometimes oppressive attitude found within the Church. Their prophetic call for recognition and liberation is not only to be heard by secular institutions. Equally important is that the prophetic call be heard within the Church. Catholics, who form a majority in many countries of the Americas are often obstacles to liberation; they are the very people who are perpetuating the sins of oppression and exploitation. Thus, it is essential that the Church join in denouncing the causes of structural sin even if she contributes to it. Through solidarity with the borderland people and the poor of society the Church can prophetically proclaim the Good News of the Gospels. For both Elizondo and Gutiérrez, denouncing the acts that lead us away from God must come first in order to remind others that the Kingdom is here in our midst. The ecumenically-oriented method of *See, Judge, Act* allows us to denounce

32. Elizondo, *Future is Mestizo*, 111.

the injustices caused by human sinfulness and to announce the reign of God by allowing us to live truly in freedom as God's children.[33]

By utilizing the method of *See, Judge, Act* method, Elizondo and Gutiérrez are able to make relevant the reign of God in the concrete lives of those residing on the edges of borders and poverty. By confronting both secular institutions for the injustices perpetuated against the most vulnerable in their midst and religious institutions for their role in maintaining and even escalating oppressive structures in the Church, Elizondo and Gutiérrez have opened the doors for others to enter into the struggles of liberation. By addressing secular institutions, Hispanic/Latino theology and liberation theology are able to dialogue ecumenically with other faiths under the banner of a shared struggle for liberation called forth by our common humanity. By addressing the attitudes and actions of their own Catholic Church, Hispanic/Latino theology and liberation theology are able to dialogue ecumenically with other Christian denominations through a common struggle for liberation called forth by the Gospel commissioning. In addressing both the secular and the religious, in denouncing and announcing, Elizondo and Gutiérrez embody "unity through freedom, ecumenism through liberation." As José Míguez Bonino has pointed out,

> In the light of our experience, it seems that freedom and unity are not mutually contradictory, nor are they mutually dependent, nor does one necessarily promote the other. Both can be genuine or false. Both can be at the service of the mission of the Church as defined by the witness and redemptive work of Christ, and both can be manipulated ideologically at the service of oppression. The measure of validity, therefore, is not either unity or freedom conceived abstractly, but that freedom and unity which corresponds to God's promised and coming Kingdom. When the Church engages herself in this mission, [she] finds unity in her struggle for liberation and that unity strengthens and deepens her commitment to freedom. Such unity and such liberation we claim, the Church can find today when she identifies with her

---

33. Although Virgilio Elizondo and Gustavo Gutiérrez both subscribe to the method of *See, Judge, Act*, the two differ slightly in its immediate application. This difference will be treated in the next section in discussing the difference between the two theologians. For present purposes, it is important to emphasize that they both embrace *See, Judge, Act* as a way of liberating their people from the bonds of inferiority and insignificance.

Lord by committing herself to and [participating] with the poor in their struggle for a new day for the whole of humankind.[34]

Liberation theology as an ecumenical theology is not without its critics. Although, ecumenical agreement appears reachable because of the common mission of liberation in oppressive situations and poverty, the early momentum is presently not bearing fruit as it once did. For example, Leslie James sees liberation theology "as a common thrust among Latin American theologians" because it represents "a theological movement with a vital ecumenical dynamic."[35] However, this upsurge in ecumenical cooperation does not have the same results today. James cites three significant reasons why the ecumenical thrust of liberation theology has not netted the interest and results of the past: first, with nearly four decades of theological reflection under its belt, the ecumenical thrust in liberation theology has been limited mainly to scholars, yet the results of these interdenominational "dialogue[s] between scholars remain still largely unknown to the laity and clergy of the respective denominations or Churches. At the ground level ecumenism has hardly begun."[36] In addition, liberation theology and its ecumenical driving force have simply lost the interest and energy of the ecclesial community. Finally, "religious and theological ecumenism is increasingly being displaced by secular ecumenism . . . an ecumenism of 'special purpose groups.'"[37]

There is no argument that the ecumenical nature of liberation theology is not what it once was. The enthusiasm and interest in ecumenical endeavors among liberation theologians have certainly been tempered as theologies of context have undergone periods of non-activity. Some may see this period of calm as detrimental to the theological enterprises that once possessed so much momentum. Others see this calm as part of the natural process of maturation, as growth can only be measured within a totality—a much longer period than we have now. In fact, the entire ecumenical outreach of the Church has been tempered after the ground swell experience following Vatican II, so liberation theology may simply be reflecting the overall attitudes of the Church. Regardless

34. Bonino, "Freedom Through Unity," 264.

35. James, *Toward an Ecumenical Liberation Theology*, 5.

36. Ibid.

37. Ibid.

of the reasons for the recent lack of ecumenical growth within theologies of context, there is no denying the importance of the potential social impact of these theologies: "This is not to claim, of course, that Liberation Theology, is no heir to historical, theological and ecclesiological developments within each communion. It is to say that a vital ecumenical dynamic is at work in this movement as perhaps nowhere else in contemporary Church history."[38]

VIRGILIO ELIZONDO AND GUSTAVO GUTIÉRREZ: DIFFERENCES IN THEIR THEOLOGICAL METHOD

The methodological similarities between the theological works of Virgilio Elizondo and Gustavo Gutiérrez are numerous and seemingly stem from a Hispanic legacy whose origin goes back to the 16th Century Spanish conquest. Through the Iberian conquest of the Americas, both the Spanish culture and language were imported to the Americas and imposed upon the indigenous people. An oppression, which began with this foreign invasion, continues to this day in various forms of oppression and oppressors, both internally and externally. This weight of subjugation—physical, emotional, psychological, and even spiritual—has produced a solidarity among theologians in the Americas. Theologies within the context of the Americas were generally aimed at overcoming internal and external oppression so as to enable people to live in freedom as God's children.

Multiple forms of persecution in the Americas also resulted in the marginalization of great numbers of the population within specific locales. Regardless of the cause or context, marginalization forced many people to the fringes of society. The marginalized for Elizondo are the border-crossers on the frontiers of Mexico and the United States, who experience marginalization in two forms. Within the Euro American culture, Mexican Americans are marginalized as foreigners sometimes within their own land, while within the Mexican culture, they are marginalized as not being "Mexican" enough because of their encounter with the English speaking population. In contrast, the marginalized for Gutiérrez are the poor in Latin America who are the majority, yet who have no voice in society. The insignificant poor located on the fringes

38. Ibid., 6.

have an existence of voicelessness and subhuman conditions and an inability to become agents of their own history.

Although Virgilio Elizondo and Gustavo Gutiérrez knew of each other early in their theological careers, their pastoral ministries and writings developed independently of each other.[39] Since meeting in the 1970s—without really understanding each other's future ecclesial presence—their lives have continued to intersect, eventually leading to many collaborative projects and mutual support as their pioneering efforts in theology matured.[40] The two, as friends, are currently serving on the same faculty at the University of Notre Dame. Although the marginalized poor in Latin America and the Mexican-American border-crossers have many commonalities, the marginalization felt by Elizondo and Gutiérrez within themselves and their people show differences in their respective theologies of context.

Another noticeable difference between the theological writings of Elizondo and Gutiérrez is in the way that they communicate their context. Although both theologians begin with a theology of context, the manner in which the context is communicated is quite different. For example, Elizondo employs a personal narrative in most of his writings; in contrast, Gutiérrez shares very little of his own personal story, bypassing his personal narrative and immediately communicating his contextual reflections through familiar theological categories. For Elizondo, personal narrative is not only the source, but also the vehicle to communicate *mestizo* theology. For Gutiérrez, the lack of personal narrative in his writings does not indicate a lack of reflection on the context of where his theology is situated; rather, his context is communicated through a different vehicle than Elizondo's. Both theologians arrive at

39. The theological endeavors of Elizondo and Gutiérrez matured independently of one another primarily because of their differing contexts. Because of ongoing immigration from Latin American countries to the United States and the attention liberation theology has received over the years, some have the impression that Hispanic/Latino theology grew out of Latin American theology. This is not to say they did not influence each other throughout their development; however, it is important to recognize that they developed independently of each other, since the maturation of both theologies was truly a response to the conditions that Virgilio Elizondo and Gustavo Gutiérrez encountered in their respective ministries.

40. Although both Elizondo and Gutiérrez attended the CELAM Conference at Medellín in 1968, they do not recall meeting one another at that time. Elizondo does not exactly remember their first encounter, only that they encountered and encouraged one another in their theological activities beginning in the seventies. See Appendix A.

the universal principles of the faith through their own context; however, Elizondo chooses to convey the personal elements of that context, while Gutiérrez remains silent. Perhaps, there are cultural or social or personal factors that have prevented Gutiérrez from this type of communication. Perhaps, his own experience of poverty and the poverty of those around him is too much to be shared at this time.

Solidarity is a difficult matter. To live in solidarity with the *mestizo*, the marginalized Mexican American people, as well as the poorest of the poor in Latin America, is a difficult challenge. However, according to Elizondo, *mestizo* solidarity is a tougher challenge to society than solidarity with the poor.[41] On the one hand, *mestizaje's* most noticeable feature is genetic makeup; on the other hand, poverty is cultural and social, but not a biological reality. Although people are born into poverty, it is still not a biological reality; however, being born a *mestizo* is a genetic reality which can never be removed. Those in poverty have the ability to "escape" their situation; however, *mestizos* can never "escape" their own being. Thus, Elizondo feels that *mestizaje* creates a greater challenge for society than poverty in terms of preferential option and solidarity.

The challenge of *mestizaje* is twofold. First, solidarity with the excluded and marginalized *mestizo* is simply not as accessible as living in solidarity with the poor and oppressed. Solidarity with the *mestizo* is not simply a decision of conscience, but a deeper reality because of its biological nature. Although, some *mestizo* solidarity can be reached when the "in-between" world is penetrated culturally and socially, biologically those outside of the *mestizo* reality can never fully comprehend it. This leads to the second challenge to those living on the "inside": *mestizos* are also affected since they always live in a reality foreign to others. Although the poor may face biological or racial discrimination, this reality is not the same as what a *mestizo* faces. The internal struggles of a *mestizo* deepen the pains of separation and further highlight the disconnect from those who consider themselves biologically "pure" or the "norm" of society. Thus, the biological factor creates both a visible and invisible, an external and internal, "barrier" and consequently a greater challenge for acceptance and solidarity.

---

41. This sentiment was mentioned during one of my many conversations with Virgilio Elizondo at the University of Notre Dame, Fall 2008.

Theology of Context in the United States

Since theology cannot escape cultural conditioning—in content and context—other differences also emerge from the same soil which birthed the theological efforts of Elizondo and Gutiérrez. Institutional leadership, both civil and religious, affected the outlook of the theologies in the Americas. The Church hierarchy in First World America has differed significantly from its Third World counterparts.[42] Although bishops in the United States produced important social documents, much of their concern has been about other matters directly affecting the laity in their jurisdictions. Thus, the lack of pastoral attention to Mexican Americans and other Hispanic/Latinos in their *frontera* reality has marginalized many immigrants from the Church. Through their frontier crossing, especially common in the Southwestern part of the United States, many Mexican Americans—with whom Virgilio Elizondo is concerned—at times have encountered an ecclesial community quite foreign to them. The history of the Church in the United States shows a hierarchy favoring Europeans over native populations especially with respect to clergy and Church leadership. Bishops often imported priests from Europe rather than nurturing vocations from the indigenous population. Thus, there has been a void in pastoral attention to the Mexican American population; this vacuum within the Church's outreach has propelled Elizondo and others to form a pastoral plan for their own people. In doing so, Elizondo has had to contend with the critical attitudes of Church leaders, government officials, as well as people in the homelands of the immigrants. "Except as people sitting passively in the pews, Hispanics had virtually no institutional representation in the Church in the late 1940's. There were few Hispanic priests because up to then little or no recruiting of Hispanic vocations had taken place. Spaniards were the largest group of Spanish-speaking priests, but their culture and that of the Hispanic people of the Southwest were not the same. The Spaniards were apt to judge the people they served as backward. After three centuries of virtual isolation, there was a cultural gap if not a chasm."[43]

---

42. The CELAM meeting at Aparecida in 2007 made greater initiatives to include the Episcopal leadership of the United States, especially since the second greatest concentration of people of Mexican descent resides in the U.S. Previously, U.S. Hispanic/ Latino bishops took an interest in CELAM, but the "signs of the times" indicate that the U.S. ecclesial leadership also has a vested interest in CELAM.

43. Sandoval, *On the Move*, 77.

The democratic capitalistic system of the United States has created a nation of great wealth and influence all over the world. In fact, most immigration stories include the desire to share in the richness of this country rather than make a radical change in the overall system of economy and government. With the opportunity for personal economic and social success, Mexican Americans have embraced a democratic and capitalistic way of life because of the opportunities and promises of this system. However, this embrace is not without limits. Although Mexican Americans live in this world, they do not fully accept it as their own nor are they accepted fully by it. For instance, the language barrier keeps some from fully engaging the American way of life. In addition, the lack of legal documentation results in a whole population not being counted in a democratic society. Millions of "undocumented" people are forced to live in a subculture of society without any vote, let alone voice, in matters of everyday life. These realities cause marginalization in both society and the Church. Even with positive views of government, economy, and Church, Mexican Americans are often underappreciated for their contribution to every sphere of life, and thus relegated to reside, internally and externally, on the borders of life. Upon this reality Elizondo expends his energies, for he knows it personally. Considering this reality as prophetic and blessed rather than outcast and despised, Elizondo and other Hispanic Latino/a theologians have sought a more just society.

It would be an understatement to say that Virgilio Elizondo is a proud Mexican American Catholic. He is appreciative of the opportunities he has received throughout his academic career; in particular, he is grateful both to Archbishop Patricio Flores for allowing him the time to develop his *mestizo* identity and theology and also to the religious community he lived with during his time of studies in Paris, France, and the faculty that supported the direction of his doctoral studies, especially his director, Jacques Audinet, who acknowledges how he has benefitted from Elizondo's dissertation. In addition, Elizondo has always taken on the pastoral challenges of ministering to Mexican Americans, as evidenced by the revival of San Fernando Cathedral and the creation of the Mexican American Cultural Center (MACC).[44]

---

44. Recently, the MACC has become a Catholic college and today the acronym stands for Mexican American Catholic College.

Elizondo loves all the countries—the United States, Mexico, France, the Philippines, and others—which have contributed to his *mestizo* identity. By gleaning the cultural diversity of both sides of the border, Elizondo has created a culturally rich atmosphere. Most of all, Elizondo is a churchman who loves the Catholic faith and the worshipping community. I recall that one of the first statements he made to me in our initial meeting was to emphasize the love he has for the Church. This love does not come without criticism, but his critique of certain Church behaviors is given so as to better what he truly loves. Finally, he is always generous and nurturing of those around him, especially the next generation. I have experienced this firsthand as Elizondo believes everyone has a contribution to make to his or her own culture and, thus, to the overall Church experience. Virgilio Elizondo is a faithful citizen and churchman who prophetically calls us to create a better reality as God's people.

Theology of Context in Latin America

The institutional systems of Latin America differ vastly from those encountered in North America. Although the United States exerts great economic and political influence in Latin America, the conditions of First World America are rarely to be found in the massive regions of Third World America. The Church hierarchy of Latin America has been plagued by biases of their own, just as the hierarchy of the United States has been influenced by European dominance. Church leadership in Latin America often come from elite oligarchies which tend to foster a rigid hierarchy protecting their upper class status and self-interest rather than embracing the most effective pastoral approach for the multitudes living in poverty. Throughout the history of the Latin American Church, there are faithful prophetic figures appearing to turn not only the hearts and minds of their people, but the entire world's attention to the massive numbers of the poor. Archbishops Oscar Romero of El Salvador and Dom Helder Câmara of Recife, Brazil, are two recent Church leaders who have called the world's attention to the impoverished situation of their people. Rising above pressures to minister only to rich elites, their examples have given others the courage to speak on behalf of those who have no significance. Gustavo Gutiérrez is one of those who appreciates the leadership and friendship of Romero and Câmara that allowed him to develop his pastoral and theological voice on behalf of the poor. This is not to say that the bishops have not also been greatly affected by Gutiérrez, for they understand the need of fieldworkers who take a prophetic stance on behalf of the poor.

During Gutiérrez's lifetime, most Latin American countries have experienced a civil war or some sort of violent uprising. Within this context of violence, Gutiérrez has witnessed a social, economic, and political system in complete disarray. During this time, the economic system and political government in Latin America came under serious questioning insofar as the adherence to democratic and capitalistic values of the Western World did not bring about a better world for many in Latin America. Rather, life got worse as corruption and oppression grew and choked off the already limited opportunities. The elite class reaped much of the rewards of the populace's hard labor, while the multitude of laborers continued in their destitute lifestyle. This desperate situation prompted liberation theologians such as Gutiérrez to infuse political liberation along with spiritual renewal in their theological endeavors.

Salvation history and human history were no longer seen as opposed to each other in Latin America but were located next to each another without being identical. In effect, political liberation meant the criticism of the democratic capitalistic system and advocating an alternative. During the 1970s, the alternative to western capitalism was socialism often imbued with Marxist influences. Because of the desperation felt in Latin America, any tools revealing economic and political oppression were embraced. Fear of Marxism quickly dissipated as Marxist analysis became a valuable tool for uncovering the underlying factors of oppression and poverty. The early writings of Gutiérrez included a denunciation of the capitalistic model of society in favor of a socialistic alternative. Over the years, however, Gutiérrez has moved beyond advocating a political system to espousing a Christian attitude towards societal reform. Gutiérrez has acknowledge this shift as a theocentric option towards liberation and not simply an anthropocentric option.[45] As Allen Figueroa Deck has commented: "In his own address, Father Gutiérrez stressed the fact that now, in hindsight, one can see that a common, popular understanding of liberation theology made the mistake of thinking that the foundations for it were anthropocentric and not theocentric. The stress given to the contextual and social analyses as

---

45. Deck, "Beyond *La Pausa*," 24.

a first moment in the process of theological reflection helps explain this anthropocentric drive."[46]

Advocating a political system as a solution for human spiritual and earthly welfare has also been addressed by Rome. In 2007, Pope Benedict XVI in his opening address to the Latin American Episcopal Conference (CELAM) in Aparecida, Brazil, rather than simply denouncing social-ism, remained neutral as he reiterated that the Christian position ap-peals neither to socialism nor capitalism:[47] "What is this *reality*? What is real? Are only material goods, social, economic and political problems *reality*? This was precisely the great error of the dominant tendencies of the last century, a most destructive error, as we can see from the results of both Marxist and capitalist systems. They falsify the notion of reality by detaching it from the foundational and decisive reality that is God."[48] Where Elizondo has labored to create a cross-cultural identity through cultural self-expression and proper faith reflection of a minority com-munity, Gutiérrez's efforts have focused on building a just society as a response to the faith reflections of an impoverished people against intra- and inter-cultural injustices. Although Gutiérrez's writings also include concern about those marginalized in society as being forgotten at the outer edges of society, he has pointed out that poverty in Latin America equals an early death for many and not simply alienation.

Denouncement, Announcement, and Fiesta

Through their pastoral and theological efforts, Virgilio Elizondo and Gustavo Gutiérrez have come to recognize not only the life-situations of their people, but more importantly, their prophetic witness in identifying the origins of oppression. Often, the sources of oppression come from within, within their own culture, people, and Church, making the stance of denouncement much more difficult and painful because it involves their own. However, both theologians realize that without denounce-ment of the current conditions enslaving their people, there cannot be any announcement of the Good News. Without identifying people and

---

46. Ibid.

47. In an interview, Gustavo Gutiérrez mentioned that Pope Benedict XVI's open-ing address was the best speech given by a pope at a CELAM gathering. Gutiérrez in-sisted that Benedict XVI's remarks were better than the comments of Paul VI and John Paul II. See Appendix B.

48. Benedict XVI, "Brazil Visit: Address to CELAM," 20.

structures that perpetuate suffering and injustice, there cannot be the necessary evangelization which brings about the Kingdom of God.

This very important position is found throughout the writings of Gutiérrez.[49] Time and time again, he emphasizes the first step in any prophetic announcement of God's reign. It is not enough to say someone is poor, but rather, it is necessary to say why they are poor by going to the causes of poverty. Without denouncement, without going to the sources of injustice, one cannot announce the Gospel message. Denouncement and announcement can never be separated for they are mutually dependent on one another. For Gutiérrez, denouncing and announcing are the constitutive elements of a spirituality of liberation.

Virgilio Elizondo echoes a similar position of denouncing in order to announce God's action in our lives. However, what is emphasized throughout his writings is the need for fiesta. In order to truly be God's people, celebrations of God's salvific actions are important.[50] True fiestas come only after the stages of denouncement and announcement; otherwise, they would be aberrations or false celebrations. Without denouncement, fiestas would simply be sentimental feelings and self-gratification. Without announcement, fiestas would simply be negative acts of debauchery. To rejoice as God's people means to celebrate the salvific act of God through the denouncement of injustice, announcement of hope, and the celebration of what God has done for us. "*Fiestas* without prophetic actions easily degenerate into empty parties, drunken brawls or the opium to keep the people in their misery. But prophetic action without festive celebration is equally reduced to dehumanizing hardness. Prophecy is the basis of fiesta, but the fiesta is the spirit of prophecy . . . It is through the two of them that the God of history Who acts on our behalf, on the behalf of the poor and the lowly, continues to be present among us bringing His project of history to completion."[51]

New Pentecost and Communidades de base

The Mexican American people on the borders of life have propelled Elizondo throughout his pastoral and theological career. For him, Mexican Americans are the bearers of the new Pentecost in the modern

49. Gutiérrez, *Praxis de Liberacion*, 56; "Latin American Perspection," 69; *Confrontations*, 16, 56.

50. Elizondo, "Mexican American Mestizo Christology," 117.

51. Ibid.

age: "In the power of the Spirit, the Galileans saw that the manifestation of Christian love involved not only their own ethnic group but all the nations and cultures of the world."[52] Therefore, it is through the Mexican American experience that bridges of different cultures found in the Acts of the Apostles come to be realized once again in our generation. "As the Galileans went to share this newly discovered love with all others, so today Mexican-American Christians, in the power of the same Spirit, must carry their boundary-transcending experience of the common mother of all the inhabitants of Mexico to all the peoples of the Americas . . . The new universalism of the Americas, which would slowly break through the barriers of caste and class, started among the "Galileans" of Mexican society of that time—the conquered Indians who lived on the periphery of power and civilization."[53]

Similarly, Gustavo Gutiérrez and other liberation theologians have shed light on the many gifts of the Church in Latin America, in particular, basic ecclesial communities. It is through the reflections of these small communities within the larger parishes of the Latin American Church that life has been given to pastors as well as theologians.

> Today in Latin America, basic ecclesial communities are an important ecclesiological element from the theological, pastoral, and institutional viewpoint. *Theologically* they express biblical elements, and aspects of the tradition and doctrine of the church, explicitly and in a new light. *Pastorally* they create and accelerate a process of evangelization and development of the faith and Christian life in a way that responds to the needs of the majority of the population. *Institutionally* they represent a paradigm of ecclesial organization different from earlier models, one which has an increasing influence on the broader institutionality of the church. Thus the basic ecclesial communities are a key element in Latin American ecclesial life and contribute to a clearer understanding of that life in the present historical moment.[54]

Unlike the renewed pentecostal gift that Elizondo has revealed through the Mexican American people, Latin America´s basic ecclesial communities are a newfound gift for the Church. "From direct contact with the basic ecclesial communities, with the people who work in them, and

---

52. Elizondo, *Galilean Journey*, 123.

53. Ibid.

54. de C. Azevedo, "Basic Ecclesial Communities," 636.

from the analysis of their bibliography, one can identify a constant in the present ecclesial consciousness: the basic ecclesial communities are a new way of being church if one compares it to the previously existing model of church, which has prevailed for the nearly five centuries of ecclesial presence in Latin America."[55] Growing out of the overall ecclesial development, basic ecclesial communities were the beneficiaries of the struggles of the twentieth century Church. This important historical root reinforces the base communities' commitment to being part of the Church—establishing a new way of being the Church of the present while leading the way as the Church of the future.

From their reflections on Vatican II, members of basic ecclesial communities understood their ecclesial commitment in a new manner reaffirmed by the universal Church. The Second Vatican Council "assumed and legitimated different tendencies that were being affirmed and were maturing since the first half of [the twentieth century]."[56] Basic ecclesial communities were further validated by the Latin American Episcopal Conferences at Medellín, Puebla and, more recently, at Aparecida as the Latin American Bishops, recognized both their own collegiality and the activities of local churches. "Made up mostly of poor people, who are the immense majority of our people, the basic ecclesial communities are a specific and living implementation of ecclesial preference for the poor. Seeing and thinking about reality from their viewpoint, being with them and serving them, the Church today is returning to the form, inspiration, and identity of Christ's own mission. He came to evangelize the poor."[57]

Finally, the current climate in Latin America has made basic ecclesial communities a necessity as the Church addresses various forms of injustices. These base communities have found themselves caught between the oppression of the colonial past and the oppressive structures of modern economic and political systems. The base communities also have struggled against the national military and oligarchic power structures of their countries and concurrently have denounced the international invasions of capital, corporations, and culture that continue and even worsen the enslavement of the poor. "In several countries the historical phase of repression acted as a profoundly pedagogical element,

55. Ibid., 637.
56. Ibid., 642.
57. Ibid.

though a painful one, with a double dimension of conscientization: on the one hand a maturation of a realistic church in solidarity with the least and poorest; on the other, evidence of a situation of social injustice that cries out to heaven, and an increasingly clear identification of the causes and processes that produce that injustice."[58]

VIRGILIO ELIZONDO: CHARACTERISTIC TOPICS

Readers of the writings of Virgilio Elizondo soon come to recognize the recurrence of a number of topics. Three that are particularly important are the Spanish conquest in the sixteenth century, the historical and theological importance of Galilee, and Our Lady of Guadalupe.

The Sixteenth Century Spanish Conquest

Much of Virgilio Elizondo's understanding of the current situation of Mexicans and Mexican Americans is derived from the beginnings of the *mestizo* people: the sixteenth century conquest of the Americas by the Spanish. Although Elizondo highlights some of the benefits of this exchange—for example, the Spanish missioners came with genuine hope for a new beginning of Christianity—much of this encounter is viewed as a physical, psychological, emotional, and spiritual massacre. It is from this deprivation that the identity of the *mestizo* people and the importance of *Nuestra Señora de Guadalupe* are derived. Commenting on the re-presentation of these historical events, Matthew Restall states: "In presenting historical interpretations of the Conquest as myths rooted in the cultural conceptions, misconceptions, and political agendas of their time, I am aware that I too am inescapably influenced by the concepts and language of my own culture."[59] Likewise, Elizondo's investigation of the sixteenth century Spanish encounter is reread through his own *mestizaje* and his devotion to *Nuestra Señora*.

Often, the story of the conquest of the Americas is told in terms of the Spaniards' superiority over the native people. Superiority during the sixteenth century encounter has customarily been defined in terms of weaponry, health, language, and culture, and in religious terminology. Without specifically distinguishing how these elements of superiority

58. Ibid., 643.
59. Restall, *Seven Myths*, xvi.

came together during the conquest, the Spaniards are characterized as being superior in all aspects of life. This belief of superiority translates to the capability to conquer the native population with ease. However, recent studies of the conquest of the New World are re-examining the traditional understanding of Spanish dominance. The rereading of this historical period, reinterpreting the evangelization of the native people by the missioners and the onslaught of the foreigners in every aspect of life, still needs further investigation for a better understanding of the indigenous culture and that of their Iberian conquerors.

In regard to evangelization, for example, there was accommodation: "The conscious decision made by the Church, formally enunciated at the First Mexican Provincial Council of 1555 but in practice earlier, was that evangelization should be carried out in the native languages. That missionary and Indian literally did not speak the same language is obvious. The problem, however, was not to translate words but concepts, to bridge the cognitive gap that separated the two cultures."[60] Simultaneously, the conquest resulted in annihilation:

> Conquest comes through military force and is motivated by economic reasons. Yet, once it has taken place, conquest is totalitarian. It imposes not only the institutions of the powerful, but also a new worldview in conflict with the existing one. This imposition disrupts the worldview of the conquered in such a way that nothing makes sense anymore. In many ways, the ideas, the logic, the wisdom, the art, the customs, the language, and even the religion of the powerful are forced into the life of the conquered . . . Yet there is not only the obvious violence of the physical conquest, but the deeper violence of the disruption and attempts to destroy the conquered's inner worldview which gives cohesion and meaning to existence.[61]

Granted that there are differing historical interpretations of the conquest of the New World, there is general agreement about Spanish dominance over the native populations. Nonetheless, historians and theologians are still discussing precisely how this "victory" came about since both secular and religious personnel were involved in the New World. "As a result, a set of interrelated perspectives soon developed into a fairly coherent vision and interpretation of the Conquest—the

60. Poole, "Some Observations," 339.

61. Elizondo, "*Mestizaje* as a Locus," 161.

sum of Spanish conquest activity in the Americas from 1492 to about 1700. While many aspects of the Conquest and its interpretation have long been debated—from the arguments of sixteenth century Spanish ecclesiastics to those of professional historians today—most of the fundamental characteristics of that vision, and a surprising number of its details, have survived."[62] The once-standard view of Spanish dominance is now viewed as a series of various factors coming together in the conquest of the Americas.

In *Seven Myths of the Spanish Conquest*, Restall is keenly aware of the "mythistory" that "seamlessly blends mythic and historical components into one epic narrative".[63] "The term "myth" is used here not in the sense of folklore, of popular narratives and beliefs featuring religious systems and supernatural characters. Rather it is used to mean something fictitious that is commonly taken to be true, partially or absolutely. Both of these meanings of "myth" have an ambiguous connection to "history"."[64] This "mythistory" has profound implications of how history is to be interpreted. Rather than debunking "mythistory," historians and theologians need to use it in order to come to a meaningful understanding of the sixteenth century Americas.

Some of the myths include: the conquest by a few influential men rather than a few hundred Spaniards aided by native armies; language barriers creating miscommunication between the conflicting parties; and the claim that the conquest reduced the natives to an absolute state of nothingness. In particular, the myth of Spanish superiority, which is attributed to all facets of European dominance, must be considered in light of the factors that produced "a perfect storm" which allowed the Spanish to conquer the Americas. Thus, for Restall, the ultimate myth is European dominance and superiority in all aspects of life upon the Spanish arrival in the New World.

According to Restall, the perfect storm came about through natural and existing factors that allowed the Spanish to conquer the New World with ease. First of all, the Spanish conquistadores had many allies during their conquest. One of these allies, largely unrecognized, was disease. Another ally, already present in the New World, was the disunity between various native groups: "The Mexica capital fell not by

62. Restall, *Seven Myths*, xv.

63. Ibid., xvii.

64. Ibid., vxi.

the force of Spanish arms, but to disease and plague. The siege of the island city cut off food supplies, but as starvation approached, defenders succumbed to plague or disease. Smallpox seems to have been the prime culprit. As Spaniards and their Nahua allies moved through the devastated city, they found pile after pile of corpses, and huddled groups of the dying, covered with telltale pustules."[65] Along with disease and divisions among indigenous groups, Spanish weaponry added to the perfect storm. However, guns, horses, and war dogs were not the overwhelming factor in the conquest; rather, the steel sword made the most difference since it provided a real advantage in close combat situations. "The one weapon, then, whose efficacy is indubitable, was the steel sword. It was worth more than a horse, a gun, and a mastiff put together. Because a steel sword was longer and less brittle than the obsidian weapons of Mesoamerican warriors, and longer and sharper than Andean clubbing weapons or copper-tipped axes, a Spaniard could fight for hours and receive light flesh wounds and bruises while killing many natives. Spanish swords were just the right length for reaching an enemy who lacked a similar weapon."[66]

In addition to disease, native disunity, and the steel sword, Restall posits two additional factors that sealed the fate of the native peoples against their Spanish conquerors—the final pieces to the perfect storm. First, the Amerindians adhered to a culture of war where ceremonial rituals preceded and accompanied battles; thus, there were no surprise encounters, since battles were announced by rituals prior to the conflict. The Spanish conquistadors had no such announcements of war nor did they respect the rituals the natives performed prior to combat, rituals which emphasized the fact that the indigenous people had much more to lose since the fight was on their home turf. "[N]ative Americans stood to lose their families and their homes and were thus quicker to compromise, to accommodate the invaders, to seek ways to avoid full-scale or protracted wars."[67] With family and other territorial concerns preoccupying native warriors, the Spanish invaders had a psychological advantage in battle.

On the other hand, the Spanish mindset was swayed by a desire for expansion found not only on the European continent, but also within

65. Ibid., 141.
66. Ibid., 143.
67. Ibid., 144.

most civilizations at that time. Much larger than just a Spanish outlook, this viewpoint encompassed the entire world as differing civilizations found themselves in an age of empire building and warding off foreigners with differing religious and world perspectives.[68] "This larger story is not one of Spanish superiority, or even Western European superiority, but is instead a complex phenomenon in world history that transcends the particulars of the Spanish Conquest in the Americas . . . But the age of expansion began with the rise of empires outside Europe, with the Mexica fanning out across Mesoamerica and the Inca dominating the Andes, and in West Africa with the rising of the Songhay empire from the ashes of that of Mali. In Europe, the Ottomans and the Muscovites began empire building before the Spaniards, as did the Portuguese—who beat their Iberian neighbors in the race for a sea route to East Asia."[69] Thus, the Spanish conquest of the Americas came about through natural and existing factors creating a perfect storm from which the natives could not recover. Through the elements of disease, native disunity, the steel sword, and the European and native mindsets of their encounter, the Spanish conquistadors embarked on a conquest in the New World, with an attitude similar to that which had motivated them in their conquest of the last Moorish kingdom in Spain in 1492.

The Historical and Theological Implications of Galilee

Virgilio Elizondo's doctoral dissertation, which focused on the region of Galilee and its significance in the life and ministry of Jesus, was both simple and profound. Simple—in the sense that what Elizondo uncovered regarding the *mestizo*-type existence of Galilee was obvious in many ways. It was a diamond in the rough others had simply overlooked, and thus no one had made any present-day connections until Elizondo's groundbreaking efforts connecting the *mestizaje* in the region of Galilee with the *mesitzaje* found in the Southwestern United States. Profound—in the sense that this simple finding regarding the cultural, social, and biological, complexity of Galilee would impact the outlook of many Mexicans, Mexican Americans, and Christians in general. The existence of the profound within the simple is a further instance of Elizondo's overall theme that the particular reveals the universal.

68. Ibid., 145.
69. Ibid.

Even with this important insight that propelled the development of Hispanic/Latino theology, Elizondo's biblical and theological extrapolations from his reading of Galilee are not without detractors both within and outside the Hispanic community. Comments regarding his groundbreaking work range from accurate scriptural portrayals to anachronistic identification between Mexican Americans and Galileans. According to Jeffrey Siker, issues abound when "racializing" Jesus and making interconnections between historical reconstructions and theological reflections.

> The racializing of Jesus points to a fundamental problem for contemporary Christian theology. The Christian claim that God became incarnate in a particular human being at a specific time in human history, the belief that God is not only utterly transcendent but also was embodied in the flesh-and-blood particularity of Jesus, inevitably gives rise to the attempt of each particular human group to show, implicitly or explicitly, how their distinctive group markers can be associated with the particularity of Jesus. Not only are they like Jesus, Jesus is like them. Each group has a self-interest, and understandably so, of not only imaging Jesus, and hence the divine, after their own image and in their own likeness. Humans may have been created in the image of God, but ever since then God has been created and recreated in the diverse images of humans, with Jesus as the focus of these incarnations within Christian tradition[70]

In addition, because Elizondo's work shifts the focus away from Jewish elitism to those who are marginalized, some have questioned Elizondo's attitude towards Judiasm as a whole and even have gone so far as to call his work anti-Semitic. In response to these critiques, Elizondo has taken these opportunities to clarify *mestizo* theology and to discuss the region of Galilee.

In his analysis of Elizondo's *mestizo* Christ, Siker first characterizes the historical reconstruction of first century Galilean Judaism in terms of *mestizaje* as problematic: ". . . perhaps most striking, is that Elizondo's historical claims about Galilee and Jesus are made without substantive foundation . . . Elizondo goes out of his way to stress the importance of the historicity of Jesus as a mestizo Galilean, but does virtually nothing to demonstrate his claim beyond generic assertion."[71] In addition, rather

---

70. Siker, "Historicizing a Racialized Jesus," 27.

71. Ibid., 38–39.

than tracing a development forward, appropriating the Galilean Jesus to the modern day notion of the *mestizo* Christ, Siker claims that Elizondo is doing exactly the opposite. "Elizondo does not map the historical Jesus onto the modern mestizo so much as he maps the modern mestizo onto the historical Jesus. This anachronistic rendering of first-century Galilee in the image of the borderlands of the American southwest can undergird Elizondo's theological project only if he is willing to advocate what increasingly appears to be an historical fiction, Galilee as the land of *mestizaje*."[72]

Another problem in Elizondo's *mestizo* theology is his attitude toward Judaism. Because the Galilean Journey is a movement to Jerusalem that challenges the centralist and elitist positions of so-called pure Jews in contrast to Jews living in Galilee, some find Elizondo's Galilean movement to be anti-Semitic: "Elizondo sets up Judaism in powerful and urban Jerusalem as a false, rigid, hollow shell of the true spirit of Judaism, again with Jesus as the primary figure to lead his disciples against the power structures of the corrupt Judaism of Jerusalem."[73] "[Elizondo] may have unintentionally incorporated anti-Semitic aspects of German scholarship on the historical Jesus and early Christianity."[74] Finally, the stress on *mestizaje* both in the past and today have led some to criticize the implication that only through the creation of a new race, exemplified in Mexican Americans, can we understand our true identities: "The denigrating description of mestizos as 'half-breed' becomes for Elizondo a badge of honor that communicates mestizos as 'most fully human' because though rejected by society they have been chosen by God."[75] "[T]he biggest problem is Elizondo's determination to draw such bold connections between *Galilean mestizaje* and *mestizaje* in the American

---

72. Ibid., 41.

73. Ibid., 43. In addition, some have noted the limited scriptural footnotes in his foundational work and criticized the sources for his Galilean *mestizaje*. Elizondo cites Ernst Lohmeyer, *Galiläa und Jerusalem*, and Walter Grundmann, *Jesus der Galiläer und das Judentum*, as scriptural references for his understanding of the *mestizo* situation of Galilee. However, Lohmeyer's eschatology claiming Galilee as universalistic and Jerusalem as nationalistic is unfounded especially in its application in the Galilean Principle and the Jerusalem Principle of Elizondo's *Galilean Journey*; Grundmann is also problematic since his Christological motifs are traced to Aryan origins; see Jean-Pierre Ruiz, "Good Fences and Good Neighbors? Biblical Scholars and Theologians."

74. Lassalle-Klein, "Guest Editorial/Introduction," 259.

75. Siker, "Historicizing a Racialized Jesus," 46.

Southwest as something more than a metaphorical connection, indeed as an historical connection. This is a move that Elizondo does not need to make in order for his analysis and description of modern *mestizaje* to stand quite well on its own. Elizondo has unfortunately tied his good analysis of contemporary mestizo existence in the American Southwest to the millstone of a parallel first-century Galilean world that most likely did not exist."[76]

Besides the critique of *mestizo* theology outside the Hispanic/Latino community, questions within the *mestizo* community have also arisen. Jean-Pierre Ruiz has pointed out the deepening chasm between biblical scholars and commented on the inaccurate scriptural portrayal by theologians, especially by Elizondo. Others within the Hispanic community have commented on Elizondo's "non-scriptural" approach:

> In using the Bible as a source for his theological system, Elizondo is not interested in biblical exegesis per se. As a matter of fact, he does little or no exegesis in his writings . . . For Elizondo the Bible, in general, and the Gospels, in particular, are "transparent"; that is, they are a window through which we can access Jesus' historical praxis. This explains Elizondo's fondness of the Synoptic Gospels, his apparent disregard of the Johannine Jesus, and the little attention paid to exegetical methods. For him the Bible is the document that faithfully records the ministry of Jesus the Galilean."[77]

As Ruiz reminds us, given the interrelatedness between exegetes and theologians, respectful interactions are needed. After all, "[e]xegesis has never been *just* exegesis pure and simple."[78] The truth of the matter is that every scriptural exegete must engage in some form of theological reflection and theologians must engage scripture for their reflection. As Ruiz rightly states: "Responsible biblical scholarship and responsible theological research call for—and call each other to—transparency and accountability. Rather than accepting at face-value—and often at second or third hand—the claims of biblical scholarship, systematic theologians who turn to the Bible as the "soul of theology" would do well to bear in

---

76. Ibid., 47.

77. Jiménez, "In Search of a Hispanic Model," 45.

78. Ruiz, "Good Fences and Good Neighbors."

mind the contextuality of all discourses as they read the discourses of biblical scholarship with a measure of care and caution."[79]

In light of these comments from both within and outside the Hispanic/Latino community, Elizondo has honed his understanding of *mestizo* theology. Accordingly, Elizondo has taken these opportunities to make *mestizo* theology relevant for all humanity by asking: "So, even for those who criticize me, I would pose the question, what for you is the theological meaning of Galilee? . . . Why do you have to be at Galilee to see Jesus? So, what is redemptive about Galilee?"[80] Interestingly, Ruiz's comments regarding Elizondo's haphazard use of scripture for his *mestizo* Galilean portrayal raised enough interest in Elizondo's work that it eventually lead to his receiving the John Courtney Murray Award of the Catholic Theological Society of America in 2007.

Expounding on his previous works, Elizondo in an essay in *Theological Studies* in 2009 further develops *mestizo* theology. Christologically, Elizondo emphasizes the Jewishness of Jesus, rather than a messianic figure that is anti-Jewish, by portraying Jesus of Galilee as a faithful Jew, calling upon his Jewish brothers and sisters in Jerusalem to be mindful of the marginalized in society especially in Galilee.[81] "The question pressed itself: Why is Jesus' ethnic identity as a Jewish Galilean from Nazareth an important dimension of the incarnation, and what does it disclose about the beauty and originality of Jesus' liberating life and message."[82] In regard to the historical interpretation of the region of Galilee, Elizondo emphasizes the *mestizo*-type situation of the region since Galilee was the borderland between the Roman Empire and the Jewish world.[83] Naturally, this encounter allowed for a *mestizo*-type interaction to occur culturally, socially and biologically. Elizondo's claim of the Galilean Jesus as a *mestizo*-type person includes all three areas of culture, society, and genetics. Regardless of Jesus' earthly biological heritage, Elizondo's claim of the *mestizo*-like person in the figure of Jesus is not limited to human terms and is further defined by the commingling of his humanity and divinity. "You want to be careful with doctrine. That's why I use "appears" or "functions as" rather than saying "he

79. Ibid.
80. See Appendix A.
81. Elizondo, "Jesus the Galilean Jew," 270 and 273.
82. Ibid., 270.
83. Ibid., 271–72.

was" . . . that is why I said Jesus certainly culturally would have been considered a *mestizo* because of his encounters. But I try to stay away from saying biologically he was, although in reality he was, because if it is about a mixed race, there is nothing more diverse than the divine and the human race."[84]

"For me, however, the point of departure has been the question described above: What was the theological significance of Jewish Galilee and its Gentile surroundings for the Gospel writers and early Christians?"[85]

Broadening the identification of the Galilean Jesus with the Mexican American people, Elizondo sees the identification of the Galilean Jesus with all those who are excluded and marginalized. "I think being a Galilean he was marginalized. Being a Galilean, he would be in constant contact with other. The constant contact with others would function as a *mestizo* society."[86] The Mexican American experience has allowed Elizondo to experience his own exclusion and marginalization, thereby allowing him to identify more closely with the historical Jesus of two thousand years ago. However, this experience does not prevent Elizondo from seeing the natural progression of a globalized world becoming more and more *mestizo* in non-violent ways as encounters between people increase. Even with this natural evolution through the encounter of others, exclusion, and marginalization continue in society. Thus, the need to connect the present situation with the past as illustrated in Elizondo's work of bringing identity and hope to those excluded and marginalized becomes increasingly more important on this global stage. *Mestizo* theology is then a way of theologizing for all people, for all situations, as cultures continue to encounter one another. "Eliminating the boundaries or blurring the boundaries—that to me is the Kingdom of God—when you constantly ease the boundaries that keep us apart. It is not a "super race," but a more inclusive expression of humanity. A *mestizo* child is not something "super," but is something new from the parents."[87]

---

84. See Appendix A.

85. Ibid.

86. Ibid.

87. Ibid.

Our Lady of Guadalupe

Virgilio Elizondo's lifelong reflections about Our Lady of Guadalupe have not only afforded Mexicans and Mexican Americans the opportunity to recapture their identity through the beauty and richness of the sixteenth century apparition, but also have allowed those outside of the culture and tradition to discover an intricate and beautiful aspect of the Catholic faith as well as of our humanity. By exploring the theological meaning of Mary beyond traditional Marian categories (e.g. *Theotokos*, Immaculate Conception, Assumption, etc.), Elizondo and others seek to make Guadalupe relevant to the present by examining "the Guadalupe image, apparitions account, and its historical context as a means of exploring the collision of civilizations between the Old and New Worlds and the ongoing implications of this clash for Christianity in the Americas and beyond."[88]

Nevertheless, Elizondo's interpretation of *Nuestra Señora de Guadalupe* does not exhaust the revelation found within the *mestiza* Madonna. In fact, as Elizondo's good friend and colleague, Timothy Matovina, points out, there are many interpretations of Guadalupe throughout different periods of history. Of particular note are the colonial and nationalistic interpretations that predate new perspectives that arose after the Second Vatican Council.

> In sharp contrast with the colonial and nationalistic interpretations of previous centuries, these contemporary analyses do not conclude that Guadalupe sought to obliterate all indigenous traditions, nor that she formed a covenant relationship with Mexico parallel to the biblical covenant between Yahweh and Israel. Rather, they look at Guadalupe's love and respect for the conquered indigenous peoples and, by extension, her compassion for the downtrodden in other times and places. The tendency to concentrate on the *Nican mopohua* in theological studies of Guadalupe reflects a wider trend among scholars to accentuate the indigenous origins of Mexican culture and traditions.[89]

Elizondo's reflections, especially in *Guadalupe: Mother of the New Creation,* are indicative of the new Guadalupan perspective following Vatican II where pastoral theologians have interpreted the sixteenth century event in modern-day terminology. Even Pope John Paul II, "whose

88. Matovina, "Theologies of Guadalupe," 62.
89. Ibid., 78–79.

ardent Marian and Guadalupan piety led him to make more theological pronouncements on Guadalupe than any other pope"[90] utilized *la Virgen* to emphasize the connection between the local and universal elements of evangelization especially in the Americas. "John Paul's emphasis on Guadalupe's evangelizing role first in Mexico and subsequently in the wider American hemisphere reflects the tension between the particular and the universal in Guadalupan theologies, and indeed in theology and religious traditions more generally."[91] However, this perspective which relates the local and universal dimensions of Guadalupe, is only one of many interpretations that Matovina illustrates throughout history. "Contemporary scholars offer a range of insights on the criteria for assessing the liberationist endorsement of living Guadalupe's message in a way that uplifts the poor and marginalized, the feminist insistence that Guadalupe be engaged in a manner that affirms the full humanity of women, the doctrinal measure of an interpretation's faithfulness to Catholic teaching and tradition, and the *sensus fidelium* criterion that perspectives on Guadalupe be consistent with the core conviction of the past and present Guadalupan devotees."[92]

Prior to the Second Vatican Council, the events at Tepeyac were interpreted in nationalistic or colonial terms. Beginning with Juan Diego and the *Nahua* people, *Nuestra Señora de Guadalupe's* significance is derived from their cultural heritage. In particular, the encounter between Juan Diego and Our Lady at Tepeyac was narrated in *Nahuatl* in the *Nican mophua*. Thus, the initial reception of the Guadalupan message was received within a specific context and culture of the indigenous people. With the widespread embrace of the *mestiza morena* throughout Mexico, Europeans in the New World took liberties in interpreting the Guadalupe event to include their own existence in the New World. Utilizing Scriptural interpretations and European traditions, priests in Mexico City during the seventeenth century interpreted the Guadalupe events in well-known Scriptural and devotional language for the purpose of communicating the Guadalupan story as an ongoing cosmic battle over the souls of Mexico.[93] "And just as Elizabeth expressed her joy

90. Ibid., 86.

91. Ibid., 88.

92. Ibid., 90.

93. The most notable of the clergy in Mexico City who developed the Guadalupe theme beyond the *Nican mopohua* were Miguel Sánchez and Luis Laso de la Vega in

that Mary had come to her, so too the faithful of the New World respond to Guadalupe through their prayers, processions, writings, orations, dedication of Churches and altars, and now through offering the Mass, divine office, and official title patroness of New Spain which Benedict XIV providentially designated to her."[94]

During the nineteenth century, Guadalupan theology shifted the colonial mindset and its use of traditional biblical and devotional imagery of the sixteenth century to nationalistic interpretations praising people of a *mestizo* heritage. For example, "Guadalupe's preference of the indigenous neophyte Juan Diego as her chosen messenger and her speaking with him in his native tongue provided an example for just treatment of the indigenous people."[95] This nationalistic mindset regarding the Guadalupe event continued through the turn of the twentieth century especially during the Mexican Revolution. During this period, Our Lady of Guadalupe was hailed as the patroness of Mexico, who would bring about peace during this tumultuous period. "The call for Guadalupe to be recognized as patroness of the hemisphere and the ongoing echoes of previous Guadalupan theological themes notwithstanding, the extensive focus on Guadalupe's covenant relationship with the Mexican nation had clearly displaced an earlier emphasis on assessing Guadalupe's meaning within the context of biblical, patristic, and other theological sources."[96]

Thus, Guadalupan interpretations have varied over the years beginning with her first message to Juan Diego at Tepeyac. To devotees of Our Lady of Guadalupe from different generations and various historical circumstances—especially in regard to to their self-perceived identity as Catholics and as human beings—*Nuestra Señora* has been at the service

---

the seventeenth century; see: Miguel Sánchez, *Imagen de la Virgen María* (Mexico City: Viuda de Bernardo Calderón, 1648), reprinted in *Testimonios históricos Guadalupanos*, edited by Ernesto de la Torre Villar and Ramiro Navarro de Anda (Mexico City: Fondo de Cultura Económica, 1982) and Luis Laso de la Vega, *Huei tlamahuiçoltica omonexiti ilhuicac tlatocaçihuapilli Santa Maria totlaçonantzin Guadalupe in nican huei altepena-huac Mexico itocayocan Tepeyacac* (*By a Great Miracle Appeared the Heavenly Queen, Saint Mary, Our Precious Mother of Guadalupe, Here Near the Great Altepetl of Mexico, at a Place Called Tepeyac*), reprinted as *The Story of Guadalupe: Luis Laso de la Vega's Huei tlamahuiçoltica of 1649*, edited by Sousa, Poole, and Lockhart.

94. Matovina, "Theologies of Guadalupe," 73.

95. Ibid., 76.

96. Ibid., 77.

of people, helping them regain their dignity by connecting the present with the events of the past. These connections have allowed people to interpret the Guadalupe event of the sixteenth century as a meaningful symbol for the present. *Nuestra Señora de Guadalupe* continues to bring hope and dignity to her children throughout history. Thus, the work of theologians such as Virgilio Elizondo after the Second Vatican Council can be seen as a continuation of the tradition of making *la Virgen* relevant in the lives of those living in the Americas while at the same time unpacking the historical richness of the original encounter between Juan Diego and *Nuestra Señora*.

Although many share in the hope-filled message of Our Lady of Guadalupe, some deny the authenticity of the sixteenth century Marian apparition. Stafford Poole, a Vincentian priest, has criticized the uses of Guadalupe and Juan Diego within the Catholic faith tradition. Poole is uncomfortable with the lack of historical data validating the alleged communication between Juan Diego and *Nuestra Señora*. Mindful of the careful attention to detail the Spanish had in documenting their activities in the New World, Poole is concerned that there is no evidence of the Guadalupe event in either religious or secular documents at the supposed time of the apparitions. The historicity of Juan Diego's encounter is based on the *Nican mophua* which Poole claims is a later document and insufficient as historical data: "Though 1531 is the traditional date given for the apparitions, the story was first published in 1648 by Miguel Sánchez, a Mexican priest. His account came as a complete surprise to the people of Mexico City who had either never heard it before or believed that it had been forgotten in the course of time. Sánchez admitted that he had been unable to find any documentary evidence for his account. This has been a great stumbling block for Guadalupe."[97] Poole emphasizes that if the sixteenth century events of Guadalupe at Tepeyac were real, then Bishop-elect Fray Juan de Zumárraga and his household would have documented the events, especially in light of such miraculous conversions.

In addition, there were controversies about Juan Diego's canonization. Without historically accurate documentation passing through the proper channels in Rome, Poole is suspicious of the whole process; as a historian, Poole finds little evidence of the existence of Juan Diego.

97. Poole, "Did Juan Diego Exist?," 9.

From the beginning the process was under the control of its sponsors and advocates, with the congregation playing a reactive role. At no time were opponents of the process invited to join in the proceedings nor were their opinions sought. None of the persons who led the cause were historians or had historical train-ing. All the historians who were consulted by the Congregation for the Causes of the Saints were from Roman universities. The consultors were willing to accept the most dubious evidence, with special reliance on the Codex Escalada and incorrect dating and authorship for the *Nican mophua*. Finally, there is the fact that the 1982 report on the image which showed it to be a work of human hands that had not been miraculously preserved over the centuries was totally ignored.[98]

Poole's disagreements with theologians who extol the virtues of Guadalupe is not a theological matter; as a historian, he is concerned with the way historical data are represented to support modern day beliefs. Historical accuracy concerns Poole, who sees the discussion re-garding Our Lady of Guadalupe lacking any academic merit.

In sum, on the one hand, not everyone agrees with Elizondo's un-derstanding of the *la morena* and how the events of the past relate with the events of today. On the other hand, not everyone agrees with Poole's position, which insists on historical evidence for theological investiga-tions. Although debate continues over the historical data and represen-tation of *Nuestra Señora de Guadalupe* and Juan Diego, what cannot be denied are the millions of faithful who consider her their Mother.

GUSTAVO GUTIÉRREZ: CHARACTERISTIC TOPICS

Readers of Gustavo Gutiérrez's writings soon come to recognize the re-currence of a number of topics. Four that are particularly important are the distinction of planes, Bartolomé de Las Casas, scriptural interpreta-tion, and theological interpretation. In the four corresponding sections below, the first two consider specific issues in Gutiérrez's writings that have been raised by others. The latter two consider general concerns fac-ing liberation theologians about which I will offer my assessment of how Gutiérrez would respond to these issues.

98. Poole, "History Versus Juan Diego," 12.

The Distinction of Planes: A Dialogue with Joseph Ratzinger

During the 1980s, there were many debates regarding the orthodoxy of liberation theology, in particular, its use of Marxist analysis. Pope Benedict XVI, then Cardinal Joseph Ratzinger, as the Prefect of the Congregation for the Doctrine of the Faith, published two documents, *Libertatis nuntius* (1984) and *Libertatis conscientia* (1986), which detailed the Vatican's concerns regarding liberation theology in Latin America. In turn, Gutiérrez published his personal thoughts, emphasizing how criticisms such as those of Ratzinger, have deepened over the years, and as painful as those were, have helped liberation theology to clarify certain positions.[99]

Particularly noteworthy are the similarities and differences between Ratzinger and Gutiérrez on the distinction of planes. According to James Corkery, both theologians are in agreement about maintaining the "distinction of planes" as a "distinction but not separation."[100] However, the two theologians do not stress the same aspects of the distinction of planes. Ratzinger holds the "distinction but not separation" model but emphasizes the "distinctness" between worldly progress and growth of the Kingdom of God. For Corkery, Ratzinger is consistent on this point throughout his writings, while never denying that there is a link between politics and theology: "His real concern is simply to counter an approach that he sees as virtually identifying the two. For to identify them is to make the Kingdom of God into a political reality, into something that results from human activity—in other words, into something "makeable"."[101] Within this *machbar* ("makeable") perspective, salvation would be a product of human activity and Ratzinger fears that the liberationist approach of identifying the world too closely with the Kingdom of God would undermine the "gift-character" and the transcendence of salvation. Although the two theologians maintain the same axiom, a difference is present that may seem subtle at first, but becomes a focal point in the whole discussion of liberation theology.

For Gutiérrez, the model of "distinction but not separation" is applicable because the world and the Kingdom of God are not identical since the Kingdom encompasses the fuller measure of salvation than

99. Gutiérrez, "Criticism Will Deepen," 2–7.

100. Corkery, *Human Existence and Christian Salvation*, 208.

101. Ibid., 201.

the world. "His [Gutiérrez] basic position is that, while the former [the world] can never be said to be all of the latter [the Kingdom of God], neither can it be said not to be the latter. But 'this is not an identification' of the two, he insists; the coming of the Kingdom remains 'above all a gift.'"[102] Thus, while maintaining both spheres, Gutiérrez insists that the theological evolution of the nature-grace debate supports a unified outlook rather than the dualistic perspective of the past. "The temporal-spiritual and profane-sacred antitheses are based on the natural-supernatural distinction. But the theological evolution of this last term has tended to stress the unity which eliminates all dualism."[103]

Even with this distinction, Ratzinger still feels that Gutiérrez is creating a system which fuses too closely the temporal reality with that of the Kingdom of God. No matter how the distinction is made in Gutiérrez's scheme, Ratzinger finds the two realities becoming incorporated in the end. In *Politik und Erlösung*,[104] Ratzinger asserts the similarities of the theological and the political thought in Gutierrez's approach: "theology and politics are not entirely congruent; each has its own range, with which it extends beyond the sphere of the other; but in a very comprehensive core area they are one and the same."[105] In sum, Ratzinger maintains the need to distinguish the world and the Kingdom of God: one can still distinguish between the spheres without being dualistic.

Thus, the theological difference between Ratzinger and Gutiérrez relates to where they place their emphasis. Both theologians subscribe to the "distinction but not separation" of our earthly activity and heavenly gift. However, the emphasis either on the "distinction" or on the "not separation" is what differs in the two theologians' approach. On the one hand, Gutiérrez maintains he is not making the two planes identical while emphasizing the unity of the model. On the other hand, Ratzinger maintains the distinctness of the model without becoming dualistic or sacrificing the unity of the planes. In the end, the differences in their position are over which aspect of the distinction of planes should be emphasized, the "distinction" or the "not separation."

102. Ibid., 190.

103. Gutiérrez, *Theology of Liberation*, 43.

104. Ratzinger, *Politik und Erlösung*.

105. Ibid., 192, German text translated by James Corkery.

Bartolomé de Las Casas

A central figure who defended the rights of the indigenous during the sixteenth century Spanish conquest, Bartolomé de Las Casas is frequently referenced as a model of evangelical missionary service. Theologians from Gutiérrez to Ratzinger have appealed to Las Casas to illustrate their theological and historical understanding of the New World. On the one hand, theologians such as Gutiérrez see Las Casas as a model defending the rights of the indigenous as his primary concern in spreading the Gospel. On the other hand, theologians such as Ratzinger see Las Casas as a prophetic voice for consciousness and conversion.[106] Although never formally canonized by the Church, Las Casas is still a saintly figure whose perspective on the New World is exemplary, especially with regard to his steadfast promotion of the dignity of indigenous peoples. Las Casas presents a universal model of missionary servanthood, upheld by many regardless of historical or theological interpretation and biases.

Seeing Las Casas as a model of prophetic conscience in missionary activities, Ratzinger emphasizes the missioner's own conversion as the key to such modeling. "Alongside the suffering conscience he represents the prophetic conscience which shakes the power of the powerful, which raises the rights of those deprived of their rights, places himself calmly between the thrones and does not cease to disturb the rest of those whose power is at the expense of the rights of others."[107] From his ambivalent beginnings in the New World as a soldier and *encomendero*, Las Casas underwent a conversion through his firsthand experience of the mistreatment of the indigenous population and the prophetic preaching about the oppressive situation by his brother Dominicans. Accordingly, Ratzinger finds in Las Casas a struggle of conscience that brings about conversion and justice: "From then on Las Casas becomes the guilty conscience of the powerful, hated, cursed, but no longer to be brought to silence."[108] This conversion of conscience reached its culmination in Las Casas' installation as a bishop in Mexico. For Ratzinger, the transformation of Las Casas while patiently enduring the injustices of the New World illustrates the power of conscience in its proper conversion by the prophetic challenges surrounding it. Ratzinger speaks of this suffering

---

106. Ratzinger, *Church, Ecumenism and Politics*, 176.

107. Ibid.

108. Ibid., 177.

in a positive light: "Only power that comes out of suffering can be power for healing and salvation; power shows its greatness in the renunciation of power."[109]

However, few others in the Church received favorably these references to Las Casas and his missionary efforts on behalf of the native population as a contemporary rationale for liberation theology. By presenting the hostile reactions to Gutiérrez's nearly seven hundred-page tome on Las Casas, Christian Smith raises two important issues. First, Smith acknowledges that some claim the demise of liberation theology and suggests the appeal to Las Casas is a retreat to the past rather than accepting the failure of liberation theology: "The 1993 publication of Gustavo Gutiérrez's *Las Casas: In Search of the Poor of Jesus Christ* merely confirmed, for many, the impression of liberation theology's demise. This massive 682-page tome by the movement's leading light is not a step forward, but backward. *Las Casas* is a retreat to the past, a defensive move . . . Gutiérrez is leading his readers to hunker down and keep hope alive by tapping into the continuity and stability of history, by taking solace in a great hero of days gone by."[110] In addition, Smith suspects that the timing of the 1993 publishing is in response to Roman authorities and theological opponents who criticized liberation theology throughout the eighties.

> *Las Casas*, it seems to me, is not most plausibly read as a defensive retreat to the comfort of the past. Rather, *Las Casas* is best read as a strategically *offensive* move that challenges Rome—indeed, the entire Catholic Church—with the imperative to reconstruct the very essentials of Christian systematic theology . . . With *Las Casas*, Gutiérrez appears to be saying that, not only is liberation theology *not* collapsing, but that it is actually prepared to continue to challenge, on more secure grounds than ever, the very logic and content of existing, established Church doctrine; that theology still does, in fact, need to be radically reconstructed from the perspective and experience of the poor, the exploited, the marginal.[111]

Smith does not hide his interests for Gutiérrez, liberation theology, and appeals to figures of the past such as Las Casas for contemporary

109. Ibid., 178.

110. Smith, "*Las Casas* as Theological Counteroffensive," 69.

111. Ibid., 69–70.

claims. His concern is twofold: first, the attempt of liberation theologians to reinvent systematic theology as a whole. By appealing to Las Casas, Smith claims that Gutiérrez is laying a foundation for systematic theology that "if one begins with the basic, inescapable Gospel commitments to love and to work for the salvation of one's neighbor, and if one then experiences firsthand the unjust slaughter of the poor by a brutal social system, and if one *then* discovers that the Church's established theology is actively legitimating this lethal social system, then one will have *no option* but to modify radically that theology so that it promotes, rather than violates, the Gospel imperatives of love and evangelization."[112] Smith believes that if one subscribes to Gutiérrez's theological reflection, then systematic theology will have to be reconstructed, rather than simply amended to include the elements of justice and liberation advocated by liberation theology. This belief stems from Gutiérrez's overall work advocating a theology of liberation as a new way of doing theology because a new context raises questions different from those of the recent past.

Smith's second concern about liberation theology is its reinvention after the fall of communism, which signaled the end of the contemporary understanding of Marxism and with it the failures of dependency theory upon which it relied. Although Gutiérrez distinguishes the two in his writings, Marxism and dependency theory, Smith emphasizes their interconnectedness in the theological reflections of liberation theology. In contrast, Gutiérrez rejected dependency theory as failing to address the situation of poverty in Latin America, thus leading to the advent of a theology of liberation. For Smith, liberation theology's attempt to reinvent itself without any Marxist influence is an effort to cleverly represent liberation theology as "user-friendly". "It is just working with the basic Gospel message and the unmerciful facts of life learned through lived experience in Latin America . . . But the regrounding of liberation theology on a foundation absent of Marxism and dependency theory represents only part of the book's clever counteroffensive strategy. The larger strategic and political brilliance of *Las Casas* resides in the fact that Gutiérrez allows the historical figure of Bartolomé de Las Casas to stand for and speak the truth that, really, he wants to and is also speaking."[113]

---

112. Ibid., 70.
113. Ibid.

Rather than seeing a process of maturation, some do not acknowledge the efforts of Gutiérrez and other liberation theologians to dialogue with Roman authorities, European theologians and each other in order to refine liberation theology. The critiques of liberation theology mainly come at its inception and germinal stages. Outside observers do not see the constant refinement (through sometimes vicious attacks) as a maturation process, but simply see the error or the demise of liberation theology. However, for Gutiérrez in particular, liberation theology is constantly undergoing refinement since theology is always the second step, a reflection of the first step, prayer of contemplation and praxis.

Scriptural Interpretations in Liberation Theology

John Meier's "fraternal correction" of the use of scripture by Latin American theologians in their theological reflection provides further examples of criticisms of liberation theology.[114] Meier criticizes the claim of theologians of liberation that "Latin American communities replicate in their experience the first Christian communities that produced the Gospels. This is simply naiveté."[115] Similarly, Meier is critical of the indivisible connection that Latin American theologians have postulated between the poor in scripture and today's economic poor. According to Meier, poverty has a much broader definition for it includes characteristics such as humility and meekness: "I am not arguing here that the vocabulary of poverty had totally left its socioeconomic moorings; many of these people were economically poor. I am simply pointing out that the theological use of terms for the poor makes an analysis of the NT data more complex[.]"[116] After pointing out some of the deficiencies in the use of scripture by theologians in Latin America, Meier emphasizes—if they want to play the academic game, they must abide by its rules.

In response to Meier's presentation, Jon Nilson questions why historical criticism should be the overriding determining factor for Latin American theologians who reflect on their own situation. ". . . our Latin American colleagues are not likely to accept Meier's "fraternal

114. Meier, "Bible as a Source for Theology," 1–14. Although Meier's comments were directed at Jon Sobrino's use of scripture in his Christology, the same criticisms can be applied to many Latin American theologians who closely associate their reality of poverty with the situation of the Gospels.

115. Ibid., 7.

116. Ibid., 11–12.

correction" nor his proposal that they broaden their base beyond the historical Jesus. . . . They know only too well that dehistoricized Christs have been turned into idols which tolerate and even legitimate suffering in Latin America."[117] Unlike Meier, Nilson finds the use of biblical sources by Latin American theologians not as amateurish. Rather, Nilson is willing to dialogue with Latin American theologians to foster mutual growth by broadening each other's perspective. On the one hand, academicians would be introduced to the world of the poor and the need to historicize Christ in the midst of suffering. On the other hand, Latin American scholars would benefit by refining their identification of their situation with that of the Gospels.

Echoing similar concerns of fusing present day horizons with scripture, James Loader illustrates the interaction that takes place between the reader and the text. "So the simultaneity of the merging of horizons is not clear. The reader, in his own situational context, decides what the canon should be, and therefore which horizon should be merged with his own. This means that we move from our situation to the next, and only then allow the horizon of one canonical text to merge with the horizon of our situation. Therefore, the "situation" or the "us" . . . takes precedence over the text."[118] By giving priority to the circumstances of one's life, the biblical text is, at times, solely read through the hermeneutics of the present, the context of the reader.

Often cited for its liberative aspect, the Book of Exodus is an example of where contemporary instances of liberation become the interpretative lens for Latin American theologians. Reading scripture in this manner creates three difficulties according to Loader. First of all, the bible becomes redundant or simply performs a rhetorical function where the presuppositions of the reader force passages to conform. The liberative aspect of the kerygma becomes the hermeneutic lens making scripture speak only of this message and little else. The second difficulty with the liberation theologians' reading of scripture is the contradiction found in reading the text from a specific life situation—the movement going back and forth from the bible to the oppressive situation. "If the liberation theologian oscillates between "Bible" and "situation" he alternatively ascribes authority to each of these poles while excluding the other. He is alternately claiming: "Exodus vindicates my theology" and

117. Nilson, "Response to John P. Meier," 15.

118. Loader, "Exodus ," 8.

"In my theology Exodus is read that way". In effect he is therefore really saying: "My theology is true because of Exodus" and: "My theology is not true because of Exodus (but because of the way I read Exodus)".'"[119] The third difficulty is with the selective use of biblical texts in liberation theology. The choice of scriptural readings conforms to the liberative kerygma and oftentimes glances over those not proclaiming the same liberative theme.

The criticisms regarding the reading of scripture by liberation theologians are not without merit. As selective texts are used to support liberative acts in salvation history—connecting events of the past with those of the present—liberation theologians can, at times, appear to have a biased reading of scripture. However, others are also quick to defend their use of scripture within a specific context. As Gutiérrez points out, the interaction is not one way, such that we strictly read scripture in its historical context; scripture also "reads us" in our present context.

Theological Interpretations in Liberation Theology

In reflecting on "The Failure of Liberation Theology," Ivan Petrella attempts to "reclaim" the legitimacy of liberation theology, which he feels is currently incapable of responding to the present situation, by highlighting four "debilitating conditions" of liberation theologies in the hope of making this kind of theology once more applicable. Although Petrella clusters North American theologies with liberation theologies of Latin America because of their common liberative aspect, his four debilitating conditions of liberation theology highlight many of the misunderstandings arising in recent theologies of context.

First, liberation theologies overly focus on special interest groups as these theologies isolate themselves in their own context and people. For Petrella, this narrow, monochromatic perspective is "the most important debilitating condition."[120] "Monochromatism is thus evident when the theologians of a particular ethnic or racial group refuse to look beyond the parameters of that group, as well as parameters of their discipline, for tools and resources useful to the cause of liberation. Theologians with monochromatism, therefore, stress the goal of liberation, but dramatically limit the pool of resources they can draw upon to actually

---

119. Ibid., 12.

120. Petrella, *Beyond Liberation Theology*, 84.

engage the task. In the end, colour of membership and membership in a professional guild takes priority over liberation from material blight."[121]

Next, Petrella is critical of liberation theologies' selective memory: "Amnesia is the most general of the debilitating conditions afflicting liberation theology."[122] Petrella does not assert that liberation theologians easily forget, but he criticizes the "compromise" that is made as "selective victories" overtake the real problems and goals of the impoverished situation. Petrella claims that liberation theologians begin with the key problem, poverty, and the key goal, social liberation; however, in the end their theological constructions address neither the key problem nor the key goal. Thus, "cultural advancement of a particular ethnic group replaces social liberation as the goal of theology."[123]

The third debilitating condition of liberation theology is gigantism: "Theologians suffering from gigantism see giant and monstrous forces oppressing the material poor . . . economic conditions and social liberation are always the main focus."[124] By strictly focusing on the political and economic reality of poverty, the task and solution become overwhelming. In the end, the magnitude of the political and economic reality causes paralysis rather than constructive progress towards liberation.

Finally, Petrella finds liberation theologians and current theological reflection naïve. Although the prior three problematic areas are unrelated, naiveté is "[i]ntimately related to amnesia, monochromatism, and gigantism" and is "often a consequence of these."[125] "If you choose your sources according to colour or guild you are prone to naiveté; if you forget to include sources within your theology that allow for concrete socio-economic and political analysis you should be wary of naiveté; finally, if you see an all-encompassing monster as the cause of oppression you will likely fall prey to naiveté . . . Look for it when liberation theologians suffering from previous conditions try to outline paths of society reform or means of resistance to an unjust status quo."[126]

Although Petrella's critique of liberation theology is not a direct critique of Gutiérrez's theology, his comments raise the question of how

121. Ibid., 84–85.
122. Ibid., 93.
123. Ibid.
124. Ibid., 100.
125. Ibid., 104.
126. Ibid., 104–5.

Gutiérrez would address these four allegedly debilitating conditions of liberation theology? To the charge of monochromatism, Gutiérrez would find that the poor and the situation of poverty transcend the racial "ghettoism" implied within that term. To side with the poor is not a detriment to theological reflection; but to engage in a preferential option means that those on the margins will always be highlighted. As Gutiérrez has often stated, preference does not mean the exclusion of those who are not poor. Rather, he underscores that only in universal acceptance and the inclusion of all of God's children can preference or a priority of the poor be properly located.

In response to amnesia or selective memory that does not address the key problem and the key goal, Gutiérrez would insist that history must be rewritten through the perspective of those on the underside. Rather than remembering events of the "victors," Gutiérrez has insisted that real solutions to poverty cannot be addressed unless we remember and act through the perspective of those living on the underside of history—those most forgotten by the world. For Gutiérrez, his question, a simple one, of asking how we are to speak about God as Father to those who are considered subhuman, unable to be considered sons and daughters, has brought about a generation of reflection on the poor.

In regards to gigantism debilitating theological reflection, Gutiérrez would argue that Latin America has not been paralyzed by the enormity of the issue of poverty, but its grassroots movements reveal that each act in accordance with the Gospels produces much fruit. *Las comunidades de base*, the ecclesial small base communities, have shown that in the face of great poverty, people are willing to act on behalf of their faith no matter how great the forces of opposition. In addition, the episcopal conferences in Latin America have shown Church leadership by actively engaging and addressing the issue of poverty rather than accepting a defeatist attitude.

Finally, how would Gutiérrez address Petrella's charge that Latin American liberation theology is permeated with naïveté? In reply, Gutiérrez would find Petrella's own understanding naïve since Gutiérrez has never romanticized the poor and the world they live in. First of all, Gutiérrez has insisted that although the poor should receive preference simply by their state in life, he has insisted that the poor must make their own option as well. Too often, the poor make an option for the rich and do not continue to see the world through the eyes of those most in need. Second, only through spiritual poverty can we truly become sons and daughters of God. The detachment of the poor in material things is only a reflection of the detachment to which we are called in all matters. Although, Gutiérrez has acknowledged the error of liberation theology in its early anthropocentric view of poverty and liberation rather than a theocentric understanding, the naïveté that Petrella finds appears to be the growing pains of a theology in its germinal stages.

DEVELOPMENTS IN THEOLOGIES OF CONTEXT

The theological method of Virgilio Elizondo and Gustavo Gutiérrez has had a wide impact beyond their immediate locales. Not only are the poor and marginalized consoled by the voice that has been given them, the theological community as a whole also is able to benefit from the method of theologies of context. Obviously, a theology of context did not originate with the theologies of Elizondo and Gutiérrez, but their efforts revealed the way theology needed to be done by addressing revelation found in scripture and tradition and context that not only receives revelation from the past, but also communicates the meaning of that revelation today. Accordingly, the theological methods of Elizondo and Gutiérrez allow others to understand the dynamics of a theology of context and to develop a theology within their own context. Such developments outside of *mestizo* theology and liberation theology are found in other theologies of context such as African American, Asian American, feminist, dalit, and others throughout the world.

A concern of both *mestizo* theologians and liberation theologians is the future of their respective theologies and contexts. It is clear that these two theologies have impacted and borne fruit in other contexts, especially in the current generations facing oppression, poverty, and marginalization. However, subsequent generations have not always been eager to subscribe to, and carry forward, the theological endeavors of Elizondo and Gutiérrez.

In the case of *mestizo* theology, the realities of the border-crossers have at times failed to resonate with the up-coming generation in the United States, sometimes called *Generación Ñ*, insofar as this generation is removed from the immigrant process and has gained the status and wealth through their education and career achievements that their parents' generation could not. People of *Generación Ñ* maintain their identities derived from two worlds, but transcend to some degree the economic and societal non-acceptance of their parents. "What differentiates them from Generation Xers is their attempt to simultaneously live within two worlds, one Hispanic and the other Euroamerican, without losing anything in the "translation." Ñs are bicultural in the fullest sense of the word, largely bilingual, more often fluent in English. Many are well educated and possess economic clout in the marketplace."[127] By living in both worlds and successfully juggling both cultures, the feeling of marginalization—emphasized by Elizondo—is no longer a central issue. Their new Ñ existence challenges the generational limitations of Hispanic/Latino theology as their presence transforms their context: ". . . Hispanics in the United States are still predominately Catholic, and in this respect, the Ñs are no different. As cultural Catholics, they honor and respect Catholic traditions without necessarily practicing them. Their practices, or lack thereof, are beginning to affect Latino/a theology, which attempts to "do" theology from the grassroots . . . The Generation Ñs phenomenon has contributed to the dismantling of the romanticization of the oppressed, has facilitated the assimilation to Euroamerican mores for a privileged segment of Hispanic culture, and has resisted the pan-ethnic Hispanic identity many scholars attempt to construct."[128] Thus, removed from the realities of the borderlands, subsequent generations of the original immigrants may lose any desire to build upon *mestizo* theology. Nonetheless, a new phenomenon is emerging as some "return home" and discover their *mestizo* roots —some, but only a few thus far.

Similarly, recent generations in Latin America have not viewed their impoverished realities in the same manner as those in Gustavo Gutiérrez's generation. One could argue that economic conditions have improved making liberation not as imperative. Perhaps this situation is attributable to the politics and stigma associated with liberation theology. Working on behalf of the poor in Latin America is still a priority for many; however, being labeled a liberationist seemingly causes too many complications for the current generation. Those engaged in ministries emphasizing the preferential option for the poor do not want the connotations that liberation theologians endured during most of their

127. De La Torre and Aponte, *Introducing Latino/a Theologies*, 142–43.

128. Ibid., 143.

ministries.[129] Rather than fighting as to whether their theological reflections are orthodox, those on the frontlines of the impoverished world would rather expend their energies in service of the poor. They may not take up the banner of liberation theology, but their efforts embrace its preferential option.

There are many reasons why some people would want to avoid the label of liberation theology. In contrast to *mestizo* theology, which is not considered "dead" or "obsolete," liberation theology has been characterized as a theology past its time and no longer relevant. In short, many have pointed to the demise of liberation theology, especially in light of world events. Another reason for avoiding liberation theology is the manner in which Vatican officials have portrayed liberation theology. With several notifications and penalties silencing theologians, liberation theology appears to have been condemned by Rome, as well as stringently critiqued by theologians. However, the recent activities of CELAM at Aparecida in 2007 affirmed the legacy of liberation theology as being orthodox and valuable to the development of both the Latin American Church and society.

On the one hand, *mestizo* theology and liberation theology have motivated others in oppressive, impoverished, and marginalized situations to develop a theology reflecting their reality within the framework of salvation history. On the other hand, once these theologies have reached some maturation, subsequent generations have not been able to carry on the theological reflection mainly because their situations no longer fully resonate with that of the preceding generation. Does this ability to speak to the current context of suffering, oppression, and marginalization, but inability to speak to subsequent generations nullify or lessen the theological reflections of Elizondo and Gutiérrez? Even if the particular theologies of Elizondo and Gutiérrez are not readily transferable to the next generation, nonetheless, each generation needs to reflect on its own specific moment in salvation history just as these pioneering theologians have spoken about God in their own local situations.

Developments in Mestizaje

Although theologically speaking, *Generación Ñ* has not fully embraced *mestizo* theology, the theme of *mestizaje* has been developed in other

129. This sentiment was relayed to me at a 2008 Amazonian priests' gathering in Brazil.

fields. For example, John Phillip Santos, a journalist and novelist, has used the theological category of *mestizaje* in a literary manner. "Indian mothers gave birth to the new race of Mestizos. *Mestizos*, literally meaning "the mixed ones," combined the blood of the Old World and the New. Indian and Spanish, Indian and African, Indian and Asian. With the emergence of the Mestizo world, Mexico became obsessed with this mixing of the world races, finding exotic names for each racial combination."[130] More than just a theological understanding, *mestizaje* is a hermeneutic lens in literature as well as in social sciences. Utilizing Elizondo's work, which uplifts the situation of *mestizos*, Santos formulates the history and meaning of his own life story. *Mestizaje* provides perspective and meaning to his existence. Thus, Santos is able to retrace his genealogy with pride and gratitude with his *mestizo* understanding of his life and his people, in contrast to the shame and ignorance felt by many of mixed-heritage. "This is a story that took place long ago in a homeland far from where I live today, in a land whose first, forgotten names were never meant to be written down . . . I am a descendant of the people of this forgotten tale, but nothing of their lives was ever told to me by my elders . . . Nonetheless, centuries on in the tale, their story has come to me for telling, their lost story of a lost world[.]"[131] Through the perspective of *mestizaje*, Santos quickly realized that his heritage is much broader than just the lineage of his parents as he discovered a much broader *mestizo* world. "*Follow the lineages back as remotely as you can, relations spreading out wider into the past like a genetic radio broadcast, and soon it is apparent that we are from everywhere.* Eventually, we are implicated by the whole human story. But you have to begin somewhere. The Lopez and Velas began their New World story in Spain, en la madre tierra incognita."[132]

In order to recreate his *mestizo* heritage, Santos investigates all the elements that contributed to his current existence. Knowing San Antonio as his only homeland, Santos like others who are caught on the borders of two worlds without having any history of immigration, had to journey and experience life in the worlds creating this tension—Spain, Mexico, and the United States.

---

130. Santos, *Places Left Unfinished*, 73.

131. Santos, *Farthest Home*, 1.

132. Ibid., 25 (italics in original).

My mother's family are Tejanos from the deep time of Nueva
España, when San Antonio represented one of the northern-
most outposts of civilization in the sprawling desert wilderness
that reached all the way south to Querétaro, the colonial town
to the northwest of Mexico City. The long history of the Lopez
and Velas in south Texas and the borderlands left them with that
aloof quality that comes from seeing many nations come and go
as would-be masters of the land. The United States of America
was only one incarnation. They knew there had been other
worlds before this one, even if they might not be able to name
all of them.[133]

Santos also had to discover the impact of the Catholic faith throughout
the various historical periods influencing his existence today. However,
he realized this discovery is not just the fairly recent period of the birth
of the southwestern *mestizo* population of the United States: "Was it not
enough to learn of the family's descent through history, going back almost five hundred years? Wasn't that the original curiosity?"[134]

Traveling to Israel, the birthplace of Christianity, and European
centers of Catholicism, Santos came into contact with the various places
around the world that make up his current world. The more he discovers
about his *mestizo* heritage, the more he is curious about his beginnings:
"But who knows where we began? In truth, the story is only unfolding
now, and no one knows where it will end."[135] His life in New York as a
journalist ends in his return to his hometown of San Antonio to continue his reflections on his *mestizo* heritage in the place where he began
his earthly *mestizo* existence.

Developments in Liberation Theology

While some theologians have downplayed the importance of the theologies emerging from the Americas, others have simply wondered
about the lasting impression these theologies would have on the theological and ecclesial landscape. In 2002, a conference at the University
of Notre Dame[136] examined what observers of liberation theology had

133. Santos, *Places Left Unfinished*, 75.

134. Santos, *Farthest Home*, 266.

135. Ibid., 267.

136. The *Option for the Poor* conference at the University of Notre Dame in 2002
was hosted by Daniel Groody and Virgilio Elizondo.

called, *la pausa*, "a decline in interest and influence and a 'pause' in the production of new liberation theology texts."[137] Instead of discouragement or defeat, what emerged from the Notre Dame conference was a new-found respect for the direction in which theologies of context in the Americas are headed. Rather than seeing *la pausa* as a negative, this pause in the development of Latin American theology was seen as the necessary silence allowing the movement to settle in for critical reflection, especially on the preferential option for the poor. Whether one is engaged in liberation theology, Hispanic/Latino theology, feminist theology, black theology, or any other theology of context, this conference confirmed that the foundational element for the theological efforts of the Americas is the preferential option for the poor. "A constant theme of the Notre Dame gathering was that the option for the poor today is deeply functional, with an apostolic spirituality of service with and for the marginalized of this earth."[138]

During this conference, Gustavo Gutiérrez highlighted three interrelated aspects of liberation theology as its ongoing contribution to the universal task of theology: (1) it offers a basis for ongoing theological development in specific areas of systematic theology, such as the theme of Jesus the Liberator in Christology; (2) it emphasizes the social-pastoral aspects of Christian praxis; and (3) it highlights the spiritual aspects calling us to service to others out of gratuitous love.[139] Much of liberation theology's contribution in these three areas of ecclesial life is also true of Hispanic/Latino theology, insofar as both these theologies have changed the landscape of how theology is done and whom it addresses. Therefore, the fruitfulness of the theologies emerging from the Americas is not only seen internally, but also for its external impact. Liberation theology has given meaning and perspective far beyond Latin America; in fact, theological reflection in Third World conditions has nurtured many other theologies of context. "After having undergone a period of reflective calm–*la pausa*–liberation theology lives. Its method and message have taken root in the lives and passions of too many people in too many places and in too many ways."[140]

137. Deck, "Beyond *La Pausa*," 21.

138. Ibid., 22.

139. Ibid.

140. Ibid., 23.

THEOLOGY OF MIGRATION:
A THEOLOGY OF CONTEXT ILLUSTRATING ELIZONDO'S AND
GUTIÉRREZ'S THEOLOGICAL CONTRIBUTIONS

The fruitfulness of Hispanic/Latino theology and liberation theology is not only found in their own context of marginalization and poverty, but also in other oppressive situations needing liberation throughout the world. In particular, these two theologies of context have afforded feminist, indigenous, and Asian theologians the ability to relay God's message of salvation within concrete situations of oppression. Most recently, a theology of migration has captured the imagination of many throughout the world since a faltering globalized economy, still in the grips of neocolonialism, forces many to migrate to other lands out of sheer social advancement, economic necessity, or political security. "The International Organization for Migration (IOM) calculates that at the beginning of the twenty-first century there were 175 million migrants. Among them, about 10.4 million are refugees, that is, 1 out of 35 persons is involved in some type of human mobility . . . Of the 175 million migrants about 65 million live in industrialized countries or in those where oil is the basis of economy, while the rest remain in the south."[141]

Regardless of their reasons for migration, many migrants find themselves displaced in their host countries as well as disconnected from their native homelands. Many migrants face unprecedented abuse and mistreatment by the dominant groups as they attempt to gain a foothold in the new land.

> As a movement in the interior of a country it is called *displacement*; as a movement out of a country, it is called *emigration*; and as introduction into a new territory it is called *immigration*. But the migratory process does not end with the arrival into a new territory, the second stage begins, which we can call an *inter* space, which is the space of struggle between the native culture and the resident culture. This space could be cultural, sociopolitical, economic, or religious, all of which contribute to the process of forming a new identity. The third phase deals with building a new life and new identity in a new and often different land."[142]

141. Guerra, "Theology of Migration," 246. Statistics from the 86th session of the International Organization for Migration, Migration in a Globalized World conference on October 10, 2003.

142. Ibid., 247.

Because of the great numbers of those experiencing exclusion and marginalization as immigrants, a theology of migration seeks to recognize the *convivencia* of all migrants—"the creation of common and harmonic spaces that make true encounter between human beings possible."[143] "Very far from being a fashion, the centrality that the theme of migration is given in theological reflection comes from an organic development, where a Christian attitude and spirit have been accompanied by practices that are prophetic, communal, hope-filled, and based on *convivencia* and solidarity."[144]

A theology of migration in its germinal stage is still rooted in the developments of liberation theology, while at the same time it moves beyond the scope of liberation by focusing on the two worlds encapsulating the migrant, a reality already witnessed in Hispanic/Latino theology. In many ways, the theological reflections of Elizondo and Gutiérrez continue as the model for theologies of context being done today in different places. In particular, a theology of migration, as a recent and ongoing model of a theology of context, exemplifies the relevance of Elizondo's and Gutiérrez's work. In fact, a theology of migration fits nicely within the two theological frameworks as liberation theology provides a foundation for such a theology, while Hispanic/Latino theology provides a vision of where such a theology is moving. As with all theologies of context, the task of each unique theology of context is to not only to discover the subject within a context of oppression, poverty, exclusion, or marginalization, but also to emphasize that theologies of context must also include an aspect of liberation.[145] As a theology owing its foundation to liberation theology in the way it identifies those receiving God's preference, theology of migration moves beyond this liberative aspect:

> A theology of migration is not simply an update or a reelaboration of the theology of liberation. A theology of migration is inspired by the liberating and martyr legacy, and wants to contribute to the liberation of all creation from its specific subjects, the migrants . . . A theology of migration values the so-called Medellín heritage, which calls for the option for the poor and interprets it as the option for and with the migrants, and for the formation of societies of *convivencia* . . . A theology of migration

143. Ibid., 265, footnote 2.
144. Ibid., 243.
145. Ibid., 249.

values the understanding of God systematized by the theology of liberation: God of the poor, God of life, God of the victims, and puts them again in context as the pilgrim God, who does not remain on the other side of the border. Likewise, it captures the meaning of Christ the liberator as the migrant Christ, and the Holy Spirit as the strength that inspires a welcome in solidarity, unity, and mutual understanding, and the plan of salvation of the reign of God as a hope that gives courage to struggle for intercultural *convivencia*.[146]

Today's global world with all its human movements presents a complex vision of the human person within his or her environment. Thus, in the case of a theology of migration, the context has a two-fold similarity to the context of Hispanic/Latino theology addressed by Virgilio Elizondo. "The migrant is the person that after initiating his or her history of migration, in a forced or voluntary way, has assumed different identities (emigrant, immigrant) and now in a new territory must build his or her identity as migrant."[147] *Convivencia* is created, not only through an oppressive situation, but in this instance also through the internal struggles as a migrant. This space, unique to those who have left their homeland in search of another, becomes the privileged place Gutiérrez speaks about in terms of preference and Elizondo speaks about in terms of *mestizaje*. "A result of the process of transformation of identity—as we will describe later—is what is called double belonging, the experience of being *in-between* and *in-both*, or in other cases double denial, belonging neither to the territory of origin nor to the territory of destination."[148]

On the one hand, a theology of migration seeks liberation for those facing unjust situations as migrants. On the other hand, the focus is on migrants and not just the poor. Therefore, a theology of migration is rooted in liberation theology's commitment of liberation but at the same time differs from it by focusing on the fluctuating situation brought about by human movement. "Today, from the diverse contexts of migration, theology turns to the migrants and springs up again from them, from their *sensus pauperum* and *sensus migratorum*. For this reason it is a theology that tries to be an expression of the human situation of the

---

146. Ibid., 249–50.
147. Ibid., 248.
148. Ibid.

migrants[.]"[149] Although many modern day theologies of context owe a great debt of gratitude to the work set forth by liberation theologians, the liberative aspect of Latin American theology is still not enough to meet many migrants in their newfound context. Liberation is the starting point of theologies of context, but only in accounting for the specific situation can liberation fulfill the salvation called forth by God. Therefore, "a theology of migration proposes for theological reflection a specific content, one therefore different from the context that up to now has been central for liberation theology . . . The theology of liberation has made clear the importance of a sensitized openness to context."[150] "Liberation theology . . . offers analytical and methodological instruments to capture the sociopolitical situation of the victims, to value the liberating practice and the faith present there, and to contribute to the transformation of reality. In the face of the phenomenon of migration those instruments are not sufficient because we are before a new context that presents new problems."[151]

As the issues plaguing migrants are further investigated, the difference between migrant theology and liberation theology begins to appear more intensely in the *inter* spaces—the "in-between" or "in-both"—caused by the coming together of two worlds: the country of origin and the new host country. Just as liberation theology is incapable of addressing the needs of the migrant because of its limited context, a theology focusing only on the context of origin is also incapable of fully addressing this *inter* space. "A theology of migration emerges as a theology that wants to deal, in a Christian way, with the "in-between" situation of the migrants, situated between the reality of origin and the reality of the society where they arrive. At the same time a theology of migration pays attention to the places of "in-both" that mediate social, cultural, political, and religious realities of communion."[152] To address the "in-between" and the "in-both," a theology of migration cannot limit itself to the context of origin, but at the same time it cannot limit itself to the context of the destination country. Calling itself an intercultural theology, a theology of migration delicately balances the dialogue between two cultures, two worlds—the one left behind and the new one

149. Ibid., 251.
150. Ibid., 253.
151. Ibid.
152. Ibid., 254.

encountered. The goal of a theology of migration "is to facilitate the dialogue-communion through the acknowledgement of the otherness and affinities in a relational way. It deals, then, with a transforming dialogue-communion, where identities are not changed or exchanged but reciprocally sensitized through the practices of proximity. It is from there that the process for intercultural transformation begins in society and the Church."[153]

The tasks of a theology of migration are to announce by recognizing migrants as bearers of the Good News, to denounce by condemning the injustices facing migrants, and finally to engage in the dialogue in the *inter* space, *convivencia*. Annunciation in a theology of migration occurs when the dreams and hopes are identified in migrants, especially in their difficult and, at times, dangerous transitory existence. Human mobility is motivated in a large part by the impoverished situation in the country of origin. By escaping a previously paralyzing situation, migrants reveal their faith, hope, and love in their families left behind, in themselves as they undertake a treacherous journey, and in God who, they feel, journeys with them. The migrants in our midst, like the poor in Latin America of whom Gustavo Gutiérrez speaks and the *mestizos* of whom Virgilio Elizondo speaks, are a constitutive aspect of our reality. The migrants of today bear the Good News in two ways. First, by the dreams of a more humane life that is part of their migrating and liberative stories. Second, by being the poor and lowly ones in our midst, migrants bear the Good News in the preferential space the Gospels speak about where God is found.

The Good News accompanying the migrants in a foreign land is rarely received in an amicable manner. Negatives also arise as the dreams and hopes of migrants are met with fear, racism, and intolerance. Accordingly, denunciation is necessary, as structural and individual biases which migrants experience must be addressed. The poor and lowly ones have been despised from the time of Jesus and continue to be despised to this day. Thus, the work of Christ continues as we denounce the unjust situation where society considers the newly arrived as inferior. The work of Christ continues by reaching out to migrants as an act of solidarity and as an act of denouncing the situations which place migrants in inferior situations.

153. Ibid., 255.

Finally, to address this double aspect of the migrants, one of the most important tasks of a theology of migration is to foster an environment conducive to dialogue with, and commitment on behalf of, migrants. By leaving their countries of origin and arriving in their country of destination, migrants live in a privileged space of *convivencia*, an *inter* space. Initially, *convivencia* is not readily available because a migrant is in a foreign world—familiar at times, but not fully recognizable by either the origin or host country. Initially disheartening due to the non-acceptance of either the origin or host countries, upon further reflection, *convivencia* is acknowledged as a privileged space because of its identification with what the Gospels address. A preferential notion exists in this *inter* space because of the poverty and lowliness contained within it. In addition, *convivencia* allows dialogue to occur in two forms. Intercultural dialogue occurs naturally as migrants become members of two cultures, two worlds. Their being, their presence, naturally fosters a dialogue about societal and cultural practices. Interreligious dialogue also occurs by "reaching out to the human condition of the migrants, their life, expectations, and religious perception, and pursuing a collaborative work for the most humble and needy migrants".[154] The extension of oneself to others in need, especially in the face of today's global migration, requires transcending religious affiliation to meet the human person in their journey crossing borders.

Not only are there parallels between the theological efforts in a theology of migration to that of liberation or *mestizo* theology, but more importantly, a theology of migration further illustrates the theological method of connecting the *loci theologici* of scripture, tradition, and context. What is also valuable in using a theology of migration to illustrate a theology of context is that it highlights Elizondo's and Gutiérrez's own theological methods. Theologies of context are liberative in nature because of the connection between our history and that of salvation history. Accordingly, a theology of migration begins with this liberative aspect as it acknowledges its roots in liberation theology. However, a theology of migration becomes specific to its own context by identifying the preferential option in its own reality. For migrants, this preference is found in the *inter* space, *convivencia*. The focus on this reality of being "in-both" and "in-between" two worlds is closely connected to the work of Elizondo's description of the *mestizo* situation of Mexican Americans.

154. Ibid., 263.

The difference between a theology of migration and Elizondo's *mestizo* theology is that not all Mexican Americans are immigrants: some were native inhabitants of the southwestern region of the United States. However, the theological reality of *convivencia* in migration is similar to the *mestizo* situation and in many ways *mestizaje* becomes the vision, a goal of a theology of migration. Therefore, a theology of migration as another illustration of a theology of context and the ongoing work of incorporating the three *loci theologici* constitutive to all theological methods further illustrate the efforts of Elizondo and Gutiérrez by highlighting the magnitude of their pioneering theological reflection.[155]

SENSE OF IDENTITY

Identity is a constitutive element in any theology. Without a sense of oneself and one's environment, proper theological reflection cannot occur. Therefore, who we are truly matters! Elizondo and Gutiérrez were able to formulate theological concepts and terms which speak to the poor and marginalized because they understood better than anyone else what it meant to be poor, marginalized, or both. Without their identification of *mestizaje* and marginalization, Elizondo and Gutiérrez could never have become the spokesmen of their generation. Precisely because they were what they proclaimed made them credible to speak on behalf of the majority facing exclusion and poverty.

In a personal conversation with Elizondo, I raised the issue regarding the formation of identity, a national consciousness of a people such as Mexican Americans.[156] His recollection of the Mexican American consciousness reached a pinnacle in the sixties where flagrant racial injustices persisted in society. Two particular events came to mind:

155. Although a theology of migration is presented here as a middle ground, or a connector, between a theology of liberation and *mestizo* theology for strictly illustrative purposes, this is not the only possibility since theologies of context have other parallels as well. A theology of context may have several similarities in its theological method because of its uses of the *loci theologici* apparent in all theologizing; however, the uniqueness of a theology of migration is that it acknowledges portion of its theologizing are indebted to the theological efforts of theologians such as Elizondo and Gutiérrez. In this schema of a theology of migration, the roots acknowledge the liberative aspects in Gutiérrez's theology while the direction of this theological method acknowledges the *mestizaje* of Elizondo's theology.

156. See Appendix A.

first, World War II or rather events after the war raised awareness of the mistreatment of soldiers of Hispanic/Latino descent; their return home did not bring about the celebrations their white-counterparts enjoyed. Second, the Civil Rights movement raised further awareness of the unacceptable attitudes towards minorities. Societal injustices and racism became major factors in forming the consciousness of a people. Elizondo rode this wave as he developed a theological approach that spoke to the formation of the Mexican American people.

The sense of identity is nothing new in theology or society. Modernity's turn to the other and postmodernity's turn to the other on the margin have put our identities under close scrutiny.[157] As we realize our own identity in relation to the other, the question becomes who is the other in our midst? In a similar way to the Gospel of the Good Samaritan—"and who is my neighbor?"—our Christian identity, our humanness, is defined by standing before the other. In this respect, Elizondo's and Gutiérrez's work is extremely valuable in understanding ourselves through the other—the poor and marginalized. "[T]here is another perspective whose distinctiveness is often overlooked at the end of modernity. The horizons are broadened not just from a postmodern perspective, but also from the experience of people on the margins of the postmodern world . . . The liberation perspective goes beyond the pluralism of postmodern thought, claiming not merely respect for people who are different but a special concern for those who are marginalized and oppressed."[158]

Following Enrique Dussel's philosophical understanding of Latin American historical development, Jorge Rieger argues that modernity for Latin America did not begin with the Cartesian—"I think therefore I am"—but rather with Christopher Columbus' arrival a hundred years earlier in the New World. Similar to modern and postmodern thinkers, Rieger finds the basis for the self only through the other. However, because of the revised understanding of modernity in Latin America, the other can only be found in the margins, those who were oppressed because of Columbus' "I conquered." "People on the margins add a decisive point to this postmodern awareness, especially where they remind us that our success is often built on the back of others—on their labors and efforts and, at times, even on their misfortune and suffering. The

157. Rieger, "Theology and the Power," 180.
158. Ibid.

amazing success of Europe and the United States, for instance, cannot truly be understood without the histories of conquest, colonialism, and slavery that provided both inexpensive raw materials and the labor forces necessary to build empires."[159]

The real issue for Rieger is the "lessening" of challenge from the margins in today's postmodern world. Postmodern recognition of the other, in particular, the differences among us, creates a pseudo-atmosphere of tolerance and respect. "Postmodern pluralism thus tends to create a safety net that keeps people from plunging into the awareness of social conflict, the tensions between rich and poor and between those in power and those without power."[160] Because our view of the world is so intricately tied in with the economics of life, it is difficult to critique, adequately and honestly, an oppressive or unjust situation because of the repercussions it has on our lifestyle. "Here a new challenge emerges—revealing the asymmetries of a pluralistic society in which the powerful are still powerful and the powerless are still powerless."[161] "The reality of the other, of people at the margins, is not a mere accident—a colorful addition to a "tossed salad" (a popular image among pluralists) and something that just happens to be there—but one of the creations of modernity in collaboration with the free market that has not disappeared in postmodernity."[162] Thus, the search for identity requires an understanding of the other who is marginalized. Upon further reflection, the marginalized are seen as not only the poor and those oppressed by some extraneous forces; more importantly, the poor and oppressed are understood to be in their situation through the interconnectedness of our lives. In the end, we are responsible for their poverty and alienation because of the global economy affecting us all; thus, our identity can only be found in asking who the other, the marginalized, are, and why they are in that situation for which we are responsible.

> The reality of the other, the marginalized, is not a given or a mere accident. The realities of life on the margins are in many ways the creation of modern market economy, industrialization, colonization, and efforts at civilization—processes which have changed form but have not necessarily ended in postmodern times. In

159. Ibid., 182.
160. Ibid., 190.
161. Ibid., 191.
162. Ibid.

this context, references to the other are not only politically and socially but also theologically useless if they do not at the same time raise the question of who and what put (and is holding) this other in its place of repression even in the postmodern world."[163]

The theological contributions of Elizondo and Gutiérrez allow us to see the other in the poor and *mestizo*. Furthermore, in their theologies, proper reflection on context has been emphasized. However, this emphasis on context is not a vague intellectual speculation but rather a close examination of our own identity derived from the other before us. "Contextual theologies often proceed as if the context were already clear. To make theology contextual . . . means to relate it first of all to what concerns me or other people like myself."[164] The others who afford the contextual nature in theology, according to Elizondo and Gutiérrez, are the poor and marginalized. Hence, through the poor and the *mestizo*, we are reminded of the Gospels' concerns. Although the poor and *mestizo* may not always appear in the same manner as Elizondo's or Gutiérrez's, to do proper theological reflection requires that we consider those who are the least in our midst. The preferential option for the poor and the life of the Galilean Jesus requires this of us and nothing less.

The inclusion of the other as described by Gutiérrez is what makes liberation theology so unique. Distinguishing liberation theology from other theologies of context, Rieger claims the "biggest difference" is that liberation theology becomes more specific through the poor with whom it is associated. "This does not mean that contextual theology is completely unaware of suffering, pain, and structures of oppression. But contextual theology tends to see those structures as exceptions, anomalies, merely deviations from the normal course of things. Liberation theology, on the other hand, understands that suffering, pain, and oppression are not merely accidental but point to a deeper truth about the dominant contexts.[165]"

In the case of Elizondo, the contextual nature of theologizing about the plight of Mexican American border-crossers has revealed a much more complex view of the poor. "Lately, Hispanic theology for instance has reminded us that the struggle for liberation is yet more complex, arguing that our reflections need to include the aspects of culture and

163. Ibid., 193.
164. Rieger, "Developing a Common Interest Theology," 128.
165. Ibid., 129.

identity as well."[166] This is not to say that Latin American liberation theology does not take into consideration culture and identity, but rather, Hispanic/Latino theology has uncovered the complex dimensions of those in impoverished situations. Through the work of Elizondo and Gutiérrez, the contextual nature of theology has not only been emphasized but the deepening of context through one's identification and solidarity with the poor and excluded has been highlighted. Thus, the continuing challenge in theology, as posed by Elizondo and Gutiérrez, is how to speak about God in the world of the other. The greatest of these challenges lies with those on the underside of history and those who are *mestizos* biologically.

Both biological *mestizos* and those on the underside of history present a complex reality to address theologically. However, Elizondo argues that the *mestizo* challenge is much more difficult because of its biological characteristics. *Mestizaje* presents a more challenging complexity than just poverty. However, Gutiérrez's poor provide greater understanding to Elizondo's *mestizo* reality, and Elizondo's challenge of biological *mestizo* acceptance further reveals the world of those Gutiérrez calls the insignificant ones. In many ways, the two situations found in Latin America and in the United States complement one another by addressing their current status or "non-status" in life and by interpreting the Gospels' understanding of the least among us.

Just as Vatican II and CELAM gave hope to theologians such as Elizondo and Gutiérrez in developing a theology of their own, CELAM continues to do so by affirming their lifework on behalf of those who are voiceless in our midst. According to Gutierrez, Pope Benedict XVI's address to the Latin American bishops was the best the episcopal conference has heard over the years. Furthermore, affirmation of the theologizing of the past has safeguarded the legacy of not only the theological reflection in this part of the world, but more importantly, safeguarded the way theologians are to do theology in all parts of the world.

> Both Aparecida's preparatory document and its final statements give evidence of this distinctive aspect of Latin-American theology. Western theology is often produced by individual scholars, but most Latin American theology has emerged collectively. The Vatican did insist on making some changes in the final document, but the substance of Aparecida remains intact. It reaffirms the

166. Ibid., 130.

general theological approach and methodology used at Medellín and Puebla: *ver, juzgar, y actuar*—see, judge, and act. One cannot do theological reflection in a vacuum or design effective pastoral plans simply by reiterating previous Church teachings. To evangelize today, the Church must immerse itself in the realities of the times, and in the spirit of *Gaudium et spes*, it must heed the cries of society's victims.[167]

The preference for the poor and excluded was highlighted by both Benedict XVI and the bishops at CELAM.

Aparecida marked the first occasion where both United States and Canadian bishops were included as voting members because of the number of Churchgoers of Latin American descent in both countries.

> One of the most beautiful passages of the Aparecida document personalizes this option for the poor. The point is not to exclude people but to include everyone. It is not about protest marches but about friendship. For the preferential option begins by seeing the poor not as objects of pity but as brothers and sisters. Only then can we "recognize the immense dignity and their sacred value in the eyes of Christ who was poor and excluded like them." The option for the poor is not merely a matter of doing social work but of creating relationships of love that will bring about social, economic, and cultural change. Precisely because they are our brothers and sisters, we must become advocates and defenders of the poor.[168]

In reclaiming their heritage of the previous forty years, the Latin American bishops affirmed the local church's solidarity with the poorest of the poor. In doing so, Aparecida also affirmed the connection between the recent events in Latin America after the Second Vatican Council and salvation history. No longer can the ecclesial developments of the Americas be seen as an anomaly or aberration, but rather, the liberative events on behalf of the poor and marginalized are seen as the work of the Holy Spirit in accordance with the traditions of the universal Church.

> Aparecida—is Medellín in another language—is 40 years after but it is very close to it. For example, preferential option for the poor is a very important affirmation of Aparecida, because the Pope, especially at the beginning of the conference, was very clear about preferential option of the poor. He says this is implicit

167. Elizondo, "Collaborative Theology," 8.

168. Ibid., 9.

in the Christological faith and that it is, to say, the center of the Christ of Faith . . . Aparecida repeated the relevance of the option of the poor. When some people ask me about the presence of liberation theology in the Church, I say well, 90% of it is very present in the preferential option for the poor today. It is one point of the ecclesial magisterium. Option for the poor is coming from Latin American, from liberation theology, and now is a universal affirmation of the Churches because several evangelical Churches also [affirm it].[169]

169. See Appendix B.

Epilogue

M ANY LAYERS OF SELF-DISCOVERY have emerged during my research and writing on the pastoral and theological endeavors of Virgilio Elizondo and Gustavo Gutiérrez. On a pastoral level, Elizondo and Gutiérrez have inspired me not only through their writings but also through personal contact, mentoring me to work pastorally and academically on behalf of my own people. Since their theology is a reflection on praxis, their method has naturally led me to investigate further my own *Sitz in Leben* and that of my fellow immigrants of Korean descent here in the United States. Elizondo's and Gutiérrez's approach to pastoral ministry and theological reflection has encouraged me to continue ministering to Korean American communities across the United States during my doctoral studies. Thus, on a personal level, I have been able to discover more of who I am as a Korean American and further to identify the needs of Korean American communities.

My visits to Korean American communities in various parts of this country have also further strengthened my priestly ministry to those who are often neglected. Although immigrant groups as a whole are often overlooked by mainstream society, the parent group or initial generation of immigrants is able to create an insular community shielding themselves from the foreign environment surrounding them. However, succeeding generations are not always so lucky. In my pastoral ministry, I have encountered groups of Korean Americans who are the marginalized and neglected within my own people. We are the children who immigrated to the U.S. at an early age or began our lives here in this country. We are the ones struggling between our parent's culture and lifestyle and that of the dominant English speaking society. These newly formed minorities within minority groups are often splintered internally and externally. Internally, we struggle with identity as we attempt to reconcile our Korean heritage while living in a non-Korean environment. Externally, we struggle with language, either our parent's tongue or the one to which we have become accustomed. The internal and external conflicts are fully realized in our appearance as our efforts to enter mainstream society are hindered by our distinctly Asian physical features. Even the Church, where our parents have found so much solace and shelter, has become a stranger for so many across the U.S.

Originally, our immigrant parent group established Korean American Churches for many reasons. First, these ethnic religious communities afforded displaced immigrants some continuity with their homelands as native speaking clergy often accompanied their people. Within the Church structure, Korean speakers who could not interact with their English-speaking environment were able to create a social and religious society that recognized them. Since immigrants often fail to enter the social arena of their host country, the ethnic Church provided a venue where they could build an insular community for support and stability. For example, many Korean American communities have as one of their goals to build their own Church building rather than sharing a space with their English-speaking counterparts. They are willing to contribute great amounts for this "dream." What I have realized in my ministerial travels is that this willingness to give to the Church but not to other worthwhile causes in society reflects the first generation's dilemma. Giving financially connotes ownership.

Immigrants are not so apt to give to society at large because they do not feel like the host country is theirs. Rather, they give to causes they feel are theirs, such as the ethnic Church they attend. For subsequent generations, the challenge is to give of oneself to society in order to claim one's place. The difficulty facing the next generation is that neither the Church nor society allows them the opportunity to give in order to make it theirs. The Korean American Churches continue to minister to the parent generation and to the ongoing influx of immigrants; however, the passing on of the Church to the next generation has yet to be realized.

On a theological level, rather than engaging solely with a philosophical Christ, the theological reflections of Elizondo and Gutiérrez reveal the necessity for an incarnational Christianity where specific moments in history and the human condition matter in God's communication with creation. Even with its unique history of Catholicism where the laity evangelized themselves through books and other religious articles brought over from China, the Church in Korea eventually broadened due to the arrival of European missioners who expanded the native conception of Christianity. Korean Christians, inspired by the martyrs, embraced much of the theological reflection of Europe without regard to their own contribution to the universal Church. This attitude has also migrated across the Pacific as Korean Americans still look to the dominant structures in Church and society for self-identity and meaning. Without accounting for the richness of their immigration experience to the universal Church and overall society, Koreans sometimes harbor an inferiority complex brought about through displacement. This stigma often precludes them from looking within their new situation as immigrants and minorities and finding that they have much to contribute. To them, the host countries are seen as having much more to offer materially and spiritually.

Due to this lack of appreciation for one's own being as a Korean American, contributions to the wider society and Church are often underestimated. Therefore, the reflections of theologians such as Elizondo and Gutiérrez have encouraged even those outside of their cultural and ethnic spheres to discover richness within the labeled impoverished and marginalized existence. In order for one to follow the path of Elizondo and Gutiérrez, several developments need to take place. The two primary movements of any group understanding their privileged position must be based on a particular group's understanding of Jesus' humanity and where the humanity of Christ can be encountered today. Having spent several months examing Elizondo's and Gutiérrez's theological method of context, I conclude that my understanding of their works boils down to this: a Christocentric approach which allows us, as a people living in a specific moment of history in a particular locale, to use a unique hermeneutical lens to encounter both the historical Jesus and the Christ of faith.

Elizondo brings this approach to life through his re-conception of the Galilean *mestizo*-type Jesus who is one like them today in the *mestizo* existence of Mexican Americans living in Southwestern United States always on the border of two worlds. Gutiérrez portrays the Old Testament figure of Job as the prefiguration of Christ as a suffering servant, one suffering in solidarity with all those who suffer unjustly. Once again, the poor in Latin America resemble the oppressed and impoverished of the past where Christ becomes real for the world. The Christocentric approach to the theology of context proves a further challenge for discipleship where the Gospels are reread in light of one's present reality to comprehend further the Jesus of history, thus allowing those who have faithfully reflected on incarnation to encounter the Christ of faith in their midst.

The starting point of the historical figure of Jesus, rather than a philosophical Christ, demands we account for our present context in all theologizing. The revelation of God in the incarnation in Galilee two thousand years ago is still relevant for us today and we, in turn, are relevant in continuing the transmission of our faith. Within one's encounter with the historical Jesus through one's own *Sitz in Leben* lies the fundamental truth that every group has a radical and unique contribution to make within salvation history. Thus, not only is the historical period of the incarnation important to our faith life and not only is our present day reality also important, but every period and generation has a significant contribution to make. Elizondo appeals to Our Lady of Guadalupe for his ecclesial connection to highlight and further elucidate his *mestizo* reflections, while Gutiérrez appeals to Bartolomé de las Casas as evidence within the ecclesial tradition of defending the poor. In summary, the challenge of a theology of context for any individual is to encounter the Christ of faith in and through others. Whether this encounter is through a religious devotion, a saintly figure, or an ecclesial event, the Christological encounter is necessary to solidify the encounter with the historical Jesus and Christ today.

What I hope to have accomplished through this book is to provide a foundation for a theology of context by following the examples of Virgilio Elizondo and Gustavo Gutiérrez. By taking their theological method and making it my own, I have applied the same elements they used to address Korean Americans, especially the next generation, as their needs go unnoticed and unaddressed. What Elizondo and Gutiérrez illustrate in their theological methodology is the importance of identifying the insignificant, the non-person, the marginalized, and the excluded. To begin anywhere else is incompatible with the Gospels since Jesus' life and ministry was spent with these people. This identification of those who receive God's preference requires us to reread scripture through their perspective. In doing so, a deeper understanding of the historical Jesus is realized. This unique relationship between

Jesus and those to whom He ministers allows us to see where Christ is today and whom He addresses as the favored ones in the reign of God. In addition, this relationship is further affirmed and elucidated within our salvation history through Church figures and ecclesial events. For Korean Americans and any other groups in the infant stages of theologizing their unique cultural and religious experience, the challenge is to recognize the lowly ones and to reimagine Christ who becomes the poor, marginalized, and excluded within our own. This task is difficult as our Confucian heritage does not support a theological method where lowly ones hold a privileged position.

Furthermore, once we recognize this unique relationship between the cornerstone that has been rejected and his people, Elizondo and Gutiérrez remind us of the need for solidarity through the threefold act of announcement, denouncement, and *fiesta*. Our solidarity with those who are displaced and have no voice requires us to announce the blessings held within the people, to denounce the injustices cast upon those who are unable to defend themselves, and finally to rejoice through the celebration of the Eucharist and *fiesta* with all peoples. Due to the insular lifestyle Korean Americans have created for themselves for survival in a foreign land, and the Confucian principles such as always having to save face, we have not been able to embrace solidarity let alone identify the poorest of the poor among us. Korean Americans historically have no time to denounce unjust structures since overcoming oppression and other negative forces must be accomplished through education, wealth, and other forms of worldly success. Without the announcement of the significance of the poor who embody the Good News and without the denouncement of injustices facing immigrants and minorities, especially minorities within minorities, our Eucharistic celebrations and Korean cultural celebrations are becoming less relevant as the Church is unable to address the situations most vexing to Korean Americans. Rephrasing Elizondo's and Gutiérrez's question for our own: How are we to speak about God to Korean Americans who are minorities within a minority?

The strength of the theological method utilized by Elizondo and Gutiérrez is that it empowers a community of faith to reflect properly on scripture, tradition, and context. This reflection requires a comprehensive understanding of the entire human person in order truly to comprehend God's communication. Through this process, dignity is restored as the once overlooked or despised elements in society are incorporated into the sacred. The communal aspect of this theological investigation reveals that theology cannot be done in isolation. As pastors first, theologians second, Elizondo and Gutiérrez understand that theological reflection is always done as a communal exercise. This theological method reconnects the pastoral with the academic as the Church's evangelical mission of preaching the Gospel to all nations demands that all nations further deepen revelation through the contribution of one's own unique humanity. This dynamic interchange puts an interesting demand on discipleship as it empowers us not just as recipients but also as integral agents for understanding and communicating God's grace. Thus, the theology of context as utilized by Elizondo and Gutiérrez reminds us of the demands of discipleship in a twofold manner. First, this theological method requires we take seriously the cultural, social, and political life events surrounding us. Second, it requires that a significant contribution be made in unfolding the revelation to humanity through the hermeneutical lens arising out of one's own context.

As much as the theological method of Virgilio Elizondo and Gustavo Gutiérrez prophetically reminds of us of our own contributions and our mandate to be part of the theological effort, this method also contains divisive elements in need of reconciliation. By highlighting the uniqueness of one's own culture and people, antagonistic tendencies surface against the dominant groups in society for they are often seen as the oppressors, the ones benefitting from the current unjust social structures or as those knowingly or unknowingly maintaining the present course in both Church and society. Healing is needed between the dominant and minority groups once injustices against the latter are recognized. Certain gestures also are needed from the dominant group to recognize the contribution the overlooked and neglected can make to both Church and society. However, more than mere gestures are needed to address and correct injustices as dominant groups tend to benefit and to perpetuate such systems. Solidarity means that those who have benefitted materially and who have a voice in society must act on behalf of those who have not and do not.

The challenge then is twofold. On one hand, the poor, marginalized, and excluded must find their dignity through their positive contribution to Church and society. On the other hand, solidarity is needed from everyone else: a willingness to let go of one's comforts and status so that the contributions of the others are fully realized. The latter becomes much more difficult than the former, partly due to the fact that the announcement and denouncement Elizondo and Gutiérrez speak of must come eventually from those outside the poor, marginalized, and excluded. Just as God entered an impoverished humanity in Galilee and continued to live in solidarity on the fringes of society, we too must constantly work to enter into the lives of the poor, marginalized, and excluded, and to advocate on their behalf. The prophetic announcement and denouncement cannot only come from within but must also come from elsewhere. Those who are able must help to give voice to the voiceless, announce the Good News held within them, and denounce the structures of societal injustices. With these acts we are not doing for the other, but in our prophetic announcement and denouncement we are allowing others to do for themselves.

Although the poor, marginalized, and excluded have been the subject of much deep theological reflection, the requirements of solidarity have not been adequately addressed. To do so is divisive since prophetic responsibilities burden many sitting passively in the pews. The poor are constitutive elements of conversion and salvation; however, it is not enough for the poor, marginalized, and excluded to call others to be generous. The call to conversion on behalf of others must come from one's own. Just as Elizondo and Gutiérrez have worked tirelessly on behalf of their neglected people, others in society must call those like them to enter the world of the other and prophetically challenge themselves.

This book is the foundation of my lifework. As a descendant of Korean heritage with a clerical position in the Church, a theology of context illustrated by Hispanic/Latino theology and liberation theology provides the framework and inspiration to pursue a theological reflection on behalf of my own. Already germinating through this writing and the pastoral activities during my studies, a Korean American theological reflection is being realized. I have learned through my research and writing the need of minority groups to look to other minorities for guidance and leadership. Theologically, Elizondo and Gutiérrez have provided a way for me to theologize about my own situation, both in their writings and through personal contact. Pastorally, the successful models of evangelization found within different ethnic groups must be replicated as much, if not more, than the replication of the dominant methods so that the uniqueness of one's own may emerge. Personally, this period of ongoing formation as a Korean American and a disciple through my studies has passionately impelled me to look more creatively into my own heritage while compelling me to uncover and encourage the contributions of Korean Americans to Church and society.

Appendix A

Interview with Virgilio Elizondo
July 26, 2010

On your first encounter with Gustavo Gutiérrez . . .[1]

Gustavo and I are not sure when we first met, so we are not sure whether we met there [Medellín] or not, because we met so many people. At that time I was a nobody, so he would not have remembered and he wasn't well recognized either. I would suggest you say that since the early encounters in the 1970s, because neither one of us is sure. I mean, we couldn't say we didn't, but we also couldn't say we did. Neither one of us are sure, we think we might have, but there were so many people there, but both of us at that time were unknown to each other. He wasn't famous and I was a nobody. I was there just as a secretary to my archbishop. I wasn't even there as a theologian.

Could you once again refresh us on how you use mestizo and mestizaje in your work since you take them from the Mexican and Mexican American experience, but then apply it as a universal theme?

My process begins with the pastoral in trying to make sense of the ongoing question of my own self personally and my people. We were considered Mexicans in the U.S. and we were very, very Anglo-cized. In Mexico, they considered us as "other"—whatever name they gave us— but here we were still Mexicans, so I had to deal with that in-between. I

---

1. In Italics are my paraphrased statements or questions to give context to Virgilio Elizondo's answers.

think that's why I started digging into and then going back to almost discovering the original *mestizaje* as it applies to Mexico in the encounter between the Europeans and the natives and how the process had gone through several stages. First of all, there were simply the children of the Spaniards. Then later on when the population gets too big, people get scared of it—in this country, the fear, the incredible fear of race-mixing, even the taboos and laws against it. I was reading the laws and legislation against mixed-marriages. Because of who we were—the mixed race, the mestizo people, we were Christians—we were put down by both sides. So we asked the questions: who are we, where do we go? So, it was reclaiming the term that was used in a derogatory way by others. Reclaiming it by saying this is who we are and it is not bad. It is not bad to share two great cultures. As one person put it, we can have twice as much fun. We have fun the Mexican way; we have fun the Anglo way. It was almost turning something that was looked down by others and turning it inside out to say, "hey, it's not bad, it's great." We are sharing in two great traditions. Let's not be ashamed of the Indian side of us, let's not be ashamed of the Mexican side and let's not be ashamed of the Anglo side, we were very Anglo-cized in many ways. And really seeking the ultimate meaning of all this, which as Christians we found it in the Gospels and that's what lead me to the whole Galilean Journey theme.

In your comments, you wanted me to be cautious about calling Jesus a mestizo.

You want to be careful with doctrine. That's why I use "appears" or "functions as" rather than saying "he was."

Yet, you use mestizo in a much broader sense than just biological.

Oh yes, that is why I said Jesus certainly culturally would have been considered a *mestizo* because of his encounters. But I try to stay away from saying biologically he was, although in reality he was, because if it is about a mixed race, there is nothing more diverse than the divine and the human race. So, in a way you could say it, but I think it is better to avoid it.

Would you speak of Jesus as mestizo or just marginalized?

I think being a Galilean he was marginalized. Being a Galilean, he would be in constant contact with others. The constant contact with others would function as a *mestizo* society.

Can you speak more about your vision of a "new creation" or "new humanity"?

Eliminating the boundaries or blurring the boundaries—that to me is the Kingdom of God—when you constantly ease the boundaries that keep us apart. It is not a "super race," but a more inclusive expression of humanity. A *mestizo* child is not something "super," but is something new from the parents.

Some have mentioned that your portrayal of Jesus is anti-Jewish?

I have been accused of that, I don't think I am. I didn't realize that in the early days of the rise of the Nazi mentality where they were trying to separate Jesus from the Jews, they used the Galilean identity to claim he was not a Jew. So, they almost opposed it to justify anti-Judaism. But I never opposed it because I consider myself a Mexican but not just from Mexico. I've been more careful in later years to avoid that.

Would Mary's background be similar to what is said about Jesus?

I would say that being in the environment of Galilee, they would have certainly had *mestizo*-type experiences. Mary we know very little about, but Jesus growing up in Galilee—culturally, there is no doubt in my mind about the *mestizo* encounters.

Can you speak about the contributions of mestizaje?

The contribution *mestizos* make is to break down the separations at the most sacred level, the level of the sexual.

It seems that mestizaje is a universal concept, because it is a natural progression of humanity.

We are finding out more and more with DNA studies this progression.

For me, it seems to be a way of being more human.

For me too—absolutely, for me it is a step toward the final eschatological identity. When you see the ethnic divisions and hatreds of people, I think it becomes more and more urgent. But how to accept the newness, without rejecting, being ashamed of the parent groups. That to me is one of the big challenges even now. Lot of our Hispanic kids, they try to hide the Mexican side.

There's an interesting paradox happening in the Korean American community, we haven't had the Korean American role models, so everything in Korea seems good and here things appear second class.

We went through that and we are still there somewhat. We had a fellow who believed everything Mexico is great and pure, beautiful and nothing's wrong. He was a dark-skinned person and when he went to Mexico he was treated really badly because he couldn't speak Spanish correctly and he was very Indian-looking. He came back totally disillusioned because the Mexico he created in his mind doesn't exist. The first moments of the Chicano movement almost idealized just the Indian. They would have rejected my idea of *mestizaje*, because they rejected everything Spanish. It was just the Indian. My conviction is that every single group has expressions of grace and expressions of sin. I mean, there is cultural sin and cultural grace.

Lots of your work speaks to the first generation immigrants, do you see it influencing the next generation as well?

I think somewhat, but I don't know how much. One of the testimonials you might say of how I am influencing the next generation to come are the books of a secular author, John Phillip Santos, who has really taken up this *mestizaje* theme in his books and he credits me as being his mentor. In fact, he quotes me in his books a few times and he's not a theologian, he's a novelist. And he's very much the new wave, you might say of U.S. Latinos, who is somewhat reclaiming their Mexican roots—not wanting to go back to Mexico in any way and not wanting to impose, but rather celebrating his roots.

In my classes at Notre Dame I find young Latinos who desire to really know where we come from beyond just our own parents. The fact that we never study about Latino stuff in schools in the United States, the people who take my courses are regular 2nd, 3rd, and 4th generation Latinos fascinated by it. Many speak about it as liberation. So, I think there is an interest.

On your scriptural interpretation of Galilee . . .

It [historical-criticism] doesn't always point to it [*mestizo* encounters], but there is very serious scholarship that does speak about it. Even in the Gospel Jesus is constantly crossing borders, constantly going to Decapolis and the cities. And the fact that it's estimated that many of the Jewish people in Galilee worked as day laborers. I think there is enough evidence to think of Galilee as a region of encounters. There may have been very strong Jewish towns; they were commercial crossroads going through them. I don't agree with the criticisms. In hindsight, I try to be very careful, aware of the criticisms, especially when I wrote the article for *Theological Studies* and I had a couple of people go through it with a real fine comb. But I think I'm on firm grounds. I have worked with Sean Freyne, who is one of the leading experts on Galilee. I found his comments have led me to be more precise, but I don't think he's led me to take a different opinion. I also think there are different ways of reading the scriptures. The catechism brings it out. Even Pope Benedict in his book, *Jesus of Nazareth*, there is the critical-exegetical, but there is also the spiritual-analogical. What I take very serious even though it was after my first work was written is Pope John Paul II first encyclical that because of the incarnation, every detail of the life of Christ was part of the revelation. So, even for those who criticize me, I would pose the question, what for you is the theological meaning of Galilee? Which they haven't have answered. That's what my doctoral board, and I had a very good Christologist on the board, Christian Duquoc, he's a Frenchmen, not very well-known in this country, but a very good French theologian. He was the one who really grilled me, very strongly, in the defense about why I made Galilee a major theological point. Where did you get the idea to make it a theological point? Finally, I said it was my own stuff. The reason he was pushing me on the point because as far as he knew it, it has never been said before, but it was so self-evident. Regardless of how you interpret it, the fact that it is so consistently used has to have theological significance. So what is it? My point is that I have found a way to interpret Galilee, which I think is correct when you analyze it, but my point of departure for using Galilee as you know is; one, in the first sermon of Peter in the Acts of the Apostles, the stone rejected, the whole rejection-acceptance theme and I take the other theme from one of the earliest creeds in Philippians, he, in his divine condition empties himself. What does it mean to empties himself and becomes one among so many? He was so insignificant that nobody noticed him until he started doing his miracles. So, he becomes the insignificant one. Then the third point is the whole resurrected Lord who sends us back to Galilee, so there we will see him. Why do you have to be at Galilee to see Jesus? So, what is redemptive about Galilee? That is why I started to put together in terms of Jesus walking on to the Kingdom, yet he becomes one who can suffer in the flesh the pain of rejection. Therefore he knows the pain; therefore he works with the rejected. Those are what kind of led me to use Galilee. Is it exactly, historically correct? I don't think anybody knows, because I don't think there is agreement among the scholars and in my latest article I consulted the best scholarship and yes, it helped me to make precise my ideas, but not to change it.

When I read Jean Pierre Ruiz's article, the talk he gave at the CTSA meeting, it didn't seem like you were just the main focus of his criticisms. Unfortunately, he used you as an example for the point he was trying to make between the biblical scholars and systematic theologians, in particular, separating the conference and moving in different directions.

Actually, I don't know if you know the long term result of that. I received the academy's award for theology because so many that didn't know my work became knowledgeable of it. The long term result was very good, because I got the John Courtney Murray Award.

Mary Boys also made some comments regarding your anti-Jewish stance...

I never read her criticisms, but she felt that I was anti-semitic. It appeared to her that I was opposing Galilee to Jews, which I wasn't. That is why in my later writings I insist on Jesus being a Jewish Galilean.

On your latest article in Theological Studies . . .

I think it's just to criticize, I think that is what theology is about. But if anything it did help me to try to be more precise and it did help me to write the article for *Theological Studies,* I spent a lot of time going through the recent literature and I found nothing that would lead me to change my interpretation, although it did help me to become much more precise.

Could you talk a little about how a consciousness of a people comes about? You walked through the whole gamut as reflected in the creation of the cultural center here. This is something that personally interests me, the rise of a group consciousness.

I think it is one of those things that nobody controls. I think, generally speaking, the collective consciousness arises gradually through the historical process and we find certain common points whether it is certain historical dates we celebrate or certain songs we sing or certain foods we consider traditional or humor. I think there are diverse elements that we don't normally speak about, but we share, we kind of feel a sense of us—for example, when you hear a particular song like Mexican soul music or the feast of Our Lady of Guadalupe. Certain events give us a sense of collective consciousness. During the World Cup when Spain won is the only time in history when all the people trying to break away from Spain were celebrating Spain. So there is something to events like a football game, like a particular feast day, or like in the United States, the collective tragedy of 9/11. I think everyone was super-united. So, how does that come about? I think the historical consciousness gradually emerges. I think it can be helped. It is helped by certain heroes involved, whether they are movie stars or football players or certain people that in a way epitomize who we are. I think things like that bring out a sense of being.

What was the tipping point for Mexican American consciousness?

There have been several moments. I would say for a Mexican American consciousness, probably before World War II there was a Mexican consciousness. Regardless of whether there were several generations before being U.S. or not, basically the Spanish-speaking had a sense of being more Mexican. I think with WWII, many of our young men and women went into the military and had great pride of being in the military, a great sense of patriotism. With WWII, there begins to be a sense with returning veterans, a sense of Mexican Americans. Therefore, you find the beginning of movements that want to simply establish that they are just like other Americans. Movements started to show that we might be of Mexican heritage, but we are just like any American, we are just like you.

The next big wave was with the beginning of the civil rights movement, the César Chávez movement and all that where we started to affirm our cultural characteristics. Hey, we have language, we have foods and we don't want to lose them. The Chicano movement started to have a cultural sense, a cultural identity. The first sense was, we are going to speak English like everyone else, we are going to be just as American as you. The second movement was the cultural affirmation movement. I think we are still somewhat into that one now. I think now it is a combination of the two.

On the MACC . . .

I think MACC served a very important role in the Church. You hear from many people who went through here, from bishops and people in the academy. I think MACC made a contribution to the awakening of the positive contribution that Latinos can make in this country. That is one of the great things MACC did, to show that we are not just a problem to be solved, but a gift in the Church. I think MACC had a great impact.

For example, I don't know of any seminary that teaches a course, a serious course on the evangelization of Mexico. It is one of the most marvelous moments in Church history since the apostolic era. The creativity, the way they brought things together to form something new. It is just fascinating. I don't know any university teaching that at the seminary level. So, I am afraid that we are losing as we get a lot of Latin American seminarians who know neither their own history nor the history of the

United States nor the history of the Latino struggles. They are triply ignorant. Good fellows, likeable, but they have not been taught their own history in Latin America.

On liberation theology today in the Hispanic/Latino community . . .

A lot of people in this country are scared about liberation theology, but Hispanic evangelicals have assumed it completely. They have pushed the English-speaking evangelicals to be more socially minded. That's an indirect thing how liberation theology has transformed evangelicals.

On native vocations . . .

We are falling into the same trap. Instead of fostering native vocations we looked to Ireland. I have nothing against the Irish. But my point is, rather than fostering local vocations we went elsewhere. We are doing that with Latin America now. We are bringing priests from other places. The Church is still failing to really foster native vocations. I think that is the failure of the local Church. The Church is not really established without its own clergy.

Appendix B

Interview with Gustavo Gutiérrez
December 8, 2009

Is it an iPhone?[2]
Yes. It is an iPhone. Yes, I know it's not in line so much with my option for the poor.
[Laughter] Is this the new generation of iPhone?
Um, no. I find it helpful when I travel because I can record on it like this conversation.
Okay.

So, am I leaving out anything in your theological method in writing it from the perspective of the preferential option for the poor? It seems like everything that you are saying whether from scripture or Church teachings is always from the perspective of the poor.

Well, maybe I can start further back because, before the name of liberation theology, some years before '68, I was working the method in theology and speaking about, over this definition as you know this very well—theology and reflection, all praxis in the light of faith—it is before the name liberation theology. Another point before the name of liberation theology was the question of poverty in the bible. In 1967, one year prior to '68, before Medellín—these two big points were older points— we called this liberation theology. The name of liberation theology came later, after the meaning of poverty, and for us the question and for me,

2. Our conversation was recorded on an iPhone. My remarks and questions are paraphrased and in italics to give context to Gustavo Gutiérrez responses.

248

the question of reflection or praxis is the key point . . . actually means the life, means spirituality, is the right reason to follow Jesus Christ. For this reason spirituality was so central in liberation theology from the very beginning.

It seems that the difference I noticed between your writings and your European counterparts is that the European theologians have a difficult time putting together praxis with contemplation, which together is prayer—where for you, you speak of prayer as both worship and practice.

I say praxis is prayer and commitment because prayer is a practice. I am doing something, and well, some Europeans theologians were very important at that time in the beginning like Fr. Chenu, a Dominican. For him . . . to understand theology we must go to spirituality. Spirituality as a source [of theology], this idea was very important for me. Another Theologian putting the accent in praxis was Schillebeeckx, another Dominican.

But you mentioned that your work in theology has always been very different since the theology being done in Latin America addressed the non-person, where Europeans were addressing the non-believer.

Exactly.

So, the works of Chenu and Schillebeeckx could only go so far for you?

Well, they were Europeans theologians but very open to human history, on this side we are close [to each other]. They were not speaking exactly as liberation theology today, but with some ideas very relevant and important for me and other persons.

Did protestant theologians influence you too like Moltmann?

Moltmann, a little bit, but not so much, not so much . . . I am almost a contemporary of Moltmann . . . Metz was relevant also in political theology. But clearly for them the interlocutor was another mentality for Moltmann and for Metz, clearly.

Do you think they ever got to the point of seeing theology from your per-spective, from what you were trying to do?

I would say yes, through my pastoral work, a work . . . very marked by the concrete and daily problems of the poor persons. Because I was a parish priest for forty years, my first appointment as professor in a theological institute was here eight years ago, before that I worked as a professor in only one theological center.

You write many times that you are priest first, theologian second in your spare time.

It was very useful for me you know, because I find pastoral work very stimulating, theological speaking.

I see similarities on this point with Virgilio's work as he too is walking with his people first.

Virgilio, he was pastor for a long time. You know, Chenu, he was a very committed pastorally, very close to the problems of the people . . . Chenu was a very important influence for me. I knew him personally, very well actually, and at the same time, I have tried to do a theology looking for biblical foundation, I was always dealing with the bible. And often in this country, this democratic theology is not biblical. Well, it depends, there are always exceptions, but often more philosophical. I have tried to go to the biblical foundations. It is always risky but it is necessary.

How do you see scripture scholars scrutinizing liberation theologians for their use of scripture?

Well, it is their right; they can criticize. Other scripture scholars are in favor. For example, Norbert Lohfink, a Jesuit, he has written a small book called *Option for the Poor* or another person Ulrich Luz, author of a big commentary . . . open to liberation theology. It depends, not all American scholars were against [us]. Leon Duffy . . . was open to liberation theology. Also other American scholars: Pablo Richards, Elsa Thomas—they are biblical scholars.

One of the things that I enjoyed reading is when you talked about where you were when certain things happened. When you talk about the close of Vatican II, you were sitting in your room in Rome, listening to it on the radio and, in one sense, you were feeling happy with what the Church did, but at the same time, you were also sad.

[laughter] You have read this . . . I was [studying] the poor section of the Council and I was very happy there. I was learning a lot. Many of my professors of theology were there working in the Council as experts, but at the end of the Council, in the two days of the final session, yes I was exactly this, happy and at the same time [sad because] the big problems of my country, my continent were not present. Well, it is not a critique of Vatican II, it is only to see it is the case, how it was so. Vatican II was doing a very good work, very beautiful work, but I was very—French people call this *sentiments mélanges*, feeling mixed or mixed feelings.

You also write that once you became a priest that you are no longer insignificant and that you too had to live out your option for the poor. What has been some of the struggle with that?

In our context, we say poverty is not only an economic issue, poverty is also to be insignificant for several reasons; one is economic, or the color of the skin is another reason, or to speak badly—the dominant language of our country is another reason, to be a woman is another reason. With this point of view of insignificance, I cannot say that here or in my country a priest is an insignificant person—it is not true. I could be poor economically maybe, but I am not insignificant, my family background is poor in the global view, but I was studying, being a priest doing theology—I am not insignificant. But you know, to be clear, my intention is not to do a comparison here, but Romero was not insignificant. An Archbishop in a small country, one of the most important persons in the country, but he was giving his life to the poor, this is the first thing.

On commitment to the poor . . .

You know, to be committed to the poor is not to try to imitate the concrete poverty of the poor because it is impossible. The commitment is solidarity—that is the true commitment. But you know, this discussion

about Jesus Christ—was he poor, was he not poor, was the family poor—
he is not insignificant. People called him rabbi, he is not insignificant in
this perspective. He is not poor, but committed to them. They crucified
him for this reason.

Commitment as being friends with the poor . . .

This is very important—the question is not only to fight for the rights of
the poor, but personal friendship. As Jesus [says] in the Gospel of John,
chapter 15—I don't call you servants, but friends—because friendship
supposes a kind of equality. We share our lives with friends, this is the
point.

On theology and context . . .

Any theology has a context. Any theology, when Europeans and North
Americans people say contextual theologies, it is a very bad expression
because any theology is contextual. The theology of gravity is contextual,
but they say that contextual theology is not that important, theology that
is the idea.

You write that theology bears the mark of historical time in an ecclesiasti-
cal context. They live basically as long as the conditions that gave their
origins exist. Is this also the case for liberation theology?

At the same time, we cannot ask a theology to change the world. This
role of poverty and unfortunately is so deep and so radical and so serious. But liberation theology has recalled the place of the poor in the
Christian message. Because when we say preferential option for the
poor, the sentence is new, the content is very old, the content of the poor
are the first seen in the bible in both testament—is not new, only the
sentence is new.

Where do you think we are at this moment in the Church? Are we matur-
ing after progressing from Vatican II to Medellín to Puebla?

Well, it is very complicated, in some points we have some gains, some progress, but some backwards also. But if we take the vision, the vision of the Latin American conferences, the last one is very good.

Aparecida?

Aparecida—is Medellín in another language—is 40 years after but it is very close to it. For example, preferential option for the poor is a very important affirmation of Aparecida, because the Pope, especially at the beginning of the conference, was very clear about preferential option of the poor. He says this is implicit in the Christological faith and that it is, to say, the center of the Christ of Faith . . . Aparecida repeated the relevance of the option of the poor. When some people ask me about the presence of liberation theology in the Church, I say well, 90% of it is very present in the preferential option for the poor today. It is one point of the ecclesial magisterium. Option for the poor is coming from Latin American, from liberation theology, and now is a universal affirmation of the Churches because several evangelical Churches also [affirm it].

In one of your comments on Puebla, you were critiquing the PD, the pre-paratory document. What happened during that time from Medellín to Puebla that that document took a different direction and what was your direct involvement?

Because we had had some people very critical of Medellín, especially the person who [was] also the secretary of the CELAM, Alfonso Lopez Trujillos, [became] Cardinal after and is dead now. He was very critical of Medellín and to some experts, the authors of the preparatory document, their intention was to distance [themselves] from Medellín . . . Puebla, rather speaking about preferential option for the poor, it was not in the perspective of this critique of Medellín. Santo Domingo is a very weak document, some points are good, and Medellín was excellent, but many points underlined by liberation theology are today present every-where in the Church. Not necessarily original points of liberation theol-ogy, but liberation theology—we were speaking, for example, above all, having one history not a religious history and human history . . . Others question the social science in Medellín. We [consider] poverty [as a] social thing. Some people were very critical saying, "no, no, no," [it] does not exist, only personal thing. Well, we were speaking about the social measure of personal thing. But after the document of John Paul II about this question, [it] finished the discussion [as] social thing today is [real] . . . World history is very important, the use of social science to know reality, we were very criticized also, but today biblical studies are full of social science, the time of Jesus social context and so, again, is not original idea, but it was present in our points and, in this sense I think, Aparecida is taking many points about the spirituality. Also the speech of the Pope was very good in Aparecida, very good.

It changed some of the tone that the Vatican has taken.

Oh certainly, I think the speech of Benedict is the best speech addressed today in the Latin American Bishop Conference—is better than the speech of Paul VI; is better than the speech of John Paul.

Pope Benedict's?

Pope Benedict's is the best. Opening the conferences [were] Paul VI, John Paul II and Benedict—Benedict's is the best. The speech—it was a surprise for many people . . . You know he is a very intelligent man, very good theologian, very European person also. And he is able to change . . . and I think thirty years ago, twenty-five years ago, he was not clear about our point of view about theology, but he has learned.

Now, people close to you say that he wrote a personal letter to you after he became Pope thanking you for your work in Latin America, is this true?

Personal letter to the Dominican Superior yes, not to me . . . No, no, it was a very beautiful letter but addressed to the Superior of the Dominican order about myself. The content of the letter was my work and a very open letter.

In a positive light?

Very positive letter, but this is very ecclesiastical, he was writing to my superior not [to me] personally. But I met him several times, over the years several times. I know him well, well relatively.

You already mentioned some things about personal sin, social sin, but in liberation you talked about first social liberation, the human liberation, and then sin.

The sin dimensions of liberation.

Which correlates with the poverty?

No, it correlates with world history . . . Only one liberation—sin dimension of this statement, of this statement has zero dimensions, it's only one statement. Liberation is only one, but liberation is also from all oppression, is also . . . personal liberation.

Because for some, they cannot understand why liberation from sin is the third, thinking it as a hierarchy or a priority instead of seeing it as one.

That is true. But you know, the third liberation or third dimension is the root. [It] is the root, because to oppressed, other persons—first liberation, the root is the sin, is to refuse to love, but the idea is to say is we have one liberation, because everything happens in history for us. You know, [it] is a matter to take seriously our dogmatic affirmation about Incarnation. Incarnation is this, is that everything is here, and for these questions, and certainly the history, another aspect—eschatological aspect, is beyond history the communion with God, full communion. But the Kingdom is already present. Look it is very noble. This sentence is already present—very, very classic—already present.

You also talk about how assimilation has been destructive, assimilation then and now.

Yes, in the colonial perspective . . . We are living a very interesting moment because never in our humanity, not the whole humanity, but many people were so conscious about the relevance of, to be different, the idea of the other. This is the question, to respect for other cultures, the persons, and to assimilation means, in the case of my continent. For the European people, there was to be European and it was the idea. And Las Casas has reacted against this. You have read my book of Las Casas? Is the last one there, he has a concept, one theologian from Paris, Scottish but teaching in Paris, "if you were Indian, your views would be different," because the point of views are very important. It was Las Casas defending the Indians against worse domination and so with respect for their culture and it was, even today, many persons are thinking this—the best way to be modern.

Do you see the Church doing a better job at that now? Has it improved?

Well, yes, in one sense, but there are many reactions against. The Church is too big and we have several currents and trends inside. Certainly, many things have changed in the history of the Catholic Church, what we call the martyrdom in Latin America is one expression. First time in four centuries, people are killing Christians because they are Christians, even killing bishops, and the killers are baptized. First time, it is a very painful expression of this change. Romero was killed for this reason, because for them it was a danger, and he was a bishop. We have at least three bishops in Latin America killed. Before Romero, was Angelini in Argentina and after Romero, Gerardi in Guatemala. It is incredible, a Christian continent killing bishops, priest, lay persons, nuns, hundreds, hundreds. Something must be changed, to arrive to this manner, to these assassinations. Well, but these older aspects are difficult but you know the Church has never changed the world in some years, slavery in the 19th century, and we cannot ask to this perspective today—liberation theology to change Latin America because we are not the only factor. The economy in this country is very important there, military people are very important—so many, many factors there.

Do you feel that your theology has changed over time?

Oh normally, normally, because if the definition of theology is a reflection on praxis, it means history in the light of faith. History is aerobic, is reflection of praxis, not reflection about one concept, concepts are not changing. But praxis changes, a reflection about dynamic reality normally changes, we cannot just repeat. At the same time, the basic intuitions are there, but new problems, globalization was not present for us 40 years ago. And we know better today the complexity of poverty better than the beginning.

Has that helped though?

Yes, I think there are many progress and many other difficulties also. How to do global is usually very difficult. But we have many Christians today, Catholics and others, very committed to the poor. We did not have this half a century ago, 50 years ago. This is a progress, but this is not enough to change reality, but this is the case.

When I read your writing in the 70's and the 80's, there is always hope and passion in your writings, even in your anniversary edition of your A Theology of Liberation you write your theology is a love letter and cannot change it. Do you still have the same hope and passion?

Yes, it was my answer to a journalist. Because people were asking me several times "You are ready to write your book today in the same way than twenty years ago?" Sometimes, I say no because my book is the same [since] I am still alive . . . [I cannot] write a retraction, but is impossible to write the same way . . . One day, this journalist put [to] me this question. I said "my friend are you married?"; "yes,"; "do you love your wife?"; "yes,"; "are you ready to write a love letter in the same term as twenty years ago?"; "no." The love is the same.

And is the same today too . . .

But I need to change my manner, for me, is very serious. For me, to do theology is to write a love letter to God, to my Church, and to my people. This is to do theology to me.

And you still have the same passion today?

Certainly and psychologically, I am very passionate. I passionate, but I avoid to criticize easily other person or to enter in polemics because I think is not interesting, but personally yes, because I lived it, because

I was very close to the poverty, because for my family in the beginning and after as a priest and theologian.

I believe it is in the God of Life, *you cite some works of Virgilio about the mestizo, mestizaje, and the Galilean Jesus.*

Yes, at one point.

Do you have any other comments about his work? Do you remember how you two met?

Well, I think Virgilio has opened ways for the reflection of the Hispanic or Latin people of this country, and the point of the *mestizaje* is very important. I know *mestizaje* a little differently because of the *mestizaje* in Latin America.

In what ways is mestizaje *different for you?*

Because here in this country, it means being Hispanic and American, it is not exactly our case there. But it is very interesting because they are Hispanic people but living here, born here, citizens of this country, and Virgilio has taken into account this, to keep it in mind. I think that this perspective of *mestizaje* is not easy, and you know *mestizaje* today, it is a planetary reality . . . The people are communicating in the language English today, [also] present in Spanish today in Latin America, very present. And so it is normal, but at the same time we need to respect cultures. But to respect is not to keep cultures in the same ways, but the values. Hospitality, for example, is not so big here with this country, very individualistic mentality, so I think some cultural values are very important. Virgilio was the first person in the Hispanic community, Mexican Americans. It is a *mestizaje*, Mexican Americans, that has open ways and taken the perspective of the elitist to reflect.

Liberation theology elsewhere . . .

But you know, never in my life was my interest to have liberation theology in other countries, because there are, kind of, different. For me, the point is to take the perspective of the least, this is important. The name liberation or not [is] secondary.

And I think that is yours, both you and Virgilio's gift, that I can take your work and make it my own.

Exactly! . . . Another theology was in the Philippines, a Filipino theology. Very radical in one moment, but I think our realities are so different, . . . in very different manners, our reflection. But the questions, because it is Biblical, is not Latin American, but biblical, it is to start from the least, the last person, the people that you know, the dalit, the last. This is the point. The content of liberation theology was born, and I have recorded this, before the name liberation theology. With all the poor, liberation before the name . . . because liberation is salvation, [since,] salvation is a central notion in the recent research. But, because it is not to apply a theology born in one context in another context, this is not the question. The question is to reflect again . . . I was taking many points from some European theologians; I have no shame for this . . . . I have learned a lot from them . . . I cannot say I have applied Congar's theology, this is not true. The acts of Congar are different . . . our realities are not against one another. To be against Europeans in order to be Latin American does not make sense. This is a risk sometimes we try to [avoid] so in this country [and] Europe also, people are asking me do you think it is possible [for] liberation theology here, and I say here it is possible a theology that starts from the poor. Well, to put another name is no problem. This is possible to start from the poor. In Europe today ignorance, migration today is terrible.

I think that has very good ecumenical value, because you are not talking about starting from Christian and non-Christian beliefs, but starting from the poor.

And the non-Christians could be sensitive to this, because for human reasons non-believers understand the suffering of the poor, they understand this. And in Mexico, the Mexican Revolution in the beginning of the 20th century, we had ideology against the Church it was very strong in Mexico. And one day, I receive one letter asking me to write one article about liberation theology in one review, Mexican review, but a political social, political philosophical, nothing to do with religion. I was surprised. But the whole issue was catered to liberation theology. But they are not Christian . . . They were fighting against the Church supporting justice and so according to them, was this liberation theology or another name, well, I have no problem. He put liberation, liberation theology is not Latin American, is biblical. The meaning of liberation varies and we have a family today. Black theology in this country is contemporary to liberation in Latin America, is not influenced because we are at the same time and we are the same, different accent. Racism is very important for black theology. Or today Indian theology in Latin America, we have an Indian theology; we have black theology in Brazil, feminist theology certainly, dalit theology— this is a family—it is coming from reality, it is not coming from one book of theology. It is coming from the Bible and from reality.

Is your institute in Peru still going strong there?

Yes, but it's not only theology . . . Theology is only one section . . . the idea is to reflect, the idea is to reflect on praxis as a Christian, but it is an interdisciplinary institute. We have sociology, economy, psychology and theology.

Are you still involved with the Institute?

Yes, yes, yes, I am always there. We have no formal courses there, we have workshops or conferences. Informal courses also one week or so.

And when you go back to Peru, do you go back to the parish?

I cannot now, but I was there 20 years in my parish, because today, the priest in charge is not a friend. I am going to my neighborhood to see my friends, not exactly to the parish.

Bibliography

PRIMARY LITERATURE

Works by Virgil Elizondo

"The African Way." *The Tablet* 245 (1991) 253–54.

"America's Changing Face." *The Tablet* 242 (1988) 832–34.

"Analysis of Racism." In *Migrants and Refugees*, edited by Dietmar Mieth and Lisa Sowle Cahill, 52–59. London: SCM, 1993.

Anthropological and Psychological Characteristics of the Mexican American. San Antonio: MACC, 1974.

L'Avenir est au Mestissage. Translated by J. Pierron. Paris, France: Novelles Editions Mame, 1987; English version, *The Future is Mestizo: Life Where Cultures Meet*. Bloomington: Meyer Stone, 1988; reprint, New York: Crossroad, 1992; reprint, San Antonio: MACC, 1998.

"Benevolent Tolerance or Humble Reverence? A Vision for Multicultural Religious Education." In *Multicultural Religious Education*, edited by Barbara Wilkerson, 395–406. Birmingham: Religious Education, 1997; reprint in *Beyond Borders: Writings of Virgilio Elizondo and Friends*, edited by Timothy Matovina, 87–97. Maryknoll, NY: Orbis, 2000.

"Biblical Pedagogy of Evangelization." *American Ecclesiastical Review* 168 (1974) 526–43.

"The Biblical Pedagogy of Evangelization." In *Colección Mestiza Americana*, 1–19. San Antonio: MACC, 1975.

"A Bicultural Approach to Religious Education." *Religious Education* 76 (1981) 258–70; reprint in *Beyond Borders: Writings of Virgilio Elizondo and Friends*, edited by Timothy Matovina, 62–71. Maryknoll, NY: Orbis, 2000.

"By Their Fruits You Will Know Them: The Biblical Roots of Peace and Justice." In *Education for Peace and Justice*, edited by Padraic O'Hare, 39–65. San Francisco: Harper & Row, 1983.

"A Catechetical Response for Minorities." In *Colección Mestiza Americana*, 92–109. San Antonio: MACC, 1975.

"The Catechumen in the Hispanic Community of the United States." In *Becoming a Catholic Christian: A Symposium on Christian Initiation Organized and Directed by Christiane Brusselmans*, edited by William J. Reedy, 51–57. New York: Sadlier, 1979.

"A Challenge to Theology: The Situation of Hispanic Americans." *Catholic Theological Society of America Proceedings* 30 (1975) 163–76.

"A Child in the Manger: The Beginning of a New Order of Existence." In *Proclaiming the Acceptable Year*, edited by Justo L. González, 64–70. Valley Forge: Judson, 1982.

"Christian Challenge and the Disadvantaged." *Linacre Quarterly* 50 (1983) 242–45.

"The Christian Identity and Mission of the Catholic Hispanic in the United States." In *Hispanic Catholics in the United States*, 61–71. New York: Spanish-American Printing, 1980.

Christianity and Culture: An Introduction to Pastoral Theology and Ministry for the Bicultural Community. San Antonio: MACC, 1999.

"Collaborative Theology: Latin American Bishops, The Pope & The Poor." *Commonweal* 135, no 2 (2008) 8–9.

"Conditions and Criteria for Authentic Inter-Cultural Theological Dialogue." In *Different Theologies, Common Responsibility: Babel or Pentecost?*, edited by Claude Geffré, Gustavo Gutiérrez, and Virgilio Elizondo, 18–24. Edinburgh: T. & T. Clark, 1984.

"Cultural Pluralism and the Catechism." In *Introducing the Catechism of the Catholic Church*, edited by Berard L. Marthaler, 142–62. New York: Paulist, 1994; reprint in *Beyond Borders: Writings of Virgilio Elizondo and Friends*, edited by Timothy Matovina, 72–86. Maryknoll, NY: Orbis, 2000.

"Culture, Church and." In *New Catholic Encyclopedia* 17, 167–68. New York: McGraw Hill, 1979.

"Culture, the Option for the Poor, and Liberation." In *The Option for the Poor in Christian Theology*, edited by Daniel G. Groody, 157–68. Notre Dame: University of Notre Dame Press, 2007.

"Documento Final de la Semana Internacional de Estudios sobre Medios de Comunicación Social y Catequesis." *The Living Light* 6 (1969) 78–87.

"Ecumenism: An Hispanic Perspective." *Ecumenist* 22 (1984) 70–74.

"Educación Religiosa para el México-Norteamericano." *Catequesis Latino-americana* 4 (1972) 83–86.

"El idioma de la resistencia, la supervivencia y la liberación." In *Vida y reflexión: Aportes de la teologia de la liberación al pensamiento teologico actual*, 235–48. Lima: Centros de Estudios y Publicaciones, 1983.

"Elements for a Mexican American Mestizo Christology." *Voices from the Third World* 11 (1988) 97–117.

"Evangelization in the Americas: Santo Domingo from the Perspective of U.S. Hispanics." In *Santo Domingo and Beyond: Documentation and Commentary*, edited by John Eagleson and Philip Scharper, translated by John Drury, 202–11. Maryknoll, NY: Orbis, 1993.

"Evil and the Experience of God." *The Way: Contemporary Christian Spirituality* 33 (1993) 34–43; reprint in *Beyond Borders: Writings of Virgilio Elizondo and Friends*, edited by Timothy Matovina, 225–32. Maryknoll, NY: Orbis, 2000.

"Expanding Horizons in Ministry." In *Colección Mestiza Americana*, 83–91. San Antonio: MACC, 1975.

"Foreword." In *El Cuerpo de Cristo: The Hispanic Presence in the U. S. Catholic Church*, edited by Peter Casarella and Raúl Gómez, 9–20. New York: The Crossroad Publishing Company, 1998.

"Foreword." In *Mañana: Christian Theology from a Hispanic Perspective*, edited by Justo L. González, 9–20. Nashville: Abingdon, 1990.

Galilean Journey: The Mexican-American Promise. Maryknoll, NY: Orbis, 1983; 2nd edition, 2000.

A God of Incredible Surprises. Lanham, MD: Rowman & Littlefield, 2003.

"Guadalupe: An Endless Source of Reflection." *Journal of Hispanic/Latino Theology* 5 (1997) 61–65.

Guadalupe: Mother of the New Creation. Maryknoll, NY: Orbis, 1997.

"Guadalupe: The Birth of American Mestizo Christianity." *Louvain Studies* 26 (2001) 295–312.

"The Hispanic Church in the U.S.A.: A Local Ecclesiology." *The Catholic Theological Society of America Proceedings* 36 (1981) 155–70.

"Hispanic Theology and Popular Piety: From Interreligious Encounter to a New Ecumenism." *Catholic Theological Society of America Proceedings* 48 (1993) 1–14; reprint in *Beyond Borders: Writings of Virgilio Elizondo and Friends*, edited by Timothy Matovina, 278–86. Maryknoll, NY: Orbis, 2000.

"The Human Quest: A Search for Meaning through Life and Death." *Our Sunday Visitor* (1997).

"I Forgive But I Do Not Forget." In *Forgiveness*, edited by Casiano Floristan and Christian Duquoc, 69–79. Edinburgh: T. & T. Clark, 1986; reprint in *Beyond Borders: Writings of Virgilio Elizondo and Friends*, edited by Timothy Matovina, 208–16. Maryknoll, NY: Orbis, 2000.

"Incarnation and Culture." *Momentum* 28 (1997) 67–69.

"Jesus the Galilean Jew in Mestizo Theology." *Theological Studies* 70.2 (2009) 262–80.

"Le mestissage comme lieu theologique." *Spiritus* 24 (1983) 349–75; translated and republished as "*Mestizaje* as a Locus of Theological Reflection." In *The Future of Liberation Theology: Essays in Honor of Gustavo Gutiérrez*, edited by Marc H. Ellis and Otto Maduro, 358–74. Maryknoll, NY: Orbis, 1989; reprint in *Mestizo Christianity: Theology from a Latino Perspective*, edited by Arturo J. Bañuelas, 7–27. Maryknoll, NY: Orbis, 1989; reprint in *Frontiers of Hispanic Theology in the United States*, edited by Allan Figueroa Deck, 104–23. Maryknoll, NY: Orbis, 1992; reprint in *Beyond Borders: Writings of Virgilio Elizondo and Friends*, edited by Timothy Matovina, 159–75. Maryknoll, NY: Orbis, 2000.

"María de Guadalupe: Star of the First and New Evangelization." *Ephemerides Mariologicae* 56 (2006) 353–59.

"Mary and Evangelization in the Americas." In *Mary, Woman of Nazareth*, edited by Doris Donnelly, 146–60. New York: Paulist, 1989.

"Mary and the Poor: A Model of Evangelising Ecumenism." In *Mary in the Churches*, edited by Hans Küng and Jürgen Moltmann, 59–65. New York: Seabury, 1983.

"Mary in the Struggles of the Poor." *New Catholic World* 229 (1986) 244–47.

Mary the Compassionate Mother. Chicago: Loyola Univerity Press, 2007.

Mestizaje: The Dialectic of Cultural Birth and the Gospel. San Antonio: MACC, 1978.

"Mestissage: La naissance d'une nouvelle culture et d'une nouvelle chrétienté." *Lumière et Vie* 208 (1992) 77–90.

"Mestizaje: The Birth of New Life." In *Frontier Violations*, 47–53. London: SCM, 1999.

"'Mestizaje' Theology: As a Promising Cultural Future." *Erasmus Colloquium* (2005) 1–21.

"Mexamerica: Une Galilée des Nations." *Catéchèse* 102 (1986) 99–107.

"The Mexican American as Seen from Within." In *Prophets without Honor: An Anthology on the Hispano Church of the United States*, edited by Antonio M. Stevens Arroyo, 5–7. Maryknoll, NY: Orbis, 1980.

"Ministry in Education from a Pastoral-Theological Perspective." In *Ministry and Education in Conversation*, edited by Mary C. Boys, 45–73. Winona: Saint Mary's Press, 1981.

"The Ministry of the Church and Contemporary Migration." *Social Thought* 13 (1987) 120–32.

La Morenita: Evangelizer of the Americas. San Antonio: MACC, 2001.

"A New Humanity." *North Dakota Quarterly* 59.4 (1991) 17–20.

"The New Humanity of the Americas." In *1492–1992: The Voice of the Victims*, edited by Leonardo Boff and Virgilio Elizondo, 142–47. London: SCM, 1990; reprint in *Beyond Borders: Writings of Virgilio Elizondo and Friends*, edited by Timothy Matovina, 272–77. Maryknoll, NY: Orbis, 2000.

"On the Streets of a Fragile World." In *Walking with God in a Fragile World*, edited by James Langford and Leroy S. Rouner, 47–55. Lanham, MD: Rowman & Littlefield, 2003.

"Our Lady of Guadalupe as a Cultural Symbol: 'The Power of the Powerless.'" In *Liturgy and Cultural Religious Traditions*, edited by Herman Schmidt and David Power, 25–33. New York: Seabury, 1977; reprint in *Beyond Borders: Writings of Virgilio Elizondo and Friends*, edited by Timothy Matovina, 118–25. Maryknoll, NY: Orbis, 2000.

"Pastoral Opportunities of Pilgrimages." In *Pilgrimage*, edited by Virgilio Elizondo and Sean Freyne, 107–14. London: SCM, 1996; reprint in *Beyond Borders: Writings of Virgilio Elizondo and Friends*, edited by Timothy Matovina, 133–39. Maryknoll, NY: Orbis, 2000.

"Pastoral Planning for the Spanish Speaking in the United States." In *Prophets without Honor: An Anthology on the Hispano Church of the United States*, edited by Antonio M. Stevens Arroyo, 183–87. Maryknoll, NY: Orbis, 1980.

"Pastoral Planning for the Spanish-speaking in the United States." In *Colección Mestiza Americana*, 57–69. San Antonio: MACC, 1975.

"Politics, Catechetics, and Liturgy." *Religion Teacher's Journal* 10 (1976) 30–32.

"The Pope's Opening Address: Introduction and Commentary." In *Puebla and Beyond*, edited by John Eagleson and Philip Scharper, 47–55. Maryknoll, NY: Orbis, 1979.

"Popular Religion as Support of Identity: A Pastoral-Psychological Case-Study Based on the Mexican American Experience in the USA." In *Popular Religion*, edited by Norbert Greinacher and Norbert Mette, 36–43. Edinburgh: T. & T. Clark, 1986; reprint in *Beyond Borders: Writings of Virgilio Elizondo and Friends*, edited by Timothy Matovina, 126–32. Maryknoll, NY: Orbis, 2000.

"Popular Religion as the Core of Cultural Identity Based on the Mexican American Experience in the United States." In *An Enduring Flame: Studies on Latino Popular Religiosity*, edited by Anthony M. Stevens-Arroyo and Ana María Diaz-Stevens, 113–32. New York: Bildner Center for Western Hemisphere Studies, 1994.

Popular Religious Practices of the Mexican American and Catechesis. San Antonio: MACC, 1974.

"Pueblo de Dios en Marcha." In *Visión Profética: Reflexiones Pastorales sobre el Plan Pastoral para el Ministerio Hispano*, edited by Soledad Galerón, Rosa María Icaza and Rosendo Urrabazo, 44–52. Kansas City, MO: Sheed & Ward, 1992; reprint in *Prophetic Vision: Pastoral Reflections on the National Pastoral Plan for Hispanic Ministry*, edited by Soledad Galerón, Rosa María Icaza, and Rosendo Urrabazo, 218–26. Kansas City, MO: Sheed & Ward, 1992.

"Religious Education for Mexican Americans." In *Beyond Borders: Writings of Virgilio Elizondo and Friends*, edited by Timothy Matovina, 58–61. Maryknoll, NY: Orbis, 2000.

"A Report on Racism: A Mexican American in the United States." In *The Church and Racism*, edited by Gregory Baum and John Coleman, 61–65. New York: Seabury, 1982.

"Response to the Article by C. Peter Wagner." *International Bulletin of Missionary Research* 10 (1986) 65–66.

"Response to Theological Education and Liberation Theology Symposium." *Theological Education* 16 (1979) 34–37.

"The Response of Liberation Theology." In *Pentecostal Movements as an Ecumenical Challenge* 51–56. Maryknoll, NY: Orbis, 1996.

"Retrieving the Dream: One Priest's Story." *Priests and Community: Their Stories, Their Future. Proceedings of the Annual Meeting of the National Federation of Priests' Councils* (1992) 17–25.

"The Sacred in the Latino Experience/Lo sagrado en la experiencia latina." In *Americanos: Latino Life in the United States/La Vida Latina en los Estados Unidos*, edited by Edward James Olmos, Lea Ybarra, and Manuel Monterrey, 20–23. Boston, New York, London: Little, Brown, 1999.

"The San Antonio Experience: Transformation of the Meaning and Function of Borders." *Colloque International: "Europe et Christianisme"* Université de METZ (1990) 1–12.

"Significado de Medellín para la Iglesia latinoamericana." In *Profecía y evangelización: Bartolomé de Las Casas; Medellín*, 77–97. Lima: Centro de Estudios y Publaciónes, 1978.

"Theological Education." *Theological Education and Liberation Theology: A Symposium* XVI:1 (1979) 34–37.

"A Theological Interpretation of the Mexican American Experience." *Perkins Journal* 25, no. 1 (1975) 12–21.

"A Theology of Evangelization." In *Priest's Councils/USA: Ministry-Evangelization-community*, 7–20. Chicago: National Federation of Priests' Councils, 1979.

"Theology's Contribution to Society: The Ministry of the Theologian." In *From the Heart of Our People: Latino/a Explorations in Catholic Systematic Theology*, edited by Orlando O. Espín and Miguel H. Díaz, 49–53. Maryknoll, NY: Orbis, 1999.

"Toward an American-Hispanic Theology of Liberation in the U.S.A." In *Irruption of the Third World: Challenge to Theology*, edited by Virginia Fabella and Sergio Torres, 50–55. Maryknoll, NY: Orbis, 1983.

"Transformation of Borders: Border Separation or New Identity." In *Theology: Expanding the Borders*, edited by María Pilar Aquino and Roberto S. Goizueta, 22–39. Mystic: Twenty-Third Publications, 1998.

"Transformation of Borders: *Mestizaje* and the Future of Humanity." In *Beyond Borders: Writings of Virgilio Elizondo and Friends*, edited by Timothy Matovina, 176–86. Maryknoll, NY: Orbis, 2000.

"Transmission of the Faith in the U.S.A." In *Transmission of the Faith to the Next Generation*, edited by Virgilio Elizondo and Norbert Greinacher, 100–105. Edinburgh: T. & T. Clark, 1984.

"Unmasking the Idols." *SEDOS* 24, no. 5 (1992) 131–40; reprint in *Beyond Borders: Writings of Virgilio Elizondo and Friends*, edited by Timothy Matovina, 217–24. Maryknoll, NY: Orbis, 2000.

The Way of the Cross of the Americas. Maryknoll, NY: Orbis, 1992.

"What Good Can Come Out of Galilee?" *Church & Society* 93.4 (2003) 56–64.

Collaborated Works with Elizondo

Arroyo, Stevens, Antonio M., and Virgilio Elizondo. "The Spanish-speaking in the United States." In *Prophets without Honor: An Anthology on the Hispano Church of the United States*, edited by Antonio M. Stevens Arroyo, 7–13. Maryknoll, NY: Orbis, 1980.

Boff, Leonardo, and Virgil Elizondo. "Ecology and Poverty: Cry of the Earth, Cry of the Poor." In *Ecology and Poverty: Cry of the Earth, Cry of the Poor*. London: SCM, 1995.

———. "Editorial." In *Convergences and Differences*, edited by Leonardo Boff and Virgil Elizondo, vi–xv. Edinburgh: T. & T. Clark, 1988.

———. "Epilogue." In *The People of God Amidst the Poor*, edited by Leonardo Boff and Virgil Elizondo, 108–9. Edinburgh: T. & T. Clark, 1984.

———. "Theology from the Viewpoint of the Poor." In *Option for the Poor: Challenge to the Rich Countries*, edited by Leonardo Boff and Virgil Elizondo, ix–xii. Edinburgh: T. & T. Clark, 1986.

———. "The Voices of the Victims: Who Will Listen to Them?" In *1492–1992: The Voice of the Victims*, edited by Leonardo Boff and Virgilio Elizondo, vii–x. Edinburgh: T. & T. Clark, 1984.

Elizondo, Virgilio, editor. *The Way of the Cross: The Passion of Christ in the Americas*, translated by John Drury. Maryknoll, NY: Orbis, 1992.

Elizondo, Virgil, and Norbert Greinacher. "Between Conformity and Rejection: The Difficult Path of the Church in the Second World." In *Churches in Socialist Societies of Eastern Europe*, edited by Norbert Greinacher and Virgil Elizondo, xii–x. Edinburgh: T. & T. Clark, 1984.

———. "Do We Really Have Third World Churches?" In *Tensions Between the Churches of the First World and the Third World*, edited by Norbert Greinacher and Virgil Elizondo, vii–ix. Edinburgh: T. & T. Clark, 1980.

———. "Editorial: Handing on the Faith to the Next Generation." In *Transmission of the Faith to the Next Generation*, edited by Virgilio Elizondo and Norbert Greinacher, ix–x. Edinburgh: T. & T. Clark, 1984.

———. "Has Men's Liberation Gone Too Far?" In *Transmission Women in a Men's Church*, edited by Norbert Greinacher and Virgil Elizondo, vii–viii. Edinburgh: T. & T. Clark, 1980.

———. "Stages of Practical Theology." In *Twenty Years of Concilium – Retrospect and Prospect*, edited by Paul Brand, Edward Schillebeeckx, and Anton Weiler, 20–26. New York: Seabury, 1983.

———. "Thou Shalt Not Kill." In *Church and Peace*, edited by Norbert Greinacher and Virgil Elizondo, vii–viii. Edinburgh: T. & T. Clark, 1983.

Elizondo, Virgilio, and Timothy Matovina. "From the Guest Editors." *Journal of Hispanic/ Latino Theology* 5 (1997) 3–5.

———. *Mestizo Worship: A Pastoral Approach to Liturgical Ministry.* Collegeville: Liturgical, 1998.

Elizondo, Virgilio, Timothy Matovina, and Allan Figueroa Deck. *The Treasure of Guadalupe.* Lanham: Rowman & Littlefield, 2006.

Elizondo, Virgilio, and Alan Oddie. "San Antonio International Study Week of Mass Media and Catechetics: A Report." *Living Light* 6 (1969) 67–74.

Elizondo, Virgilio, et al. *A Retreat with Our Lady of Guadalupe and Juan Diego: Heeding the Call.* Cincinnati: St. Anthony Messenger, 1998.

Espinosa, Gastón, Virgilio Elizondo and Jesse Miranda. "Introduction: U.S. Latino Religions and Faith-Based Political, Civic, and Social Action." In *Latino Religions and Civic Activism in the United States,* 3–16. Oxford: Oxford University Press, 2005.

———. "Conclusion: Assessing and interpreting 150 years of Latino faith-based civic activism." In *Latino Religions and Civic Activism in the United States,* 307–14. Oxford: Oxford University Press, 2005.

Linskens, John, and Virgilio Elizondo. "Pentecost and Pluralism." *Momentum* 6 (1975) 12–15.

Works by Gustavo Gutiérrez

"25 Years in the Theology of Libertion." *LADOC* 14 (1984) 14–17. "Quehacer teológico y experiencia eclesial." *La Iglesia Popular, Entre El Temor y La Esperanza.* Madrid: Ediciones Cristiandad, 1984; reprint in *La densidad del presente,* 21–27. Salamanca: Ediciones Sígueme, 2003; English Version, "The Task of Theology and Ecclesial Experience." In *La Iglesia Popular: Between Fear and Hope,* edited by Leonardo Boff and Virgil Elizondo, 401–406. Edinburgh: T. & T. Clark, 1984; reprint in *Christ and Context: The Confrontation Between Gospel and Culture,* edited by Hilary D. Regan, Alan J. Torrance, and Antony Wood, 78–87. Edinburgh: T&T Clark, 1993; reprint in *The Density of the Present: Selected Writings,* translated by Dinah Livingstone 169–75. Maryknoll, NY: Orbis, 1999.

"Speaking about God." In *Different Theologies, Common Responsibility: Babel or Pentecost? Concilium,* edited by Claude Geffré, Gustavo Gutiérrez and Virgilio Elizondo, translated by Paul Burn, 27–31. Edinburgh: T. & T. Clark, 1984.

Assessment, edited by W. Dayton Roberts, 41–47. Monrovia: MARC, 1987.

"A Spirituality for Liberation." *Other Side* 21.3 (1985) 40–43.

"A Spirituality of Liberation." In *The Theology of Liberation,* edited by Alberto Rossa, 46–50. Diliman: Claretian, 1986.

"Aporte". In *Hambre de Dios, Hambre de Pan: I Congreso Teológico Internacional,* 88–94. Chimbote: Diócesis de Chimbote, 1987.

"Bartolomé de Las Casas, combatiente por la justicia en América Latina." In *Profecía y evangelización: Bartolomé de Las Casas; Medellín,* Colección Páginas Series 2, 17–25. Lima: Centro de Estudios y Publicaciones, 1978.

"Bartolomé de Las Casas, libertad y liberación."In *Profecía y evangelización: Bartolomé de Las Casas; Medellín,* Colección Páginas Series 2, 26–45. Lima: Centro de Estudios y Publicaciónes, 1978.

"Bartolomé de Las Casas: Defender of the Indians (his theology)." *Pacifica* 5 (1992) 263–73.

"Bartolomé de Las Casas: memoria de Dios y anuncío del evangelio." In *La densidad del presente*, 129–52. Salamanca: Sígueme, 2003.

Beber en su propio pozo: en el itinerario espiritual de un pueblo. Lima, Peru: Centro de Estudios y Publicaciónes, 1983. Translated by Matthew J. O'Connell as *We Drink From Our Own Wells: The Spiritual Journey of a People.* Maryknoll, NY: Orbis, 1984.

"Buscar el Reino." *Páginas* 79 (1986) 2 & 51.

"But Why Lord: On Job and the Suffering of the Innocent." *Other Side* 23 (1987) 18–23.

"Caminando con el pueblo." *Páginas* 4 (1979) 1–11.

"Caminos de solidaridad." In *La densidad del presente*, 155–67. Salamanca: Sígueme, 2003.

"The Church: Sacrament of History." In *Liberation Theology: An Introductory Reader*, edited by Curt Cadorette, Marie Giblin, Marilyn J. Legge, and Mary H. Snyder, 170–80. Maryknoll, NY: Orbis, 1992.

"The Church and the Poor: A Latin American Perspective." In *The Reception of Vatican II*, edited by Giuseppe Alberigo, Jean-Pierra Jossua and Joseph A. Komonchak, translated by Matthew J. O'Connell, 171–93. Washington, DC: Catholic University of America Press, 1987.

"Church of the Poor." In *Born of the Poor*, edited by Edward L. Cleary, 9–25. Notre Dame: University of Notre Dame Press, 1990.

Compartir la Palabraa lo largo del año Litúrgico. Salamanca: Ediciones Sígueme, 1996. Translated by Colette Joly Dees as *Sharing the Word.* Maryknoll, NY: Orbis, 1997.

"Compassion and Commitment." *Weavings* 5 (1990) 39–40.

"Comunidades cristianas de base: perspectivas eclesiológicas." *Páginas* 29 (1980) 3–13.

Cristianismo y tercer mundo. Bilbo: Zero, 1973.

"Criticism Will Deepen, Clarify Liberation Theology." Translation of interview in *La República*, Lima, Peru, September 14, 1984. *LADOC* 15 (1985) 2–7; reprint in *Liberation Theology: A Documentary History*, edited by Alfred T. Hennelly, 419–24. Maryknoll, NY: Orbis, 1990.

The Density of The Present: Selected Writings. Maryknoll, NY: Orbis, 1999.

"Desafíos de la posmodernidad." *Páginas* 162 (2000) 36–47.

Dios o el oro en las Indias. Salamanca: Sígueme, 1990.

El Dios de la vida. Salamanca: Sígueme, 1982. Translated by Matthew J. O'Connell as *The God of Life.* Maryknoll, NY: Orbis, 1991.

"Dom Helder." *Páginas* 159 (1999) 6–11.

"Donde está el pobre está Jesucristo." *Páginas* 197 (2006) 6–22.

"Drink from your own Well." In *Learning to Pray*, edited by Casiano Floristánan and Christian Duqouc, translated by Paul Burns, 38–45. New York: Seabury, 1982.

"El concilio: una pauta espiritual." *Páginas* 136 (1995) 17–28.

"El jubileo y la misión de Cristo." *Páginas* 147–48 (1997) 6–14.

"El reino está cerca." *Páginas* 52 (1983) 2 & 39.

"En busca de los pobres de Jesucristo." *Páginas* 38 (1981) 1–12.

En busca de los pobres de Jesucristo: El pensamiento de Bartolomé de Las Casas. Salamanca: Sígueme, 1992. Translated by Robert R. Barr as *Las Casas: In Search of the Poor of Jesus Christ.* Maryknoll, NY: Orbis, 1993.

"En busca de nuestra manera de hablar de Dios." In *La densidad del presente*, 71–88. Salamanca: Sígueme, 2003.

"En el horizonte del don de la vida: Pobreza y muerte." *Páginas* 196 (2005) 6–17.

"Entre las cálandrias." In *Arguedas: mito, historia y religion*, edited by Pedro Trigo, 239–77. Lima: Centro de Estudios y Publicaciónes, 1982.

"Evangelio y derechos humanos." In *La densidad del presente*, 195–99. Salamanca: Sígueme, 2003.

"Exigencias de comunión en un mundo dividido." *Páginas* 145 (1997) 18–25.

"Faith as Freedom: Solidarity with the Alienated and Confidence in the Future." *Horizons* 2 (1975) 25–60.

"Fé, Política y Movimiento Popular: Compromiso Cristiano Hoy." *Servicio Ecuménico de Pastoral y Estudio de la Comunicación, SEPEC* (1992). Translated by Magnus Lundberg as "Faith and Politics in the Popular Movements: Christian Commitment Today." *Swedish Missiological Themes* 93.2 (2005) 175–85.

"Freedom and Salvation: A Political Problem." In *Liberation and Change*, edited by Ronald H. Stone, 3–94. Atlanta: John Knox, 1977.

"Friends of God, Friends of the Poor." *Cuadernos de Espiritualidad* 73 (1996): 47–56; reprint in *The Density of The Present: Selected Writings*, Translated by Margaret Wilde, 147–56. Maryknoll, NY: Orbis, 1999.

"From Exclusion to Discipleship." In *Mysticism and the Institutional* Church, edited by Christian Duquoc and Gustavo Gutiérrez, translated by Francis McDonagh, 80–90. London: SCM, 1994; reprint in *The Density of the Present: Selected Writings*, 157–68. Maryknoll, NY: Orbis, 1999; Original in Spanish, reprint "De marginado a discípulo." In *La densidad del presente*, 183–94. Salamanca: Sígueme, 2003.

La fuerza histórica de los pobres: selección de trabajos. Salamanca: Sígueme, 1979. Translated by Robert R. Barr as *The Power of the Poor in History*. Maryknoll, NY: Orbis, 1983.

"The Gospel of Work: Reflections on *Laborem Exercens*." In *Sobre el trabajo humano: Comentarios a la Encíclica "Laborem Exercens"*, edited by G. Gutiérrez, R. Ames, J. Iguiñiz, and C. Chipoco. Lima: Centro de Estudios y Publicaciónes, 1982. Translated by Margaret Wilde as "The Gospel of Work: Reflections on *Laborem Exercens*." In *The Density of The Present: Selected Writings*, 3–38. Maryknoll, NY: Orbis, 1999.

"Gratuidad y fraternidad: Mateo 18." *Páginas* 164 (2000) 28–36.

"Gratuidad y justicia." *Páginas* 152 (1998) 80–84.

Gustavo Gutiérrez: Essential Writings. Edited by James B. Nickoloff. Maryknoll, NY: Orbis, 1996.

Hablar de Dios desde el sufrimiento del inocente: una reflexión sobre el libro de Job. Salamanca: Sígueme, 1986. Translated by Matthew J. O'Connell as *On Job: God-Talk and The Suffering of The Innocent*. Maryknoll, NY: Orbis, 1987.

"The Hope of Liberation." *Worldview* 17 (1974) 35–37.

"Introduction." In *Between Honesty and Hope: Documents from and about the Church in Latin America. Issued at Lima by the Peruvian Bishops' Commission for Social Action*, edited by Peruvian Bishops' Commission for Social Action, translated by John Drury, xii–xxiv. Maryknoll, NY: Orbis, 1970.

"The Irruption of the Poor in Latin America and the Christian Communities of the Common People." In *The Challenge of Basic Christian Communities*, edited by Sergio Torres and John Eagleson, translated by John Drury, 107–23. Maryknoll, NY: Orbis, 1981.

"Jesus and the Political World." *Worldview* 15 (1972) 43–46.

"John of the Cross: A Latin American View." In *Gustavo Gutiérrez: Essential Writings*, edited and translated by James B. Nickoloff, 137–46. Maryknoll, NY: Orbis, 1996; Original in Spanish, reprint: "Juan de la Cruz desde América Latina." In *La densidad del presente*, 115–28. Salamanca: Sígueme, 2003.

"Joy in the Midst of Suffering." In *Christ and Context: The Confrontation Between Gospel and Culture*, edited by Hilary D. Regan, Alan J. Torrance, and Antony Wood, 78–87. Edinburgh: T. & T. Clark, 1993.

"La construcción de la vida en el Perú como identidad histórica moderna." *Páginas* 100 (1989) 125–57.

"La Koinonía Eclesial." *Páginas* 200 (2006) 18–35.

"La opción preferencial por el pobre en Aparecida." *Páginas* 208 (2007) 6–25.

"La prioridad de la vida." *Páginas* 145 (1997): 6–8.

"Las cosas nuevas de hoy: una relectura de la Rerum Novarum." *Páginas* 11 (1991) 7–22.

"A Latin American Perception of a Theology of Liberation." In *Conscientization for Liberation*, edited by Louis M. Colonnese, 57–80. Washington, DC: Division for Latin America United States Catholic Conference, 1971.

"Lenguaje teologíco, plenitud del silencio." *Páginas* 137 (Febrero 1996) 66–87; reprint *La densidad del presente*, 41–70. Salamanca: Sígueme, 2003. Translated by James B. Nickoloff and Margaret Wilde as "Theological Language: Fullness of Silence." In *Gustavo Gutiérrez: Essential Writings*, edited by James B. Nickoloff, 186–207. Maryknoll, NY: Orbis, 1996.

"Liberation and the Poor: The Puebla Perspective." In *The Theology of Liberation*, edited by Alberto Rossa, 51–92. Diliman: Claretian, 1986.

"Liberation Movements and Theology." In *Jesus Christ and Human Freedom*, edited by Edward Schillebeeckx and Bas van Iersel, translated by J. P. Donnelly 135–46. New York: Herder & Herder, 1974.

"Liberation Theology and the Future of the Poor." In *Liberating the Future: God, Mammon and Theology*, edited by Joerg Rieger, translated by Isabel N. Docampo and Fernando Santillana, 96–123. Minneapolis: Fortress, 1998.

"Liberation, Theology and Proclamation." In *The Mystical and Political Dimension of the Christian Faith*, translated by J. P. Donnelly, edited by Claude Geffré and Gustavo Gutiérrez, 57–77. New York: Herder & Herder, 1974.

"Libertad y esperanza." *Páginas* 182 (2002) 60–65.

Lineas pastorales de la Iglesia en América Latina: análisis teológico. Lima: Centro de Estudios y Publicaciónes, 1970.

"The Meaning of Development (Notes on a theology of liberation)." In *In Search of a Theology of Development* (Papers from a Consultation on Theology and Development held by SODEPAX in Cartigny, Switzerland, November, 1969). Geneva: Committee on Society, Development and Peace, Publications Department, The Ecumenical Center, 1970.

"Medellín: una experiencia espiritual." *Páginas* 210 (2008) 6–12.

"Memoria y profecía." *Páginas* 181 (2003) 22–43. Translated as "Memory and Prophecy." In *The Option for the Poor in Christian Theology*, edited by Daniel G. Groody, 17–38. Notre Dame: University of Notre Dame Press, 2007.

Mision de la Iglesia y Apostolado Universitario. Lima: UNEC, 1960.

"Monseñor Óscar Romero: Aniversario y jubileo." *Páginas* 163 (2000) 53–58.

"New Things Today: A Rereading of *Rerum Novarum.*" In *The Density of The Present: Selected Writings,* translated by Margaret Wilde, 39–56. Maryknoll, NY: Orbis, 1999.

"No reconstruir la injusticia." *Páginas* 150 (1998) 24.

"Notes for a Theology of Liberation." *Theological Studies* 31 (1970) 243–61.

"Option for the Poor." In *Mysterium Liberationis: Fundamental con Centro de Estudios y Publicaciónes of Liberation Theology,* edited by Ignacio Ellacuría and Jon Sobrino, 235–50. Maryknoll, NY: Orbis, 1993.

"Opting for the Poor: Faces of Faith." Interview by Kathleen Hayes. *Other Side* 23 (1987) 10–13.

"The Option for the Poor Arises From Faith in Christ." Translated by Robert Lassalle-Klein, James Nickoloff, and Susan Sullivan. *Theological Studies* 70 (2009) 317–26.

"A Path of Reflection, an Intent to Speak of God." In *Liberation Thinking: An Evangelical* "Liberación y desarrollo, un desafío a la teología." *Páginas* 124 (1993) 14–23; reprint *Liberación y desarrollo en América Latina: Perspectivas.* Lima: Instituto Bartolomé de las Casas y Centro de Estudios y Publicaciónes (1993) 17–29; Translated by Margaret Wilde as "Liberation and Development: A Challenge to Theology." In *The Density of The Present: Selected Writings,* 124–34. Maryknoll, NY: Orbis, 1999.

"Perdonar es dar vida." *Páginas* 89–90 (1988) 6–9.

"Peru: An Interview with Gustavo Gutiérrez." *LADOC* 19 (1988) 24–28.

"Pobreza y teología." *Páginas* 191 (2005) 12–28.

"Poverty, Migration, and the Option for the Poor." In *A Promised Land, A Perilous Journey: Theological Perspectives on Migration,* edited by Daniel G. Groody and Gioacchino Campese, 76–86. Notre Dame: University of Notre Dame Press, 2008.

Praxis de Liberacion y Fe Cristiana: Praxis of Liberation and Christian Faith. San Antonio: MACC, 1976.

"Práxis de Liberación y Fé Cristiana." In *La Nueva Frontera de La Teología en América Latina,* edited by Rosino Gibellini, 13–40. Salamanca: Sigueme, 1977. Translated by John Drury as "Liberation Praxis and Christian Faith." In *Frontiers of Theology in Latin America,* edited by Rosino Gibellini, 1–32. Maryknoll, NY: Orbis, 1979

"Premio Príncipe de Asturias de Comunicación y Humanidades." *Páginas* 181 (2003) 6–8.

"The 'Preparatory Document' for Puebla: A Retreat from Commitment." Translated by Diana Houstoun and Robert McAfee Brown. *Christianity and Crisis* 38 (1978) 211–18.

"Quién es el indio? La perspeciva teológica de Bartolomé de las Casas." *Páginas* 88 (1987) 1–6.

"Reflections from a Latin American Perspective: Finding Our Way to Talk about God." In *Irruption of the Third World: Challenge to Theology (Papers from the Fifth International Conference of the Ecumenical Association of Third World Theologians, August 17–29, 1981, New Delhi, India),* edited by Virginia Fabella and Sergio Torres, translated by John Drury, 222–34. Maryknoll, NY: Orbis, 1983.

"Reflexiones sobre la crisis de los rehenes: De la Pacificación a la Paz." *Páginas* 143 (1997) 8–10.

"Renewing the Option for the Poor." In *Liberation Theologies, Postmodernity and the Americas,* edited by David B. Batsone et al., translated by Pedro Lange-Churión, 69–82. New York: Routledge, 1997.

"Reply by Gustavo Gutiérrez to John W. de Gruchy and Stephen May." In *Christ and Context: The Confrontation Between Gospel and Culture*, edited by Hilary D. Regan, Alan J. Torrance, and Antony Wood, 102–4. Edinburgh: T. & T. Clark, 1993.

"Response by John W. de Gruchy." In *Christ and Context: The Confrontation Between Gospel and Culture*, edited by Hilary D. Regan and Alan J. Torrance with Antony Wood, 88–91. Edinburgh: T. & T. Clark, 1993.

"Response by Stephen May." In *Christ and Context: The Confrontation Between Gospel and Culture*, edited by Hilary D. Regan and Alan J. Torrance with Antony Wood, 92–101. Edinburgh: T. & T. Clark, 1993.

"Search for Identity." *Latin American Perspectives* 19.3 (1992) 61–66.

"Seguimiento de Jesús y opción por el pobre." *Páginas* 201 (2006) 6–21.

"Significado y alcance de Medellín." In *Irrupción y caminar de la iglesia de los pobres: Presencia de Medellín*, 23–73. Lima: Centro de Estudios y Publicaciónes, 1989. Translated by Margaret Wilde as "The Meaning and Scope of Medellín." In *The Density of The Present: Selected Writings*, 59–101. Maryknoll, NY: Orbis, 1999.

"Situación y tareas de la teología de la liberación." *Páginas* 161 (2000): 6–22; reprint in *La densidad del presente*, 89–111. Salamanca: Sígueme, 2003.

"Statements by Gustavo Gutiérrez." In *Theology in the Americas*, edited by Sergio Torres and John Eagleson, 309–14. Maryknoll, NY: Orbis, 1976.

"Talking About God: Reflections from a Latin American Theologian" (excerpt from *Irruption of the Third World*). Translated by John Drury. *Sojourners* 12.2 (1983) 26–29.

"The Task and Content of Liberation Theology." In *The Cambridge Companion to Liberation Theology*, edited by Christopher Rowland, translated by Judith Condor, 19–38. New York: Cambridge University Press, 1999.

Teología de la liberación. Lima: Centro de Estudios y Publicaciónes, 1971. Translated by Caridad Inda and John Eagleson as *A Theology of Liberation: History, Politics, and Salvation*. Maryknoll, NY: Orbis, 1973; reprint, 15th Anniversary Edition, Maryknoll, NY: Orbis, 1988.

"Teología y ciencias sociales." *Páginas* 63–64 (1984) 4–15.

"Theology: An Ecclesial Function." In *Gustavo Gutiérrez: Essential Writings*, edited and translated by James B. Nickoloff, 176–85. Maryknoll, NY: Orbis, 1996. Original in Spanish, reprint: "La teología, una funcion eclesial." In *La densidad del presente*, 29–40. Salamanca: Ediciones Sígueme, 2003.

"Toward a Theology of Liberation (July 1968)." In *Liberation Theology: A Documentary History*, edited by Alfred Hennelly, 62–76.Maryknoll, NY: Orbis, 1990; reprint in *1492–1992 The Voice of the Victims*, edited by Leonardo Boff and Virgilio Elizondo, 1–9. London: SCM, 1990.

"Towards the Fifth Centenary." *Páginas* 99 (1989) 7–17. Translated by Dinah Livingstone as "Towards the Fifth Centenary." In *The Density of The Present: Selected Writings*, 102–12. Maryknoll, NY: Orbis, 1999.

"Two Theological Perspectives: Liberation Theology and Progressivist Theology." In *The Emergent Gospel: Theology from the Underside of History* (Papers from the Ecumenical Dialogue of Third World Theologians, Dar Es Salaam, 5–12 August 1976), edited by Sergio Torres and Virginia Fabella, 227–51. Maryknoll, NY: Orbis, 1978.

"Un camino de justicia y libertad: El Papa en Cuba." *Páginas* 150 (1998) 6–9.

"Una agenda: La IV conferencia de Santo Domingo." *Páginas* 119 (1993) 11–19. Translated by Margaret Wilde as "An Agenda: The Conference at Santo Domingo." In *The Density of The Present: Selected Writings*, 113–23. Maryknoll, NY: Orbis, 1999.

"Una nueva etapa en la vida del país?" *Páginas* 169 (2001) 15–17.

"Una opción teocéntrica." *Páginas* 177 (2002) 6–13.

"Vaticano II: Una tarea abierta." *Páginas* 178 (2002) 14–23.

La verdad los hará libres: confrontaciones. Lima: Instituto Bartolomé de las Casas-Rimac and Centro de Estudios y Publicaciónes, 1986. Translated by Matthew J. O'Connell as *The Truth Shall Make You Free.* Maryknoll, NY: Orbis, 1990.

"The Violence of a System." In *Christian Ethics and Economics: The North-South Conflict*, edited by Dietmar Mieth and Jacques Pohier, translated by Paul Burns, 93–100. New York: Seabury, 1980.

"The Voice of the Poor in the Church." In *Proceedings of the Thirty-Third Annual Convention* (Milwaukee, June 7–10, 1978, Vol. 33), edited by Luke Salm, 30–34. New York: The Catholic Theological Society of America, 1979.

"We Cannot Do Theology in a Dead Corner of History." In Rosino Gibellini, *The Liberation Theology Debate*, 80–87. Maryknoll, NY: Orbis, 1988.

Collaborated Works with Gutiérrez

Alberigo, Giuseppe, and Gustavo Gutiérrez. "Editoral." In *Where Does The Church Stand?*, edited by Giuseppe Alberigo and Gustavo Gutiérrez, translated by Robert Ombres, vii–viii. New York: Seabury, 1981.

Gutiérrez, Gustavo, et al. *Cruz y Resurrección: presencia y anuncio de una iglesia nueva* (Colección "Teologia Latinoamericana" 7), 3–45 . Mexico City: Centro de Reflexión Teológica, 1978.

Gutiérrez, Gustavo, Rolando Ames, Javier Igiñiz, et al. *Sobre el trabajo humano: Comentarios a la Encíclica "Laborem exercens."* Lima: Centro de Estudios y Publicaciónes, 1982.

Geffré, Claude, Gustavo Gutiérrez, and Virgilio Elizondo. "Editorial." In *Different Theologies, Common Responsibility: Babel or Pentecost?*, edited by Claude Geffré, Gustavo Gutiérrez and Virgilio Elizondo, ix–xii. Edinburgh: T. & T. Clark, 1984.

SECONDARY LITERATURE

Abbot, Walter M, editor. *The Documents of Vatican II.* Translated by Joseph Gallagher. New York: Guild, 1966.

————. "Message to Humanity: Issued at the Beginning of the Second Vatican Council by its Fathers, with the Endorsement of the Supreme Pontiff." In *The Documents of Vatican II*, translated by Joseph Gallagher, 3–7. New York: Guild, 1966.

Alberigo, Giuseppe. "Vatican II and its History." In *Vatican II: A Forgotten Future?*, edited by Alberto Melloni and Christoph Theobald, 9–33. London: SCM, 2005.

Aquino, Jorge. "'Ni Blanquitos, Ni Negritos': Race, Nation, and Identity in U.S. Latino/a Theology." PhD diss., Graduate Theological Union, 2006.

Audinet, Jacques. "A *Mestizo* Theology." In *Writings of Virgilio Elizondo and Friends*, 143–49. Maryknoll, NY: Orbis, 2000.

―――. *The Human Face of Globalization: From Multicultural to Mestizaje.* Translated by Frances Dal Chele. Lanham, MD: Rowman & Littlefield, 2004.

Azevedo, Marcello de C. "Basic Ecclesial Communities." In *Mysterium Liberationis: Fundamental con Centro de Estudios y Publicaciónes of Liberation Theology,* edited by Ignacio Ellacuría and Jon Sobrino, 636–53. Maryknoll, NY: Orbis, 1993.

Balasuriya, Tissa. "Issues in the Relationship between the Contextual and Universal Dimension of Christian Theology." *Bangalore Theological Forum* 24, 3–4 (1992) 24–38.

Bañuelas, Arturo J., editor. *Mestizo Christianity: Theology from a Latino Perspective,* Maryknoll, NY: Orbis, 1989.

Benedict XVI. "Address of His Holiness Benedict XVI to the Roman Curia Offering Them His Christmas Greetings." (22 December 2005). Online: http://www.vatican. va/holy_father/benedict_xvi/speeches/2005/december/documents/hf_ben_xvi_ spe_20051222_roman-curia_en.html (accessed August 26, 2010).

―――. "Brazil Visit: Address to CELAM." *Origins.* 37.02 (2007) 17–24.

Beozzo, José-Oscar. "Medellín Forty Years On." In *Migration in a Global World,* edited by Solange Lefebvre and Luiz Carlos Susin, 121–32. London: SCM, 2008.

Berryman, Phillip. "Church and Revolution." *NACLA Report on the Americas* (1997). Online: http://www.hartford-hwp.com/archives/40/023.html (accessed May 28, 2010).

Bevans, Stephen, B. *Models of Contextual Theology.* Maryknoll, NY: Orbis, 1992; revised 2002.

Boff, Clodovis, and Leonardo Boff. *Introducing Liberation Theology.* Translated by Paul Burns. Maryknoll, NY: Orbis, 1987.

Bonino, José Miguez. "Freedom Through Unity: Liberation Through Ecumenism in Latin America." *Thought* 59 (1984) 255–64.

Borgman, Eric. "*Gaudium et Spes*: The Forgotten Future of a Revolutionary Document." In *Vatican II: A Forgotten Future?,* edited by Alberto Melloni and Christoph Theobald, 48–55. London: SCM, 2005.

Brockman, James R. "The Prophetic Role of the Church in Latin America: A Conversation with Gustavo Gutiérrez." *The Christian Century* (1983) 931–35.

Brown, Robert McAfee. *Gustavo Gutiérrez: An Introduction to Liberation Theology.* Maryknoll, NY: Orbis, 1990.

―――. *Gustavo Gutiérrez: Makers of Contemporary Theology.* Atlanta: John Knox, 1980.

―――. "What is Contextual Theology?" In *Changing Context of Our Faith,* edited by Letty M. Russell, 80–94. Philadelphia: Fortress, 1985.

Cahill, Thomas. *Pope John XXIII.* London: Weidenfeld & Nicolson, 2002.

Campese, Gioacchino. "¿Cuanto Más?: The Crucified Peoples at the U.S.-Mexico Border." In *A Promised Land, A Perilous Journey: Theological Perspectives on Migration,* edited by Daniel G. Groody and Gioacchino Campese, 271–98. Notre Dame: University of Notre Dame Press, 2008.

Cardoza Orlandi, Carlos F. "'Now You See It, Now You Don't': Mission and Ecumenism in a Hispanic/Latino Perspective." *Theology Today* 54.4 (1988) 499–506.

Cadorette, Curt. *From the Heart of the People: The Theology of Gustavo Gutiérrez.* Oak Park, IL: Meyer-Stone, 1988.

Cadorette, Curt, et al. *Liberation Theology: An Introductory Reader.* Maryknoll, NY: Orbis, 1992.

Castillo Guerra, Jorge E. "A Theology of Migration: Toward an Intercultural Methodology." In *A Promised Land, A Perilous Journey: Theological Perspectives on Migration*, edited by Daniel G. Groody and Gioacchino Campese, 243–70. Notre Dame: University of Notre Dame Press, 2008.

Chopp, Rebecca S. *The Praxis of Suffering*. Maryknoll, NY: Orbis, 1986.

Comblin, José. "The Signs of the Times." In *Vatican II: A Forgotten Future?*, edited by Alberto Melloni and Christoph Theobald, 73–85. London: SCM, 2005.

Condolo, Marta. "Ecumenism and Human Liberation." *Ecumenism* 78 (1985) 35–38.

Congregation for the Doctrine of the Faith. "Instruction on Certain Aspects of Liberation Theology." *Origins* 14.13 (1984).

———. "Instruction on Christian Freedom and Liberation." *Origins* 15.44 (1986).

Conroy, Ed. "Mestizo Identity is the Heart of Virgil Elizondo's Life and Work: An Influential Theologian Writes of Jesus, the Hispanic Experience and Himself." *National Catholic Reporter* 40.43 (2004) 19.

Consejo Episcopal Latinoamericano, *Discípulos y Misioneros de Jesucristo para que nuestros pueblos en Él tengan vida "Yo soy el Camino, la Verdad y la Vida"* (Aparecida 2007). Bogotá: Centro de Publicaciones del CELAM, 2007.

Cortez, Marc. "Context and Concept: Contextual Theology and the Nature of Theological Discourse." *Westminster Theological Journal* 67 (2005) 85–102.

Corkery, James. "The Relationship between Human Existence and Christian Salvation in the Theology of Joseph Ratzinger." PhD diss., The Catholic University of America, 1991.

Costas, Orlando E. "Liberation Theologies in the Americas: Common Journeys and Mutual Challenges." In *Yearning to Breathe Free: Liberation Theologies in the United States*, 28–44. Maryknoll, NY: Orbis, 1990.

Dahlen, Robert W. "Bartolomé de las Casas: Ethics and the Eschaton." *Word & World* 22.3 (2002) 284–94.

De La Torre, Miguel A., and Edwin David Aponte. *Introducing Latino/a Theologies*. Maryknoll, NY: Orbis, 2001.

de Lubac, Henri. *A Brief Catechesis on Nature and Grace*. Translated by Richard Arnandez. San Francisco: Ignatius, 1984.

de Prado, Consuelo, and Pedro Hughes. *Libertad y Esperanza: A Gustavo Gutiérrez, por sus 80 años*. Lima: Centro de Estudios y Publicaciónes, 2008.

Deck, Allan Figueroa. "Beyond *La Pausa*: Liberation Theologies Lives." *America* 188.3 (2003) 29–31.

Deck, Allan Figueroa, editor. *Frontiers of Hispanic Theology in the United States*. Maryknoll, NY: Orbis, 1992.

Díaz, Miguel Humberto. "A Study in U.S. Hispanic Theology Anthropology, 1972–1999." PhD diss., University of Notre Dame, 2000.

Duncan, William B. *The Political Philosophy of Peruvian Theologian Gustavo Gutiérrez*. Lewiston: Edwin Mellen, 2001.

Eagleson, John, and Philip Scharper, editors. *Puebla and Beyond: Documentation and Commentary*. Maryknoll, NY: Orbis, 1979.

Ellingsen, Mark. "Building a New Ecumenism Through Contextual Theology." *The Christian Century* (1986) 713–14.

Ellis, Marc H., and Otto Maduro, editors. *The Future of Liberation Theology: Essays in Honor of Gustavo Gutiérrez*. Maryknoll, NY: Orbis, 1989.

Erdman, Daniel. "Liberation and Identity: Indo-Hispano Youth." *Religious Education* 78.1 (1983) 76–88.

Flannery, Austin, editor. *Vatican Council II:* Volume 1: *The Conciliar and Postconciliar Documents.* Northport: Costello, 1996.

Ford, John. "¡Bienvenidos!: Welcoming Hispanics/Latinos to the Parish Community." *The Living Light* 39.2 (2002) 70–78.

———. "What is Hispanic/Latino Theology?" *Josephinum Journal of Theology* 12.1 (2005) 120–30.

Freire, Paolo. *Pedagogy of the Oppressed.* New York: Continuum, 1993.

Freyne, Sean. "Galilee, Jesus and the Contribution of Archaeology." *Espository Times* 119.12 (2008) 573–81.

———. "The Galilean Jesus and a Contemporary Christology." *Theological Studies* 70 (2009) 281–97.

———. "The Geography of Restoration: Galilee-Jerusalem Relations in Early Jewish and Christian Experience." *New Testament Studies* 47 (2001) 289–311.

Gaillardetz, Richard R. *The Church in the Making: Lumen Gentium, Christus Dominus, Orientalium Ecclesiarum.* New York/Mahwah: Paulist Press, 2006.

Geffré, Claude. "Editorial: A Prophetic Theology." In *The Mystical and Political Dimension of the Christian Faith,* translated by J. P. Donnelly, edited by Claude Geffré and Gustavo Gutiérrez, 7–16. New York: Herder & Herder, 1974.

Gibellini, Rosino. *The Liberation Theology Debate.* Maryknoll, NY: Orbis, 1988.

Gillingham, Richard. "Praxis and the Content of Theology in Gustavo Gutiérrez's Theological Methodology: A Comparative Critique." *Quodibet* 7.2 (2005). Online: http://www.quodlibet.net/articles/gillingham-gutierrez.shtml (accessed June 1, 2010).

González, Justo. "A Response to Virgilio Elizondo." *Catholic Theological Society of America Proceedings* 48 (1993) 15–17.

———. "Theology from the Barrio: Virgil P. Elizondo." In *Proclaiming the Acceptable Year,* edited by Justo L. González, 61–63. Valley Forge, PA: Judson, 1982.

Groody, Daniel G. "Fruit of the Vine and Work of Human Hands." In *A Promised Land, A Perilous Journey: Theological Perspectives on Migration,* edited by Daniel G. Groody and Gioacchino Campese, 299–315. Notre Dame: University of Notre Dame Press, 2008.

Gros, Jeffrey, and Stephen Bevans. *Evangelization and Religious Freedom: Ad Gentes, Dignitatis Humanae.* New York/Mahwah: Paulist, 2009.

Hartnett, Daniel. "Remember the Poor: An Interview With Gustavo Gutiérrez." *America* (2003) 12–16.

Hennelly, Alfred. *Liberation Theologies: The Global Pursuit of Justice.* New London: Twenty-Third, 1995.

———. *Liberation Theology: A Documentary History.* Maryknoll, NY: Orbis, 1990.

———. "Theology Through the Optic of the Poor." In *Theologies in Conflict: The Challenge of Juan Luis Segundo,* 23–37. Maryknoll, NY: Orbis, 1979.

IDOC. "Celam III: Bibliography on the Preparation of the Third General Conference of the Latin American Bishops." *IDOC Bulletin* 6–7 (1978) 3–35.

James, Leslie R. *Toward an Ecumenical Liberation Theology: A Critical Exploration of Common Dimensions in the Theologies of Juan L. Segundo and Rubem A. Alves.* New York: Peter Lang, 2001.

Jiménez, Pablo A. "In Search of a Hispanic Model of Biblical Interpretation." *Journal of Hispanic/Latino Theology* 3.2 (1995) 44–63.

John Paul II. "Address to the Indians of Oaxaca and Chiapas." In *Puebla and Beyond: Documentation and Commentary*, edited by John Eagleson and Philip Scharper, 81–83. Maryknoll, NY: Orbis, 1979.

———. *Centesimus Annus*. Online: http://www.vatican.va/holy_father/john_paul_ii/encyclicals/documents/hf_jp-ii_enc_01051991_centesimus-annus_en.html (accessed January 11, 2010).

———. "Homily at the Basilica of Guadalupe." In *Puebla and Beyond: Documentation and Commentary*, edited by John Eagleson and Philip Scharper, 72–76. Maryknoll, NY: Orbis, 1979.

———. "Opening Address at the Puebla Conference." In *Puebla and Beyond: Documentation and Commentary*, edited by John Eagleson and Philip Scharper, 57–71. Maryknoll, NY: Orbis, 1979.

———. "The Apostolic Exhortation on the Family." *Origins* 11.28 (1981).

John XXIII. "*Gaudet mater ecclesia*: The Opening Speech to the Council." In *Council Daybook*, 25–29; the Latin original is in *Acta Synodalia Sacrosancti Concilii Vatican II* (Vatican City: Typis Polyglottis Vaticanis, 1970), I/1, 166–75.

———. *Journal of a Soul*. Translated by Dorothy White. New York: Signet, 1965.

———. "Pope's Address to World: Month before Council Opened." In *Council Daybook, Vatican II: Session 1, Oct. 11 to Dec. 8, 1962; Session 2, Sept. 29 to Dec. 4, 1963*, ed. Floyd Anderson, 18–21. Washington, DC: National Welfare Conference, 1965–1966; the Italian original is in *AAS* 54 (1962) 678–85.

Johnston, Rosemary. "Theologians Ponder Meanings of Borders." *National Catholic Reporter* 33.33 (1997) 11.

Komonchak, Joseph A. "Interpreting the Council: Catholic Attitudes toward Vatican II." In *Being Right: Conservative Catholics in America*, edited by Mary Jo Weaver and R. Scott Appleby, 17–36. Bloomington: Indiana University Press, 1995.

———. "Modernity and the Construction of Roman Catholicism." *Cristianesimo nella Storia* 18 (1997) 353–85.

———. "Vatican II and the Encounter Between Catholicism and Liberalism." In *Catholicism and Liberalism: Contributions to American Public Philosophy*, edited by R. B. Douglas and D. Hollenbach, 76–99. New York: Cambridge University Press, 1994.

———. "Vatican II as an 'Event.'" *Theological Digest* 46.4 (1999) 337–52.

Kirkpatrick, Dow. "Liberation Theologians and Third World Demands: A Dialogue with Gustavo Gutiérrez and Javier Iguiñiz." *The Christian Century* 93 (1976) 456–60.

Lassalle-Klein, Robert. "Guest Editorial/Introduction." *Theological Studies* 70 (2009) 257–61.

———. "A Postcolonial Christ." In *Thinking of Christ: Proclamation, Explanation, Meaning*, edited by Tatha Wiley, 135–53. New York: Continuum, 2003.

Lee, Michael E. "Galilean Journey Revisited: Mestizaje, Anti-Judaism, and the Dynamics of Exclusion." *Theological Studies* 70.2 (2009) 377–400.

Lee, Martin A., and Pia Gallegos. "Gustavo Gutiérrez: With the Poor." *Christianity and Crisis* 47 (1987) 113–15.

Lehmann, Paul L. "Contextual Theology." *Theology Today* 29.1 (1972) 3–8.

Loader, James. "Exodus, Liberation Theology and Theological Argument," *Journal of Theology for Southern Africa* 59.1 (2006) 3–18.

Loya, Gloria Inés. "Religious Education: A Portrait Based on Virgilio Elizondo's Vision." In *Writings of Virgilio Elizondo and Friends*, 13–23. Maryknoll, NY: Orbis, 2000.

Lynch, Edward A. "The Retreat of Liberation Theology." Online: http://www.ewtn.com/library/ISSUES/LIBERATE.TXT (accessed June 1, 2010).

MacEoin, Gary. "For Elizondo, Jesus is *Mestizo*, Our Lady is First American." *National Catholic Reporter* 36.32 (2000) 13.

Matovina, Timothy. "Our Lady of Guadalupe: Patroness of América." *America* 189.19 (2003) 8–12.

———. "Theologies of Guadalupe: From the Spanish Colonial Era to Pope John Paul II." *Theological Studies* 70 (2009) 61–91.

Matovina, Timothy, editor. *Beyond Borders: Writings of Virgilio Elizondo and Friends*. Maryknoll, NY: Orbis, 2000.

———. *Virgilio Elizondo: Spiritual Writings*. Maryknoll, NY: Orbis, 2010.

Meier, John. "The Bible as a Source for Theology." *Catholic Theological Society of America Proceedings* 43 (1988) 1–14.

Muskus, Eddy José. *The Origins and Early Development of Liberation Theology in Latin America*. Carlilse, UK: Paternoster, 2002.

Nichols, David. "Virgil Elizondo: A Particular Man." In *Sources of Inspiration: 15 Modern Religious Leaders*, edited by Gene Maeroff, 86–107. Kansas City: Sheed & Ward, 1992.

Nilson, Jon. "A Response to John P. Meier." *Catholic Theological Society of America Proceedings* 43 (1988) 15–18.

Noble, Tim. "An Introduction to the Theology of Gustavo Gutiérrez." *Communio Viatorum* 43.1 (2001) 8–27.

Parratt, John, editor. *An Introduction to Third World Theologies*. Cambridge: Cambridge University Press, 2004.

Petrella, Ivan. *Beyond Liberation Theology: A Polemic*. London: SCM, 2008.

Pineda-Madrid, Nancy. "Interpreting Our Lady of Guadalupe: Mediating the Christian Mystery of Redemption." PhD diss., Graduate Theological Union, 2005.

Poblete, Renato. "From Medellín to Puebla: Notes for Reflection." *Journal of Interamerican Studies and World Affairs* 21.1 (1979) 31–44.

Poole, Stafford. "Did Juan Diego Exist?: Questions on the Eve of Canonization." *Commonweal* 129.12 (2002) 9–11.

———. "History Versus Juan Diego." *The Americas* 62.1 (2005) 1–16.

———. "Some Observations on Mission Methods and Native Reactions in Sixteenth-Century New Spain." *The Americas* 3 (1994) 337–49.

Ratzinger, Joseph. *Church, Ecumenism and Politics: New Essays in Ecclesiology*. New York: Crossroad, 1988.

Ratzinger, Joseph, with Vittorio Messori. *The Ratzinger Report: An Exclusive Interview on the State of the Church*. Translated by Salvator Attanasio and Graham Harrison. San Francisco: Ignatius, 1985.

Recinos, Harold J. "Issues in: U.S. Latino/Latina Theology." *Quarterly Review* 25.3 (2005) 323–29.

Reist, Benjamin A. "The Context of Contextual Theology." *Union Seminary Quarterly Review* XXIX.3–4 (1974) 153–67.

Restall, Matthew. *Seven Myths of the Spanish Conquest*. New York: Oxford University Press, 2004.

Rieger, Joerg. "Developing a Common Interest Theology from the Underside." In *Liberating the Future: God, Mammon and Theology*, edited by Joerg Rieger, translated by Isabel N. Docampo and Fernando Santillana, 124–41. Minneapolis: Fortress, 1998.

———. "Introduction: Opting for the Margins in a Postmodern World." In *Opting for the Margins: Postmodernity and Liberation in Christian Theology*, edited by Joerg Rieger, 3–22. New York: Oxford University Press, 2003.

———. "Theology and the Power of the Margins in a Postmodern World." In *Opting for the Margins: Postmodernity and Liberation in Christian Theology*, edited by Joerg Rieger, 179–99. New York: Oxford University Press, 2003.

Rodríguez, Rubén Rosario. "No Longer Jew or Greek But Mestizo? The Challenge of Ethnocentrism for Theological Reconstruction." PhD diss., Princeton Theological Seminary, 2004.

Rowland, Christopher. "Introduction: The Theology of Liberation." In *The Cambridge Companion to Liberation Theology*, edited by Christopher Rowland, 1–16. Cambridge: Cambridge University Press, 1999.

Ruiz, Jean-Pierre. "Good Fences and Good Neighbors? Biblical Scholars and Theologians." *Journal of Hispanic/Latino Theology* (2007). Online: http://www.latinotheology.org/2007/fences_neighbors (accessed May 28, 2010).

Russell, Letty, M. "Universality and Contextuality." *The Ecumenical Review* 31.1 (1979) 23–26.

Rynne, Xavier. *Vatican Council II*. New York: Farrar, Straus & Giroux, 1968.

Sandoval, Moises. *On the Move: A History of the Hispanic Church in the United States*. Maryknoll, NY: Orbis, 2006.

Santos, John Phillip. *The Farthest Home is in an Empire of Fire: A Tejano Elergy*. New York: Viking, 2010.

———. *Places Left Unfinished at the Time of Creation: A Memoir*. New York: Viking, 1999.

Second General Conference of Latin America Bishops (CELAM, Medellín). "The Church in the Present-Day Transformation of Latin America in the Light of the Council (August 26-September 6, 1968)." In *Liberation Theology: A Documentary History*, edited by Alfred Hennelly, 89–119. Maryknoll, NY: Orbis, 1990.

Siker, Jeffrey, S. "Historicizing a Racialized Jesus: Case Studies in the 'Black Christ,' the 'Mestizo Christ,' and White Critique." *Biblical Interpretation* 15 (2007) 26–53.

Smith, Christian. "*Las Casas* as Theological Counteroffensive: An Interpretation of Gustavo Gutiérrez's *Las Casas: In Search of the Poor of Jesus Christ*." *Journal for the Scientific Study of Religion* 41.1 (2002) 69–73.

Sobrino, Jon. *Spirituality of Liberation: Toward Political Holiness*. Translated by Robert R. Barr. Maryknoll, NY: Orbis, 1988.

Tamez, Elsa. "Gustavo Gutiérrez." In *Against Machismo*, Translated by John Eagleson, 39–48. Oak Park: Meyer-Stone, 1987.

Tanner, Norman P. *The Church and the World: Gaudium et spes, Inter mirifica*. New York/ Mahwah: Paulist, 2005.

Third General Conference of Latin America Bishops (CELAM, Puebla), "Evangelization in Latin America's Present and Future (Puebla de los Angeles, Mexico, January 27-February 13, 1979)." In *Puebla and Beyond: Documentation and Commentary*, edited by John Eagleson and Philip Scharper, 225–58. Maryknoll, NY: Orbis, 1979.

Thomson, Alan. "Bevans and Bediako: Reconsidering Text-Based Models of Contextual Theologising." *Evangelical Review of Theology* 33.4 (2009) 347–58.

Tomasi, Silvano. "Migration and Catholicism in a Global Context." In *Migration in a Global World*, edited by Solange Lefebvre and Luiz Carlos Susin, 13–31. London: SCM, 2008.

Tombs, David. "A New Way of Doing Theology." In *Latin American Liberation Theology*, 119–36. Boston: Brill Academic, 2002.

Torres, Sergio and John Eagleson, editors. *The Challenge of Basic Christian Communities.* Maryknoll, NY: Orbis, 1981.

Twomey, Gerald. "Pope John Paul II and Preferential Option for the Poor." *Journal of Catholic Legal Studies* 45.321 (2006) 321–68.

———. *The "Preferential Option for the Poor" in Catholic Social Thought from John XXIII to John Paul II.* Lewiston, NY: Edwin Mellen, 2005.

Witherup, Ronald D. *Scripture: Dei Verbum.* New York: Paulist, 2006.

Yankauer, Alfred. "Hispanic/Latino—What's in a Name?" *American Journal Public Health* 77.1 (1987) 15–17.